The Gift in the Economy and Society

Mainstream economics offers a perspective on the gift which is constructed around exchange, axioms of self-interest, instrumental rationality and utility-maximisation – concepts that predominate within conventional forms of economic analysis. Recognising the gift as an example of social practice underpinned by social institutions, this book moves beyond this utilitarian approach to explore perspectives on the gift from social and institutional economics.

Through contributions from an international and interdisciplinary cast of authors, the chapters explore key questions such as: what is the relationship between social institutions, on the one hand, and gift, exchange, reciprocity on the other? What are the social mechanisms that underpin gift and gift-giving actions? And finally, what is the relationship between individuals, societies, gift-giving and cooperation? The answers to these questions and others serve to highlight the importance of the analysis of gift in economics and other social sciences. The book also demonstrates the potential of the analysis of the gift to contribute to solving current problems for humanity at various levels of social aggregation.

This key text makes a significant contribution to the literature on the gift which will be of interest to readers of heterodox economics, social anthropology, philosophy of economics, sociology and political philosophy.

Stefan Kesting is a Senior Teaching Fellow at Leeds University Business School, UK.

Ioana Negru is a Reader in Economics at Lucian Blaga University of Sibiu, Romania.

Paolo Silvestri is Contract Professor at University of Turin, Italy; Bocconi University, Italy; and Lumière University, Lyon 2, France.

Routledge Advances in Social Economics

Series Editor: John B. Davis, Marquette University

This series presents new advances and developments in social economics thinking on a variety of subjects that concern the link between social values and economics. Need, justice and equity, gender, cooperation, work poverty, the environment, class, institutions, public policy and methodology are some of the most important themes. Among the orientations of the authors are social economist, institutionalist, humanist, solidarist, cooperatist, radical and Marxist, feminist, post-Keynesian, behaviouralist, and environmentalist. The series offers new contributions from today's most foremost thinkers on the social character of the economy.

Publishes in conjunction with the Association of Social Economics.

Welfare Economics
An Interpretive History
Roger McCain

History, Methodology and Identity for a 21st Century Social Economics
Edited by Wilfred Dolfsma, D. Wade Hands and Robert McMaster

How Social Forces Impact the Economy
Edited by Steven Pressman

The Gift in the Economy and Society
Perspectives from Institutional Economics and Other Social Sciences
Edited by Stefan Kesting, Ioana Negru and Paolo Silvestri

For more information about this series, please visit: www.routledge.com/Routledge-Advances-in-Social-Economics/book-series/SE0071

The Gift in the Economy and Society

Perspectives from Institutional Economics and Other Social Sciences

Edited by
Stefan Kesting, Ioana Negru and Paolo Silvestri

Routledge
Taylor & Francis Group
LONDON AND NEW YORK

First published 2021
by Routledge
2 Park Square, Milton Park, Abingdon, Oxon OX14 4RN

and by Routledge
52 Vanderbilt Avenue, New York, NY 10017

Routledge is an imprint of the Taylor & Francis Group, an informa business

British Library Cataloguing-in-Publication Data
A catalogue record for this book is available from the British Library

Library of Congress Cataloging-in-Publication Data
A catalog record has been requested for this book

ISBN: 978-0-367-49106-2 (hbk)
ISBN: 978-1-003-04456-7 (ebk)

Typeset in Bembo
by codeMantra

Contents

Contributors

Frank Adloff is a Professor of Sociology at the University of Hamburg, Germany, where he is the co-director of the Humanities Centre for Advanced Studies "Futures of Sustainability". His research focuses on gift-giving, conviviality, civil society and sustainability.

Paschalis A. Arvanitidis (MEng, MLE, PgC, PhD) is an Associate Professor of Institutional Economics at the Department of Economics, University of Thessaly, Greece. He is an engineer and an economist with specialisation on institutional economics, urban economics, urban development and property markets. His research interests include institutional economics with emphasis on spatial and urban issues, including the analysis of the commons and of property as an institution. He holds membership in seven professional organisations and over the last years he has participated in many EU- and Greek-funded research projects. He is the author of a research monograph published by Routledge, titled *The Economics of Urban Property Markets: An Institutional Economics Analysis*, and he has published a number of research papers in collective volumes and peer reviewed journals.

Wilfred Dolfsma trained as an economist and philosopher (1970) holds a PhD in the former. He is chairholder and professor of Business Management & Organisation at Wageningen University, the Netherlands, the world's leading university in agriculture, forestry and sustainability. Wilfred's research focuses on how firms collaborate, and how people inside of firms collaborate as well, often using and expanding insights from social network analysis, social exchange theory and institutional economics.

Stefan Kesting is a Senior Teaching Fellow at Leeds University Business School, UK. He has previously taught at Auckland University of Technology, New Zealand, University of Bremen, Germany and University of Missouri, Kansas City, USA. He studied at the Universities of Heidelberg and Bremen as well as at New School for Social Research, New York City. He obtained his MA diploma and his PhD in Economics from the University of Bremen. His main research interests include the interactive and linguistic turn in economic theory (in particular central bank communication), ethics & economics, ecological sustainability, the gift as well as post-Keynesian, feminist, social and institutional economics.

Kalpana Khanal is an Assistant Professor of Economics and Finance at Nichols College, Dudley, MA, USA. She received her PhD in Economics and Social Science Consortium from University of Missouri, Kansas City, USA, in 2014. Her research interests include institutional economics, political economy and international finance. She has presented at various national and international conferences and her scholarly works are published as journal articles, book chapters and Op-eds in various sources.

Ioana Negru is a Reader in Economics with Lucian Blaga University of Sibiu (Romania) and she has extensive experience in teaching economics within the United Kingdom (Nottingham Trent University, University of Derby, Anglia Ruskin University, Cambridge and School of Oriental and African Studies, University of London) and Romania. She is the author of *Ethical formation of Economists* (with Wilfred Dolfsma, Routledge, 2019) and she is a member of Reteaching Economics, UK. Her research interests are centred around scientific pluralism, philosophy of economics, economic methodology, sustainability and ecological economics, the gift and economics, Austrian/Post-Keynesian/Institutionalist and Feminist economics.

Marina Sakovich is doctoral candidate at the Centre of Research in Economics of Grenoble at the University of Grenoble-Alpes, France. Her research interests are financial stability, macroprudential regulation and stress testing.

Ruchira Sen is an Assistant Professor of Economics at the Jindal School of Journalism and Communication, India. She has obtained her PhD in Economics from the University of Missouri, Kansas City, USA. She has also studied at the Jawaharlal Nehru University in New Delhi, India where she has obtained an MA and an MPhil in Economics. Her main research interests are gender and the economy which includes evaluating unpaid work, global care chains and dowry systems as gift economies.

Paolo Silvestri has a Degree in Economics and Commerce and a PhD in Philosophy of Law (University of Padova). He is currently Contract Professor at University of Turin, Bocconi University (Italy) and University Lyon 2 (France). His current research interests lie at the intersection of economic, legal and political philosophy, with a specific focus on: justice, reciprocity and gift-giving in taxation; freedom and liberalism; institutional economics and gift; tax percentage philanthropy institutions; value judgements and normativity in economics and in Law & Economics; Italian tradition in Public Finance. He held visiting positions at: Cornell University (USA), University of Freiburg (Germany), London School of

Economics (UK) and Université Lumière Lyon 2 (France). He was also National Coordinator of the Cornell-in-Turin Study Abroad Programme. He received the Marie Curie Fellowship of the European Union (Freiburg Institute for Advanced Studies). He has published and edited several books and special issues in academic journals and a number of papers in collective volumes and peer-reviewed journals.

Polyxeni Strolonga teaches Greek Literature and History at the Department of History at the Ionian University, Corfu, Greece, and in the programme Greek Civilization at the Hellenic Open University, Patras, Greece. She obtained her MA degree in Classics and her PhD in Classical Philology from the University of Illinois at Urbana-Champaign, USA. Her research interests focus on the intersection between Anthropology and Classics, with particular emphasis on Greek religion, hymnal poetry and social theories of exchange and reciprocity in the ancient world. She has published on various topics such as Greek religion, reciprocity, ancient reception, narratology, neoanalysis and the hymnic genre.

Faruk Ülgen is the Director of the Department of Distance Learning Programmes and International Relations of the Faculty of Economics and Deputy Director of the Centre of Research in Economics of Grenoble at the University of Grenoble-Alpes, France. He is specialised in monetary and financial economics and in institutional and evolutionary theories. His published work focuses particularly on the theories of money and financial (in)stability and regulation, on the relationships between financial development and economic development and on the economics of organisations. His latest research agenda focuses on financial regulation and public good/public choice economics.

Rene van der Eijk studied in the Netherlands, the United States and Germany, graduating Cum Laude as an economist at the Erasmus University Rotterdam, the Netherlands. He worked as a researcher at the Department of Management of Technology and Innovation at the Rotterdam School of Management, Erasmus University. He obtained his doctorate in business administration in the area of innovation. His key research interests include person-organisation fit, entrepreneurship, knowledge sharing, performance, social exchange, social networks and innovation. He has written and published articles on innovation, knowledge sharing, social exchange and social networks.

Diego Viana is a Brazilian financial journalist and philosopher. He completed a doctorate in Philosophy at the Diversitas Research Group of the Faculty of Philosophy, Social Sciences and Literature, University of São Paulo (FFLCH-USP), Brazil. He has taught Political Philosophy at the São Paulo School of Sociology and Politics (FESP-SP) and reported for the daily Valor Econômico. He is member of the Iconomia Research Group and research director of the Iconomia Institute in São Paulo, Brazil.

Benoît Walraevens is an Assistant Professor in Economics at the University of Caen Normandy, Cherbourg Institute of Technology, France. He obtained his PhD in Economics from the University of Paris 1 Panthéon Sorbonne. He is currently a researcher at CREM, University of Caen Normandy and an associate researcher at PHARE, University of Paris 1 Panthéon Sorbonne. His field of research is the history of economic thought and economic philosophy. His works focus mainly on eighteenth-century political economy and moral philosophy, and more specifically on the issue of the morality of commercial society in French and Scottish Enlightenment.

Anna Zachorowska-Mazurkiewicz is an Associate Professor in the Institute of Economics, Finance and Management, and a director of the Doctoral School of Social Sciences at Jagiellonian University in Krakow, Poland. She holds a PhD in economics. Her research interests focus on institutional and feminist economics. She has written about the economic situation of women in the United States, EU and transition economies, especially Poland, social and economic inequalities, as well as gender in economic thought.

1 Introduction

Stefan Kesting, Ioana Negru and Paolo Silvestri

This book is the result of collaborative work of the three editors[1] and brings together a variety of diverse perspectives on the gift. With this volume, we hope to encourage further critical and conceptual engagement by social and institutional economists with the gift. Economists and anthropologists have debated the gift and its meaning for decades. However, these encounters often resulted in paradigm wars instead of fruitful interdisciplinary collaboration. This book will hopefully contribute to constructive multidisciplinary conceptual work in the future.[2]

The volume is subdivided into two parts. In Part I, we have collected the contributions of a more theoretical-conceptual nature, while Part II assembles applied, empirical or experimental case studies. This is not an entirely sharp subdivision, since all the contributions are analytical in raising questions at the intersection of theory, social reality and historical reconstruction. Moreover, the "theoretical" chapters often engage with illustrative cases and examples while the "applied" chapters challenge theoretical and conceptual issues surrounding the phenomenon of gift-giving. The book concludes with an afterword by Wilfred Dolfsma who emphasises that the puzzles around the phenomenon of the gift are far from being solved and explained.

Part I – theoretical approaches

The book opens up with Frank Adloff's *Institutional Orders and the Gift: A Macrosociological Approach*. His starting point is the fundamental observation that the phenomenon of the gift is ubiquitous and he states: "without gifts no society can exist". Nevertheless, almost all social theories have remained trapped in a dichotomous and reductionist account of this phenomenon. It is either viewed from a utilitarian or an anti-utilitarian ("normativistic") perspective. In other words, gift-giving has been reduced either to people following norms or to self-interested motives. However, these explanations cannot account for a typical and relevant characteristic of the gift: it typically embodies surplus, unconditional provision, non-equivalents and asymmetries (Adloff, 2016; Caillé, 2019; Mauss, 1990). These elements are "constitutive for the creation of sociality". "Giving" is conceived here as the condition for the possibility of any sociality and therefore, of any type of social exchange, both at a micro and macro level. By relying on the theory of a flat ontology of the social (Latour, 2005; Schatzki, 2015) and on an understanding of institutions both as "interdependence breakers" of the logic of the gift and as macro-phenomena that are also produced in concrete situations, Adloff shows how and why the gift is ubiquitous and therefore, cannot and should not be confined to micro-sociological situations such as personal relationships or face-to-face interactions. He also claims that the gift is an omnipresent background mechanism, a symbolic medium of transfer, that enables interaction within institutional orders and across institutional borders. Adloff's conclusions deserve to be mentioned in full:

> gift as a background mechanism for cooperation itself has no clear normative foundation, cannot be forced or secured by self-interest. This mechanism is only weakly institutionalised. Gifts enable manifold and flexible interactions, but these cannot be provided with guarantees and certainties. Gifts are omnipresent, allow interactions and are at the same time extremely fragile.

In his *Beneficence, reciprocity and institutions in Smith*, Benoît Walraevens does justice to the richness and complexity of Smith's thought. He goes well beyond the so-called Adam Smith problem and some biased readings or "uses and abuses of Adam Smith" (Sen, 2011). Moreover, he does not buy into those caricatures of the father of political economy that portray him as the founder of the self-interest paradigm which is at the origin of a long-lasting neglect of altruism, generosity and other regarding attitudes in modern Economics. In his endeavour to reread Smith's other great work, the *Theory of Moral Sentiments*, Walraevens casts a new light on Smith's moral analysis of beneficence and reciprocity and on the influence of institutions on the meaning and practices of gift-giving. Starting from an analysis of Smith's cardinal virtue of beneficence, seen as the "apex of human nature" and presiding over the three key social passions – kindness, generosity, charity – Walraevens reconstructs Smith's careful study of different kinds of unilateral and reciprocal "good offices". These offices arise between people and their multiple causes and make up social bonds. Walraevens dwells on Smith's insights into the notion of obligation in gift/counter gift relationships and on the determining factors and norms of gratitude and reciprocity. Moreover, he shows how, for example, contrary to Mauss' famous characterisation of the three moments of gift-giving – the triple obligation to give, to receive and to give back – Smith's beneficence is "always free" and, as such, implies that we never have any obligation to give, nor to give back. At the same time, Smith's thought presents a nuanced distinction between two forms of beneficence: the generosity of the benefactor, who makes the "initial" gift and the "reciprocal beneficence" or "counter-gift" of the recipient towards his benefactor out of "gratitude". Again, Walraevens claims (in line with Smith and Wilson, 2019) that Smith's views on positive reciprocity or reciprocal beneficence are rich and innovative and provide an alternative to social preference models based on rationality and utility maximisation (see Bolton and Oekenfels, 2000; Falk and Fischbacher, 2006; Fehr and Schmidt, 1999). Moreover, Walraevens explains why Smith thinks that the state should avoid to legally enforce "duties" of beneficence.

Diego Viana's *The gift as total social fact: from Mauss to money* provides yet another relevant theoretical approach to the relation between gift and institutions. Viana starts from a reinterpretation of the key Maussian concept of "total social fact" by examining the fundamental or sociogenic aspect of the gift and by applying this aspect to money and credit in their modern forms. Viana examines three different meanings of the concept of the "gift": (1) as an unconditional transfer, (2) as a distribution system and (3) as the origin of things that would otherwise not exist. The "total social fact" then becomes a key concept which shows the connection between the three meanings of the gift and reveals the sociogenic character of this concept. It is interesting to note how such a re-articulation of the gift as "total social fact" allows Viana to go beyond some traditional interpretations of the gift as opposed to economic "exchange", such as gift vs. commodity, gift economies vs. market economies and so forth. These dichotomies have long been subject to critique (see, for example, Akerlof, 1982). Viana writes:

> even if, given the existence of markets, the relations incarnated in money can take the shape of a commodity and thus, seem to emerge from it, this does not mean that the ontogenesis of money should be traced to the commodity or to market interactions in general.

Moreover, the total social fact is understood as a "fleeting instant" when society fills its collective life with meaning. In this regard, gift-giving ceremonies have a fundamental property: they found and reaffirm the meaning in virtue of which interactions and institutions take place in a society. Viana maintains that at the beginning and at the centre of every society and institutional framework there is a collective gesture of giving. Such an interpretation of the "total social fact" and the sociogenic character of the gift find a significant application in monetary economies. Through a critical-constructive analysis of the conceptual framework of the "French monetary institutionalists" on "monetary sovereignty" and of Richard Werner's (2014) credit experiment as an issue of money by private banks, Viana indicates where it is possible to identify the presence of the gift as that which "brings into existence".

Part II – applied, empirical or experimental case studies

Innovation is essential for a company (Daneels, 2002; Peters and Waterman, 1982; Tidd, 2000) and research and scientists' labs within firms are innovative (Autio et al., 2004; Nelson, 1959), argue Dolfsma and van der

Eijk in *Lab Scientists' Innovativeness: a Case Study of Networks and Favour Exchange.* Understanding the factors and mechanisms that motivate and foster innovativeness is of great importance (Allen and Cohen, 1969; Bouty, 2000; Cross and Cummings, 2004). This research article, employing quantitative methods of analysis, is trying to determine individual lab scientists' contribution to a firm's innovativeness, focusing both on the structure of networks of contacts between individuals (Aalbers and Dolfsma, 2015; Brass, 1984; Dolfsma and Van der Eijk, 2016) and the nature of these contacts in terms of generosity and gift (favour) exchange. In the context of network analysis, one's position in a social network and its impact on innovativeness is discussed alongside the positive moderation of one's network position by generosity (Ensign, 2009). The paper reunites structural embeddedness with relational embeddedness literature (Granovetter, 1992) two concepts conflated by Robert Merton to explain innovativeness of individual lab scientists (see: Merton, 1968, 1988 as well as Rodan and Galunic, 2004). Dolfsma and van der Eijk have produced insights into how structural and relational embeddedness are different theoretically and empirically, but related. Contrary to Merton, being perceived as generous, helps an individual lab scientist only to be more innovative if he or she also has a central position in the structure of the network.

In Arvanitidis and Strolonga's *Gift as conspicuous consumption: the case of the Odyssey,* Homer's classic Greek text is viewed through a Veblenian lens. The text shows how the gift in ancient Greek history can be interpreted as vicarious conspicuous consumption. This chapter offers a fresh introduction to Veblen's analysis of conspicuous consumption (Hodgson, 2014; Veblen, 1912[1899]; Waller, 1982, 2017) and links it convincingly to the core anthropological literature on gift-giving (Camerer, 1988; Malinowski, 1922; Mauss, 1954; Sahlins, 1972; Weiner, 1992 and others). Based on this theoretical introduction, Arvanitidis and Strolonga ask: "how exactly is such a 'pecuniary superiority' demonstrated?" Moreover, they point out that Veblen did not see the gift as a way to establish a reciprocity-based relationship, but that he stressed the unilateral nature and personal dimension of giving and its purpose of establishing and sustaining status, social position and delineating social hierarchies and strata. Arvanitidis and Strolonga are convinced that the Odyssey shows "the characteristics and behaviour of the upper (leisure) class, reflecting the morals, social values, norms, customs and institutions of the time, and provides fertile ground for studying gift-giving behaviour at the dawn of western civilization". They are not the first to observe and interpret gift-giving in the Odyssey (see: Bertelli, 2014; Domingo Gygax, 2013; Donlan, 1982, 1997; Finley, 1955); however, their Veblenian interpretation of dozens of instances reported in the Odyssey demonstrates gift-giving as a typical practice engaged in by a wealthy aristocracy along with other instances of conspicuous waste and vicarious consumption, such as feasts, entertainments, games and wedding ceremonies and less often as compensation/fine or ransom, as can be found in the Iliad. Gifts play a major role in hospitality – the ritual of xenia – and "are offered by the host to the guest, usually a foreigner, who happens to visit the host during a journey". One example is: "the case of the swineherd Eumaeus, a servant, who offers hospitality and provides his own cloak to Odysseus disguised as a beggar". Arvanitidis and Strolonga conclude: "as such, gift-giving behaviour has become a customary norm of reputability and proper behaviour for all, even though it is primarily an aristocratic practice".

Stefan Kesting's *The fluid nature of gifts and grants: an institutional application to the Marshall Plan,* is at the same time an attempt at developing the theory of gift-giving and an application of this framework to a historical case study – the Marshall Plan. The chapter starts with a comparison of Boulding's grants economics (1981) with anthropological and sociological literature on the gift (Gouldner, 1973; Malinowski, 1922/1985; Mauss, 1990[1925]; Polanyi, 1968[1947]; Sahlins, 2004[1972]). While Boulding acknowledges the institutions of altruism, sacrifice and reciprocity featured as motivations in this literature, he adds legitimate utilitarian motives for gift- or grant-giving. Kesting argues for a fluid sequential combination of these three institutions to explain gift-giving. His interpretation of the Marshall Plan shows evidence for all three institutions working in parallel or sequentially. All three: (1) utilitarian motives, (2) willingness to sacrifice and (3) reciprocity were present in this multinational foreign aid programme. It is remarkable that an interpretation based on a book (Steil, 2018) written with a clearly stated intention to show that the Marshall Plan was mainly a geostrategic instrument employed by the United States to win the Cold War can be used as a source to gather evidence for non-utilitarian motives. Moreover, the case study demonstrates that even at such a high level of aggregation, there can be gifts which are characterised not only by utilitarian institutions, but also by altruism and reciprocity.

Kalpana Khanal and Ruchira Sen provide, to quote directly the title of their contribution: *An Institutional Analysis of the Dowry System in South Asia.* While mainstream economics literature, with particular reference to neoclassical economics and formalist anthropology, discusses dowry as a groom-price, this ahistorical approach fails to account for the evolution of the pre-capitalist dowry systems in modern capitalism (Arunachalam and Trevon, 2016; Banerjee, 1999; Becker, 1981; Tambiah, 1973). In this regard, dowry in South Asia bears its own peculiarities that seem to challenge this literature for at least two reasons. First of all, dowry gifts in South Asia are in principle non-reciprocal, and this raises the question of why they are given when there is no expectation of return. However, some reciprocal reasons for the practice are discussed in the chapter. For instance, that: "dowry is seen as a way of compensating the groom and his family for the economic support they would provide to the new wife". Second, while dowry gifts have become economically irrelevant around the world, prospective South Asian grooms have continued to demand increasingly larger dowries. Such puzzles lead Khanal and Sen to search for alternative theoretical lenses, needed to provide a more accurate explanation of this phenomenon. They apply a substantivist method that combines economic history (Oldenburg, 2003; Sheel, 1999) and culture and anthropology (Prasad, 1999; Rankin, 2004; Srinivasan and Lee, 2004; Tenhunen, 2008) – based on Mauss (1990[1925]); Polanyi (1957[1944]) to explain the motives for dowry giving and the interactions between dowry and market systems in South Asia. By looking at the economy as embedded within a social, cultural and historical context, they investigate and explain the continued prevalence of dowry in South Asia despite non-explicit reciprocity and market incursions.

In this first of two policy-oriented applications of the gift, entitled: *In search of relevant financial regulation: some lessons from the gift-economics*, Ülgen and Sakovich propose to take the perspective of the gift as a source of social capital which can support reciprocity-based regulation to mitigate the risk in capitalism of: "destabilizing features of a financially liberalized and self-regulation-based economy". This kind of regulation has similarities with Minsky's (1986) institutional as well as Katona's (1975) psychological and Baddeley's (2019) behavioural perspective and is couched as an alternative to the rules imposed by governments on financial markets. This approach of implicit socially embedded regulation departs from the hypothesis "that a gift-economics approach may provide a social rules-related guide to shape individuals' behaviour within society". The argument is based on a thorough institutional analysis (Dillard, 1987; Minsky, 1982; Mitchell, 1916) of the growing financialisation of the global economy characterised by a money manager capitalism (Wray, 2009) with a tendency of instability and too loose regulation (Wray, 2011) during the last four decades. The end result of all this mismanagement was the Global Financial Crisis. This historical and theoretical exposition is followed by a detailed critique of the current framework of financial regulation (Tarullo, 2019) and an overview of the workings of reciprocity rules of "gift-economics" which could support a more prudential and sustainable finance sector. All these explorations are contrasted and drawn together to suggest: "… a restatement of the characteristics of a gift relation and its possible implementation as a systemic stabilizer within a capitalist financial framework … in search for an alternative financial regulation and supervision system". The conclusion is, in a nutshell, that gift-giving has the potential of providing stabilising norms of obligation for the financial system. However, these norms need to be supported by an organising visible hand through collective action (Lapavitsas, 2002). Such a system of stability will not arise spontaneously because "the power of reciprocity in an individualistic market society is not as strong as the social constraints and reciprocity that could be in force in a traditional society".

The second policy-oriented applications of the gift in Zachorowska-Mazurkiewicz's *Principles of exchange and reciprocity in the context of providing care* explores the question whether the mode, in which care is delivered, determines the place of care in modern economies. Founded on the works of Karl Polanyi (1957[1944]), Jean-Louis Laville (2010a, b) and Douglas C. North

(1977), the analysis starts from three modes of transfer: "(1) reciprocity and gift-giving, (2) redistribution and central authority, and (3) exchange and market". In recognising care activities as crucial for the economic system and linking institutional thought (Hodgson, 2004; Polanyi, 1968[1947]) with feminist theory (Badgett and Folbre, 1999; Folbre, 2001; Folbre and Nelson, 2000), the chapter shows how care is shaped by the institutional settings attributed to the modes of transfer. In the first section the three modes of transfer are defined, distinguished and critically discussed in detail. Particular emphasis is placed on gift-giving and reciprocity (Kolm, 2006). While engaging with contesting arguments, Zachorowska-Mazurkiewicz endorses and emphasises the Mausian perspective that "most gifting takes place in a context of reciprocity". Based on feminist economics literature (Himmelweit, 2007; Standing, 2009), the next section introduces care as an interpersonal and often intimate activity "understood as the provision of personal services to meet those basic physical and mental needs that allow a person to function at a socially determined acceptable level of capability, comfort and safety". However, care is at the same time wage labour, but also work that is often delivered unpaid and mostly by women in the family context (Himmelweit, 1995; Nelson, 1999; Tronto, 1993). Zachorowska-Mazurkiewicz follows Titmuss (1972), Sandel (2013) as well as Skidelsky and Skidelsky (2012) in stressing that dominant market exchange as a mode of delivery of care will undermine and drive out the other two modes of transfer. Since "care is a service that has been and still is predominantly transferred as a gift between family members, and is based on the expectation of reciprocity" the marketisation of it poses the risk, if not the threat of under-valuation of care and of provision of merely low-quality care.

Notes

1 Paolo Silvestri acknowledges funding from the People Programme (Marie Curie Actions) of the European Union's Seventh Framework Programme (FP7/2007-2013) under REA grant agreement no. 609305.

2 In parallel, we have also edited a symposium for the *Journal of Institutional Economics* collecting five more contributions to an economics of the gift. See: "Institutional analysis and the gift: an introduction to the symposium", DOI: 10.1017/S1744137420000223.

References

Aalbers, R. and Dolfsma, W. 2015. *Innovation Networks: Managing the Networked Firm*. London and New York: Routledge. DOI: 10.4324/9781315757520

Adloff, F. 2016. *Gifts of Cooperation, Mauss and Pragmatism*. London and New York: Routledge. DOI: 10.4324/9781315692982

Akerlof, G. 1982. Labor Contracts as Partial Gift Exchange. *Quarterly Journal of Economics*. **97**(4), pp. 543–569. DOI: 10.2307/1885099

Allen, T. J. and Cohen, S. I. 1969. Information Flow in Research and Development Laboratories. *Administrative Science Quarterly*. **14**, pp. 12–19. DOI: 10.2307/2391357

Arunachalam, R. and Trevon D. L. 2016. On the Heterogeneity of Dowry Motives. *Journal of Population Economics.* **29**(1), pp. 135–166. DOI: 10.1007/s00148-015-0544-1

Autio, E., Hameri, A. and Vuola, O. 2004. A Framework of Industrial Knowledge Spillovers in Big-Science Centers. *Research Policy.* **33**, pp. 107–126. DOI: 10.1016/S0048–7333(03)00105-7

Baddeley, M. 2019. *Behavioural Economics and Finance.* Abingdon: Routledge. DOI: 10.4324/9781315211879

Badgett, M. V. L. and Folbre, N. 1999. Assigning Care: Gender Norms and Economic Outcomes. *International Labour Review.* **138**(3), pp. 311–326. DOI: 10.1111/j.1564–913X.1999.tb00390.x

Banerjee, K. 1999. Gender Stratification and the Contemporary Marriage Market in India. *Journal of Family Issues.* **20**(5), pp. 648–676. DOI: 10.1111/j.1564–913X.1999.tb00390.x

Becker, G. S. 1981. *A Treatise on the Family.* Cambridge, MA and London: Harvard University Press.

Bertelli, L. 2014. The Ratio of Gift-Giving in the Homeric Poems. In: Carla, F. and Gori, M. Eds. *Gift-Giving and the Embedded Economy in Ancient Greece and Rome.* Heidelberg: Winter, pp. 103–134.

Bolton, G. and Ockenfels, A. 2000. ERC: A Theory of Equity, Reciprocity and Competition. *American Economic Review.* **90**(1), pp. 166–93. DOI: 10.1257/aer.90.1.166

Boulding, K. E. 1981. *A Preface to Grants Economics: The Economy of Love and Fear.* New York: Praeger.

Bouty, I. 2000. Interpersonal and Interaction Influences on Informal Resource Exchanges Between R&D Researchers across Organizational Boundaries. *Academy of Management Journal.* **43**(1), pp. 50–65. DOI: 10.2307/1556385

Brass, D. 1984. Being in the Right Place: A Structural Analysis of Individual Influence in an Organization. *Administrative Science Quarterly.* **29**, pp. 518–539.

Caillé, A. 2019. *Extensions du domaine du don. Demander – Donner – Recevoir – Rendre.* Arles: Actes Sud.

Camerer, C. 1988. Gifts as Economic Signals and Social Symbols. *American Journal of Sociology.* **94**, pp. S180–S214. DOI: 10.1086/228946.

Cross, R. and Cummings, J. N. 2004. Tie and Network Correlations of Individual Performance in Knowledge-Intensive Work. *Academy of Management Journal.* **47**(6), pp. 928–937. DOI: 10.2307/20159632

Danneels, E. 2002. The Dynamics of Product Innovation and Firm Competences. *Strategic Management Journal.* **23**, pp. 105–1121. DOI: 10.1002/smj.275

Dillard, D. 1987. Money as an Institution of Capitalism. *Journal of Economic Issues.* **21**(4), pp. 1623–1647. DOI: 10.1080/00213624.1987.11504717

Dolfsma, W. and Van der Eijk, R. A. 2016. Distances in Organization: Innovation in an R&D Lab. *British Journal of Management.* **27**(2), pp. 271–286.

Domingo Gygax, M. 2013. Gift-Giving and Power Relationships in Greek Social Praxis and Public Discourse. In: Satlow, M. L. Ed. *The Gift in Antiquity. The Ancient World: Comparative Histories.* Malden, MA and Oxford: Wiley-Blackwell, pp. 45–60.

Donlan, W. 1982. Reciprocities in Homer. *Classical World.* **75**(3), pp. 137–175.

Donlan, W. 1997. The Homeric Economy. In: Morris, I. and Powell, B. Eds. *A New Companion to Homer.* Leiden: Brill, pp. 649–667. DOI: 10.1163/9789004217607_029

Ensign, P. C. 2009. *Knowledge Sharing among Scientists.* New York: Palgrave Macmillan.

Falk, A. and Fischbacher, U. 2006. A Theory of Reciprocity. *Games and Economic Behavior.* **54**, pp. 293–315. DOI: 10.1016/j.geb.2005.03.001

Fehr, E. and Schmidt, K. 1999. A Theory of Fairness, Competition and Cooperation. *The Quarterly Journal of Economics.* **114**(3), 817–68. DOI: 10.1162/003355399556151

Finley, M. I. 1955. Marriage, Sale and Gift in the Homeric World. *Revue International des Droits de l' Antiquité.* **3**(2), pp. 167–194.

Folbre, N. 2001. *The Invisible Heart: Economics and Family Values.* New York: The New Press.

Folbre, N. and Nelson, J. A. 2000. For Love or Money – or Both? *Journal of Economic Perspectives.* **14**(4), pp. 123–140. DOI: 10.1257/jep.14.4.123

Gouldner, A. W. 1973. The Importance of Something for Nothing, Chapter 9. In: Gouldner, A. W. Ed. *For Sociology – Renewal and Critique in Sociology Today.* Hammondsworth: Pelican Books, pp. 260–299.

Granovetter, M. S. 1992. Problems of Explanations in Economic Sociology. In: Nohria, N. and Eccles, R. Eds. *Networks and Organizations: Structure, Form and Action.* Boston, MA: Harvard Business School, pp. 25–56.

Himmelweit, S. 1995. The Discovery of "Unpaid Work": The Social Consequences of the Expansion of "Work." *Feminist Economics.* **1**(2), pp. 1–19. DOI: 10.1080/714042229

Himmelweit, S. 2007. The Prospects for Caring: Economic Theory and Policy Analysis. *Cambridge Journal of Economics.* **31**(4), pp. 581–599. DOI: 10.1093/cje/bem011

Hodgson, G. M. 2004. *The Evolution of Institutional Economics; Agency, Structure and Darwinism in American Institutionalism.* London and New York: Routledge.

Hodgson, G. M. 2014. Thorstein Veblen: The Father of Evolutionary and Institutional Economics. In: Reinert, E. S. and Viano, F. L. Eds. *Thorstein Veblen: Economics for an Age of Crises.* London: Anthem, pp. 283–295.

Katona, G. A. 1975. *Psychological Economics.* New York: Elsevier.

Kolm, S.-Ch. 2006. Reciprocity: Its Scope, Rationales, and Consequences. In: Kolm, S.-Ch. and Mercier Ythier, J. Eds. *Handbook of the Economics of Giving, Altruism and Reciprocity.* Amsterdam: Elsevier, pp. 371–541.

Lapavitsas, C. 2002. Commodity versus Gift as Metaphor for Market versus Non-Market Relations. *SOAS Working Papers* No. 127. Department of Economics, University of London.

Latour, B. 2005. *Reassembling the Social: An Introduction to Actor-Network-Theory.* Oxford: Oxford University Press.

Laville, J. L. 2010a. Plural Economy, Chapter 7. In: Hart, K., Laville, J. L. and Cattani, A. D. Eds. *The Human Economy.* Cambridge: Polity, pp. 77–83.

Laville, J. L. 2010b. Solidarity Economy, Chapter 21. In: Hart, K., Laville, J. L. and Cattani, A. D. Eds. *The Human Economy.* Cambridge: Polity, pp. 225–235.

Malinowski, B. 1922/1985. *Argonauts of the Western Pacific.* London: George Routledge & Sons.

Mauss, M. 1990[1925]. *The Gift.* New York and London: Norton.

Merton, R. K. 1968. The Matthew Effect in Science. *Science.* **159**, pp. 56–63.

Merton, R. K. 1988. The Matthew Effect in Science, II – Cumulative Advantage and the Symbolism of Intellectual Property. *Isis.* **79**(4), pp. 606–623. DOI: 10.1086/354848

Minsky, H. P. 1982. *Can "It" Happen Again? Essays on Instability and Finance.* Armonk: M.E. Sharpe, Inc.

Minsky, H. P. 1986. The Evolution of Financial Institutions and the Performance of the Economy. *Journal of Economic Issues*. **29**(2), pp. 345–353.

Mitchell, W. 1916. The Role of Money in Economic Theory. *American Economic Review*. **6**(1), pp. 140–161.

Nelson, J. A. 1999. Of Markets and Martyrs: Is It OK to Pay Well for Care? *Feminist Economics*. **5**(3), pp. 43–59. DOI: 10.1080/135457099337806.

Nelson, R. R. 1959. The Simple Economics of Basic Scientific Research. *Journal of Political Economy*. **57**, pp. 297–306. DOI: 10.1086/258177

North, D. C. 1977. Markets and Other Allocation Systems in History: The Challenge of Karl Polanyi. *Journal of European Economic History*. **6**(3), pp. 703–716.

Oldenburg, V. T. 2003. *Dowry Murder: The Imperial Origins of a Cultural Crime*. New Delhi: Oxford University Press.

Peters, T. J. and Waterman, R. H. 1982. *In Search of Excellence*. New York: Harper and Row.

Polanyi, K. 1957[1944]. *The Great Transformation – The Political and Economic Origins of Our Time*. Boston, MA: Beacon Press.

Polanyi, K. 1968[1947]. Our Obsolete Market Mentality. In: Dalton, G. Ed. *Primitive, Archaic, and Modern Economies – Essays of Karl Polanyi*. New York: Anchor Books, pp. 59–77.

Polanyi, K. 1968[1957]. The Economy as Instituted Process. In: Dalton, G. Ed. *Primitive, Archaic, and Modern Economies – Essays of Karl Polanyi*. New York: Anchor Books, pp. 139–174.

Prasad, M. 1999. The Morality of Market Exchange: Love, Money, and Contractual Justice. *Sociological Perspectives*. **42**(2), pp. 181–214. DOI: 10.2307/1389627

Rankin, K. N. 2004. *The Cultural Politics of Markets: Economic Liberalization and Social Change in Nepal*. Toronto and Buffalo: University of Toronto Press.

Rodan, S. and Galunic, C. 2004. More Than Network Structure: How Knowledge Heterogeneity Influences Managerial Performance and Innovativeness. *Strategic Management Journal*. **25**, pp. 541–562. DOI: 10.1002/smj.398

Sahlins, M. 2004[1972]. *Stone Age Economics*. London and New York: Routledge.

Sandel, M. J. 2013. *What Money Can't Buy: The Moral Limits of Markets*. London: Penguin Books.

Schatzki, T. 2015. Spaces of Practices and of Large Social Phenomena. *EspacesTemps.net, Travaux*. **24**, March 2015, no pagination.

Sen, A. 2011. Uses and Abuses of Adam Smith. *History of Political Economy*. **43**(2), pp. 257–271. DOI: 10.1215/00182702–1257388

Sheel, R. 1999. *The Political Economy of Dowry*. New Delhi: Manohar Publishers.

Skidelsky, R. and Skidelsky, E. 2012. *How Much Is Enough? Money and the Good Life*. New York: Other Press.

Smith, V. and Wilson, B. 2019. *Humanomics. Moral Sentiments and the Wealth of Nations for the Twenty-First Century*. Cambridge: Cambridge University Press.

Srinivasan, P. and Lee, G. R. 2004. The Dowry System in Northern India: Women's Attitudes and Social Change. *Journal of Marriage and Family*. **66**(5), pp. 108–1117. DOI: 10.1111/j.0022–2445.2004.00081.x

Standing, G. 2009. *Work after Globalization. Building Occupational Citizenship*. Cheltenham and Northampton: Edward Elgar.

Steil, B. 2018. *The Marshall Plan: Dawn of the Cold War*. London: Simon and Schuster.

Tambiah, S. J. 1973. Dowry and Bride Wealth and the Property Rights of Women in South Asia. In: Goody, J. and Tambiah, S. J. Eds. *Bride Wealth and Dowry.* Cambridge: Cambridge University Press, pp. 59–169.

Tarullo, D. K. 2019. Financial Regulation: Still Unsettled a Decade After the Crisis. *Journal of Economic Perspectives.* **33**(1), pp. 61–80. DOI: 10.1257/jep.33.1.61

Tenhunen, S. 2008. The Gift of Money: Rearticulating Tradition and Market Economy in Rural West Bengal. *Modern Asian Studies.* **42**(5), pp. 1035–1055. DOI: 10.1017/S0026749X06002629

Tidd, J. 2001. Innovation Management in Context: Environment, Organization and Performance. *International Journal of Management Reviews.* **3**(3), pp. 169–183. DOI: 10.1109/EMR.2017.7968101

Titmuss, R. 1972. *The Gift Relationship: From Human Blood to Social Policy.* New York: Vintage Books.

Veblen, T. 1912[1899]. *The Theory of the Leisure Class: An Economic Study of Institutions.* New York: Huebsch.

Waller, W. T. Jr. 1982. The Evolution of Veblenian Dichotomy: Veblen, Hamilton, Ayres, and Foster. *Journal of Economic Issues.* **16**(3), pp. 757–771. DOI: 10.1080/00213624.1982.11504031.

Waller, W. T. Jr. 2017. Reconsidering Thorstein Veblen's Use of Instincts. In: Plotkin, S. Ed. *The Anthem Companion to Thorstein Veblen.* London: Anthem Press, pp. 39–67.

Weiner, A. B. 1992. *Inalienable Possessions: The Paradox of Keeping-While-Giving.* Berkeley: University of California Press.

Werner, R. 2014. Can Banks Individually Create Money Out of Nothing? The Theories and the Empirical Evidence. *International Review of Financial Analysis.* **38**, pp. 1–19. DOI: 10.1016/j.irfa.2014.07.015

Wray, R. 2009. The Rise and Fall of Money Manager Capitalism: A Minskian Approach. *Cambridge Journal of Economics.* **33**, pp. 807–828. DOI: 10.1093/cje/bep024

Wray, R. 2011. Minsky Crisis. *Levy Economics Institute of Bard College Working Paper,* No. **659**, March.

Part I

Theoretical approaches

2 Institutional orders and the gift

A macrosociological approach

Frank Adloff

Introduction

This chapter is guided by a simple thought: people give each other a wide variety of things. They help each other, listen to each other; they give each other objects, attention, recognition and encouragement. Beyond these everyday actions, there are also greater gifts: people forgive each other, or perhaps they give something unusual and unexpected in the form of extraordinary help. Both forms of giving are constitutive of society, for without gifts no society can exist. Yet almost all social theories have woefully neglected this dimension of human action. Gifts are either ignored or explained away. Typically, gifts are accounted for in two ways: either they are reduced to the fact that people do what norms expect of them; or they are attributed to motives of self-interest. However, there is a human tendency to the gift that cannot be explained in a normativistic and utilitarian manner – gifts embody moments of surplus and unconditionality, which are constitutive for the creation of sociality. Thus, at the base of the social – both in the micro and in the macro realm – are non-equivalences and asymmetries, because giving is not reducible to the exchange of equivalent values (cf. Adloff, 2016; Caillé, 2019; Mauss, 1990). On the contrary: even exchange is based on the fact that we are able to give without directly receiving or taking something for it. There is a gap between giving and responding, which is in part barely visible, but nonetheless very central.

Micro vs. macro? Where's the gift?

But the question is whether or not the logic of the gift is limited to the small area of personal relationships or face-to-face interactions. Or even more narrowly: perhaps in modern times the logic of the gift only applies to friends and family circles? A typical argument would be that while the gift may still play a major role in personal environments – in the private sphere – larger institutional and structural phenomena, thus social macrophenomena, lie beyond the influence of the gift. However, this point depends entirely on how one defines micro- and macrophenomena.

If one defines institutional macrophenomena as a social level sui generis, which is not ascribed to microsituations then, the criticism of gift theory may be true. However, if one rejects this view and assumes a flat ontology of the social with Schatzki (2015) and Latour (2005), without at the same time pursuing methodological individualism, the perspective changes significantly. Then institutional orders such as "capitalism" are no longer "above" microsituations, but are to be reconstructed from other specific social situations, which are located at the same socio-ontological level – such as the interaction between two children in the playground, or the conversation between a professor and a student. A macrosociological perspective will thus be outlined, which follows the idea of flat ontology and can therefore ask where the logic of the gift can come into play and where not.

All thought about macrosocial phenomena is based initially on a simple sociological intuition: in every concrete action situation, we experience that our situation is pre-shaped by "things" outside the situation. For example: we have not invented the language that we use; the worker discovers that not only is a remote company management in another country behind his employment contract, but also a whole legal tradition. Political decisions affect many more people than our everyday decisions, just like the decisions of large transnational corporations dominate our everyday situations. While we can make individual investment decisions, the financial markets seem to create structural guidelines, etc.

Bruno Latour emphasises that although we have to analyse how situations are influenced by other non-situational actors and actions, one should not however speak of the "context" of a situation. The other situations do not underlie the concrete interaction situation – they are at the same level, and the question must be how situations are linked with each other and how can it be that distant situations can have an impact on a local situation (cf. Hirschauer, 2014). Hence, "macro" does not denote a comprehensive place or overarching or low-lying structures. Macrophenomena are also created locally in concrete situations, in which linking these situations through specific media with other situations is successful. These media may be technical infrastructures, money or political power channels (see below). They are means of the spatio-temporal increase of distance (cf. Giddens, 1990). The law succeeds, for example, in all people in a given territory having to be guided by it. In this sense, "Wall Street" is not an overarching structure; it is also just as local and interactive as other interactions. It is, however, associated with many other interaction situations through chains of effect and thus "more powerful" than the interaction between a customer and a vendor.

Nonetheless, the special feature of many current situations of interaction today is that they no longer function solely as face-to-face interactions. Already writing letters or later the telephone have either pulled interactions apart temporally, or limited them to the auditory. We currently experience a variety of computer-based interactions that are no longer dependent on the physical co-presence of interaction partners. Karin Knorr-Cetina (2009) speaks of synthetic situations that are arranged on computer screens and can encompass potentially large spatial dimensions. Reciprocal, comprehensive observations of the actors' expressions are then usually no longer possible, because they write or because they communicate with each other through graphics, tables, figures, etc. In the global communication networks, physical co-presence is displaced by temporal co-presence – response presence instead of embodied presence (ibid., p. 74). However, these "global structures" only exist in specific situations. Thereby, micro- and macrophenomena are not located at qualitatively different levels, it is more a matter of gradual thus quantitative differences: namely one can assume with Randall Collins (1981) that macrophenomena capture more people, expand farther spatially, and have a longer duration.

In the process, the "more powerful" situations do not just blindly affect the other situations, they do not simply develop an objective force, by which the "macrosituation" influences other situations. The effectiveness of remote situations is always also framed and staged – and thus they are also performatively effective as macrophenomena. In everyday situations, actors also produce institutional orders and macrophenomena through abstraction and representation. For example, something is described as global and placed in the foreground – the "global" is thus produced. Sociology participates immensely in these constructions, such as when its scholars speak of "society" (Durkheim, Parsons, Luhmann, etc.). However, other actors also performatively bring along such macroentities – for instance, when they say that the middle classes want something, that nations compete with each other, or that the Catholic Church condemns this or that (cf. Coulter, 2001). Here, specific technologies of representation (Knorr-Cetina, 1981, p. 34) are applied, such as the use of econometrics or statistics to construct economic macrophenomena. Thus, the GDP is not a macrophenomenon that exists in itself, but a mathematical design by statisticians, who standardise events, free them of contexts, and apply summary procedures (cf. Cicourel, 1981).

Thus we note that the world of interactions cannot be separated from a world of institutional orders and macrostructures. Rather, social macro-orders are produced in concrete situations – either by situations extending temporally and spatially through effect chains, or by invoking macrophenomena in concrete situations and thereby creating them performatively. Nicos Mouzelis summarises this position as follows: "I argue that interactions between concrete social actors (whether or not in cases of copresence) can be micro as well as macro" (Mouzelis, 1992, p. 122). However, one should discern not only different situations in their range but also types of actors. There are actors whose actions have far-reaching consequences for other actors. For example, collective actors (parties, ministries, businesses, etc.) or very powerful individuals who have available a lot of economic, political or cultural power: "Collective actors, through their democratic or nondemocratic representatives, and mega actors, because of their privileged position within the economic, political, or cultural division of labor, often generate interactions whose consequences 'stretch' very widely in time and space" (ibid., p. 123). For this reason, Mouzelis also criticises the way Erving Goffman and Anne Rawls (1987) speak of an interaction order sui generis. For him, it makes no sense to juxtapose institutional order with interaction order.

In my opinion, however, an important point escapes Mouzelis: the gift logic of interaction orders is based largely on interaction participants being able to really engage in the logic of the situation. In contrast, an institutionally stronger, prestructured situation works as if the involved actors were remote-controlled, they follow role scripts and less the requirements of the situation. Not only synthetic situations that no longer allow fully perceiving the expressions of others, but also situations in which a role action dominates reduce the egalitarian and cooperative potential of interactions, which is based on the logic of the gift. Therefore, we can distinguish interactions according to the extent to which they can actually bring the inherent logic of the gift to bear there or not. In this respect, it is thus useful to distinguish the interaction order from an institutional and impersonal order.

Personal relationships allow the interaction partners to engage in the interaction, to be considerate of each other, and mutually coordinate their actions. They engage in the game of the gift. Impersonal relationships are primarily constituted by organisational memberships. They are based on ego no longer directly exchanging with alter, but ego exchanging with a third party (such as an organisation). If one interacts with an organisation member, he or she is bound by the organisation; she follows the rules of interaction predetermined by the organisation, without betraying much about herself. One can then no longer abandon oneself to the local dynamics of interaction, but interacts in the shadow of the organisation membership. One no longer takes the other into consideration, but the expectations of the respective organisation. Thereby, the logic of gift and reciprocity is frequently undermined. Thus, the police are not allowed to exchange favours with the traffic offender; or teachers are prohibited, for educational reasons, from making themselves dependent on the devotion of individual students.

These interdependence disruptions are only possible because organisations can either offer their members bonuses or enforce sanctions. This means that the logic of gift and reciprocity does not exist between members of different organisations, but that owing to circumstances they exist inside of organisations. Normally, exchange is spoken of here: as a member of an organisation, one exchanges freedom of action for a salary (cf. Luhmann, 1964). At the same time, the exchange with an organisation implies that one can no longer arbitrarily exchange with anyone outside the organisation. This explains the objectifying and reifying character of an interaction with members of an organisation, because they are indeed rewarded precisely for this objectification. Organisations can thus be considered primarily responsible for the breaking of solidarity of interaction situations.

This process is normatively enabled by the idea that the breaking of solidarity in everyday life is overcompensated at a different level. Because through the modern division of labour, everyone benefits, in turn, from the law, the inherent logic of administrations and bureaucracies, from the action logic of corporations, etc. Viewed in this light, reciprocal exchange no longer takes place between people, but at the level of the social division of labour (Durkheim). In this context, Peter Blau speaks of secondary exchange, which "is superimposed upon the primary one and indirect transactions become substituted for direct ones as the result of normative expectations and value orientation" (Blau, 1964, p. 5).

Inside organisations, diverse means are employed to persuade the members of cooperation and compliance (cf. Kühl, 2014). These means, however, are not to be solely interpreted as utilitarian or normative. First, coercion is only an effective motivational tool in state power organisations like armies. Second, more often members are offered attractive action targets: one motivates performance by offering objectives, with which the organisation members can identify. Third, membership bonds are produced through collegiality. One willingly accepts tasks, because otherwise their colleagues will have to do them. This clearly shows how the logic of gift and reciprocity comes into play inside of organisations. Then the inherent logic of interaction is no longer effective between representatives of different organisations, but between organisation members of the same organisation. Fourth, one offers organisation members a payment in the form of money. Finally, organisations try to make the actions to be carried out also as attractive as possible.

With these five methods (cf. Kühl, 2014), organisations ensure that when entering an organisation, members forego precisely defining their activities in advance. A margin of indifference remains, which the organisation can have at their disposal. Thereby, members provide their organisation with a blank check of sorts. They sell their labour and commitment in a very generalised way. One pledges a kind of general obedience to the concerns of the organisation. Thus, one cannot speak here of an exchange in the strict sense: the expectations of the organisation are too unspecific. And yet, members of the organisation are willing to get involved in this "deal". From my perspective, this is only explicable if one recognises that organisations rely on the motivation of people to give something and themselves. Formulated in a quasi-Marxist manner, one can also say that they exploit the human tendency to the gift. In the shadow of the formal exchange, informal relationships always emerge in organisations, which are based on the logic of the gift and without which the organisation could not survive. Without the intrinsic commitment of organisation members to give something to colleagues or the whole of the organisation, without the creativity of the members, without the maintenance of formal procedures, without collegiality, and without the tendency to want to be recognised as a giver, no organisation can manage (cf. Hodson, 1991). Even modern (capitalist) societies are built on a foundation of "communist" relationships: "communism is the foundation of all human sociability" (Graeber, 2010, p. 206). Familial and friendly relations, spontaneous cooperation, collegiality, friendly gestures, and conversations – for

David Graeber, all of these are examples of a communist everyday morality that cannot be adequately comprehended by utilitarian or normativistic social theories. Here, the gift – trust, community spirit, dedication, and love – can be decoupled from the principle of clear-cut reciprocity in a specific way.

However, the logic of the gift and reciprocity can also come into effect between organisations. Under the keyword "embeddedness", there is meanwhile a long sociological tradition that shows that personal contacts and networks across organisational and institutional boundaries are essential for the prosperity of companies and entire industries (classically: Granovetter, 1985, also: Granovetter, 2017). Thus, the studies by Brian Uzzi (1997, 1999) show that companies obtain better credit terms if they are integrated into the networks of banks, or that economic efficiency increases when companies are integrated into interfirm networks.

To conclude, the general manner of speaking about an exclusive applicability of the gift theory in the private sphere and an autonomy of macrophenomena, which have fully decoupled from gift relations, is untenable. Each macrophenomenon is produced situationally and locally. It depends on seeing where mediated "thin" interaction situations allow the logic of the gift only incompletely and where organisations also hedge the power of the gift with their role expectations as interdependence breakers. The example of the interorganisational networks shows that this is never fully done. Thus, it is essential to look empirically for where the gift comes up against institutional borders and where it is permitted and required (such as within organisations). Many contemporary environmental problems are based on the fact that negative externalities are produced with respect to third parties and no networks of egalitarian giving and responding exist with these third parties (cf. Lessenich, 2019). There, where instead mistrust prevails, the logic of utilitarian calculation takes hold. Take the example of the stagnating international cooperation in the area of climate change: here it would be essential to design the negotiating arenas, in which representatives of various collective actors (nations, corporations, NGOs, etc.) come together, such that the participants can get involved with the shared interaction situation and be caught in the situational slipstream of gift and counter-gift. This is not possible as long as they are tied to rigid role action by their home organisations and act as if remotely controlled. The organisational logic then suppresses the interpersonal logic (cf. Messner et al., 2013, p. 27ff.).

Gifts and symbolic media of communication

Wherein lies the specific binding effect of the gift compared with that of the medium of language? Only humans have indeed developed a language that they can use for the coordination of cooperation processes. Why should giving a thing have a greater binding effect than talking with each other? In sociology, there are two roughly divided views on the binding effect of language, as paradigmatically represented by Jürgen Habermas and Niklas

Luhmann. For Habermas (1987, 1996) there is an inherent telos of understanding in language. Through the exchange of arguments, we can communicate about and agree on the objective world of things, normative questions in the area of the social, and questions of truthfulness in the subjective sense; moreover, we can enter binding obligations.

Niklas Luhmann (1995, 2013), however, has stressed that language in particular unleashes potential dissent. Language creates distance from the world and produces more dissonance than consensus. Language enables us to step out of the everyday life of the taken for granted and to construct abstract worlds that are not tied back to the experience world of action. The more that is explicated, the less that remains shared as a matter of course and the more communication participants are individualised (cf. Klemm, 2015). Thus for Luhmann, language does not bind the involved parties to each other, but multiplies the perspectives and releases more potential for negation. Modern society responded to this with the development of symbolically generalised communication media, such as money, truth and power which are institutionalised in the realms of economy, science and politics. Thus, the symbolic function of money consists in symbiotically combining with the needs of people and forming a preference and motivation for possessing money. In communications media, the world-creating dimension of language is coupled with binding effects in the form of specific behavioural willingness. Language alone, however, is not aimed at the acquisition of action commitments. Language indeed enables communication, but it cannot alone guarantee the binding success of a communication.

Habermas (2012) has also approached this view in recent years. He now believes that the binding effect of the language is rather weak. For Habermas, the greatest binding force of language is apparent in the archaic entanglement of myth and ritual. Earlier religious interpretations of the world already involved the power for a linguistic understanding and opening up of the world, but maintained a close connection to ritual and drew from this its power of persuasion. Thus, linguistic binding force is rooted there in the sacred, which powerfully imposes itself especially in the ritual practice of people – just as Émile Durkheim (2008) described in his book on religion (cf. Bellah, 2005). Rituals stabilise group cohesion more strongly than narrative explanations can through the medium of language. Because with the evolution of language, the close relations between perceptions of conditions in the world, expressions of one's own affects and the associated behavioural expectations of others rupture. In the call "Fire!" these three references are conflated into a syndrome: here exist coalesced into each other a status description, an expression, and a normative request in the same moment. In contrast, more complex expressions tear the propositional, expressive and apellative meaning components apart and in this way make a binding effect more unlikely.

Habermas (2012) does not see a way back to this archaic binding effect of language (which is based on the interaction of myth and ritual). According to him, the rationalised and intellectualised modernity must live with the weak binding force of language. He sees only remainders of the binding effect of the sacral complex: with some religious communities, he observes the ability to keep their traditions alive and effective through the bond to ritual. To some extent, members of religious communities seem to have to maintain contact with archaic experiences. In this interpretation, Durkheim's legacy makes itself felt negatively. For Durkheim, binding effects of rituals could only emerge in the extraordinary moments of collective ecstasy in contact with the sacred; in contrast, the profane everyday life can develop no binding force from itself.

With Marcel Mauss (1990), we can now set the binding effect of the gift against the Habermasian (and Durkheimian) model. The gift includes a ritual side, which is universally known in every culture. It has a sacred aspect, by transporting the *hau* or an affective valuation, as well as the alienness and freedom of the giver. In it exists at a level of gesture communication – thus basically before the grammatically differentiated language – the three binding effects named by Habermas coalesced: the gift conveys the offer of a definition of the situation, it contains a strong moment of self-expression, and it acts appellatively and normatively. Objective, subjective and social aspects of the world are symbolically summarised and equipped with binding effect. Thus, the gift can be considered a symbolic mechanism for increasing the probability of acceptance of communications offerings, similar to the symbolically generalised communication media such as money or truth. Thereby, it involves a mechanism that is also able to develop a binding effect in modern society. If the gift accompanies linguistic communication, it can – thus my thesis – compensate for language's lack of binding effect, which creates distances and a multiplication of perspectives.

In what follows, I will develop the thesis that the gift represents a background mechanism, which can accompany all micro and macro communications in modern societies. Just like other communication media, it reduces the likelihood that communication offers are rejected. First, Parsons' concept of symbolic media of exchange will be considered. As generally known, Talcott Parsons (1969) constructed in his later work four social subsystems, each of which has to solve a specific functional problem: economy, politics, societal community and the cultural fiduciary system. They form the social system, and this, in turn, is together with the system of the behaviour, the system of the personality and the system of culture subsystem of the parent general action system.

Parsons assigns an institutionalised "medium" to each social subsystem: money to the economy, power to politics, influence to the societal community and commitments to the cultural fiduciary system. These media serve the intra- and intersystemic exchange processes and represent for Parsons (1975) an integrative mechanism. While initially money was the general model of his media theory, he later proceeded to prioritise the comparison of language. Accordingly, language is thus the most general medium. It uses generalised symbols that exceed the actual space-time moments. According to Parsons, media exhibit linguistic structures, namely the difference between "code" and "message". The code is based on a mostly implicitly known set of rules, while the message consists of the concrete link of some components of these rules. In terms of the developed theoretical language expressed here, this means that the code is based on the implicit mastery of constitutive rules, while the code is the individual act or move. The crucial difference between language and the other media is that the other media are internally linked to a much greater extent with sanctions as language. Media formalise and sanction communications and sharpen the participation in interactions. Media of exchange, with reference to Luhmann, solve the problem of selection and motivation. How can a selected action of alter have a motivation value for ego? A generalised medium of communication integrates the selection (to pay for the offer) with a specific motivation (to hand over a good in exchange for money). Thus money reduces the likelihood of an offer's rejection and makes its acceptance more likely. Parsons speaks of the positive sanction of money: the asymmetry between money and goods motivates the acceptance of money as a general equivalent.

Underlying the four media (money, power, influence, commitments) at a deeper level is an even more general medium, namely affect, which is for Parsons the medium of the social system. With this theory alteration in the late phase of his work, Parsons initiates a radical change of perspective (cf. Wenzel, 2001): for him, social order is no longer guaranteed by the common orientation towards values and norms, but the communicative expression of affect should now enable order. Emotional expression and the generalisation of emotions now play a key role in building social ties. As a consequence, agreements in action should come about on the basis of signs and symbols having the same emotional significance for ego and alter. Actors reciprocally present their own affects, motives and intended actions – and they must be displayed and made visible for each other. Thus, common meanings for the late Parsons have a prereflexive and affective character.

With these theoretical steps, Parsons aims to show that it is no longer cultural values that bring about social order (as in pre-modern or early modern societies), but that they must be situationally produced through the bond of affects to practices, objects and subjects. Remaining unclear in Parsons' theory, however, is what exactly is meant by affect: is it a matter of emotions or moods, do affects have an intentional object? Which affects is it all about anyway? After all, not all emotions are socially inclusive. From this unsatisfactory theory, Harald Wenzel (2001) has suggested replacing the concept of affect with that of the trust. Thereby, Wenzel draws on the criticism that Harold Garfinkel practised long before on Parsons' theory. Here, the notion of trust was assigned central importance. For Garfinkel (1963, 1967), the consensus in the action must be actively established, this occurs on the basis of constitutive rules and the trust that the actors mutually give. It can be said that giving trust has to be genuinely understood as a gift (cf. Adloff, 2016). The gift can also be refused – thus, it is an indication of generalised willingness to cooperate, which offers certain affects of bonding, but is not identical with affects. The gift is the active side of the offer of cooperation, while the concept of trust is aimed at the receptive and passive side of the action process. This perspective is important for the paradigmatic case of action among strangers: they cannot rely on a common social order, but must actively produce it; social order has to be actively fabricated by the gift, in order to make it real.

The gift serves as a kind of "backup structure" for society's other communication media. Risky advances (there is always a risk of rejection or non-response) normally accompany all interactions and represent the condition of the possibility of cooperation. The gift as a backup mechanism for cooperation does not have a normative foundation itself, it cannot be forced, it cannot be secured by self-interest. Unlike money or power, the gift is not associated with a social action sphere alone, it floats freely in society beyond the functional differentiation. The gift cannot be furnished with guarantees and certainties (cf. Wenzel, 2001, p. 370f.) – this constitutes its ubiquity, but also its institutional fragility.

Let us sharpen the previous argument: under current conditions of intercultural social constellations, cooperation is not something that relies on utilitarian or cultural-normative guarantees, but a phenomenon that has to generate itself from itself. A culture of cooperation can emerge from practices of cooperating and exchanging gifts, and these practices generate specific, stabilising affective bonds. In cooperation of mutual giving, there is a common focus of attention, which may bring about shared emotions, from which representations of commonalities can then also arise – in the form of *mana* or affective valuation. A prior, commonly shared culture in the form of knowledge stocks and common values is not needed to enable cooperation, but practices, which – by way of a common focus – create their own emotional intensity and thus, communitise.

Gift and money

Whoever talks about modern institutions, functional differentiation and media of exchange cannot be silent about money. Countless historians, economists, sociologists and cultural scientists have already dedicated themselves to this theme, and worked out both the accomplishments and the alienating effects of money in the modern world. Money is "an extremely powerful idea" (Dodd, 2014, p. 6) and a medium of exchange that converts all qualitative differences between things and activities into quantitative differences. For Georg Simmel (1991, 2004), money represents the absolute means – a means by which one can get almost everything, because it can be transformed into every commodity. With money, one can influence others in their actions, reduce uncertainties and coordinate complex operations.

Because this allows agents to buy innumerable things and activities, for Simmel it can become also an end in itself. As Heiner Ganssmann emphasises pointedly, "[a] society is fully monetized once money is what everybody always wants" (Ganssmann, 2012, p. 137). In modernity, the pursuit of more money has become an end in itself: "money is capable of standing in for any specific, concrete value in the process of exchange" (Dodd, 2014, p. 29). With this, money creates a distance between us and things and activities. From the perspective of money, everything is worth the same, which costs the same. From this perspective, everything is subjected to the logic of quantification. Simmel's sociological theory of money is one of the great narratives of money in modernity. It is based on the fact that Simmel quite simply considers money the realisation of the idea of the value. Money is abstract and realises the ideal of complete fungibility. At the same time, it is the highest expression of freedom – who has money, can free themselves from traditional ties and obligations, such as the estate-based society.

Money is often still derived theoretically and historically from exchange, and in this manner: two individuals want to satisfy their needs, have different things available and then enter into an exchange with each other. Money simplifies the exchange by providing a standard of comparison and by offering a medium of exchange (Marx speaks of the universal commodity form). This barter myth of money is nothing more than a fiction, as many historical studies have shown (cf. Dodd, 2014; Graeber, 2011). The sequence, "first exchange, then money" has never existed historically, and yet this story is repeated ritually in almost every textbook on economics.

This is confronted with a different theory on the origin of the money, which essentially traces back to Bernhard Laum. Initially, money had political and religious functions. Thus, subjects had to pay tributes to rulers in the Ottoman Empire, in Europe, China and Africa. Sacrificial practices, which can be traced back to Greek antiquity, earmarked a certain, well-defined set of values as a sacrifice to the gods. The thesis from Hubert and Mauss (1981) that "sacrifice was a means of bartering with gods" can be rediscovered and integrated here (Dodd, 2014, p. 25). From this perspective, money is based on debts to gods and rulers. Mauss' reflections on a theory of money indicate a similar direction as the theory of tributes, but also shows some significant differences. In the following, I will reconstruct Mauss' position, and in a second step, look at what we can make of his theory of money in the current situation.

In a long footnote in "The Gift", Mauss (1990, p. 100ff.) grapples with Malinowski's understanding of money and develops his own position. For Mauss, the gift and money are not in a mutually exclusive oppositional relationship. On the contrary, money is deeply interwoven in its origins with the gift. Malinowski, however, reserved the concept of money for objects that act as a measure of value and as a medium of exchange. This form of money is depersonalised and exempt from personal obligations towards others. Yet from Mauss' view, Malinowski was only speaking of one type of money – namely our modern money. According to Mauss, in all previous societies there were things like stones, shells and precious metals, which also functioned as a means of payment, but exhibited other properties – they had a magical nature and were primarily talismans: "They do indeed have very general circulation within a society and even between societies. But they are still attached to persons or clans ... Their value is still subjective and personal" (Mauss, 1990, p. 101). The stability of these values is low, but there is an important parallel to today's money. These forms of money have "purchasing power" (ibid.), and this power can be counted: "For such and such American copper object, a payment of so many blankets is due... The idea of number is present" (ibid.). The power of money is in its mana and is the power of the collective. This power is also in a position to discharge debts. Thus, something has value, which in the framework of collective processes is affectively experienced and symbolised as valuable and powerful. Money is thus a matter of faith (Mauss, 1969).

For Mauss, today's money is thus preceded by a form of money, in which certain things were precious and furnished with a magic value (collectively created affective valuation of mana), which then circulated within groups. This money did not serve the acquisition of ordinary consumer goods, but the acquisition of luxury things and the acquisition of authority over other people. For Mauss, the purchasing power of primitive money is based on the prestige of money. One helps oneself to it, to rule over others. Later, it was possible to increasingly detach these objects from people and groups, and make them into instruments for the measure of value, culminating in universal measures of value in the modern world. In contrast, Malinowski takes as a basis the modern definition of money for his anthropological search for forms of money, and thus overlooks the personalised forms of money described by Mauss.

This shift in focus by Mauss allows us to develop a different view of modern money. Because if money is not diametrically opposed to the concept of gift, if there were and can be personalised forms of money, then money does not necessarily have to be cold, anonymous and abstract, as the monetary theorists of modernity (such as Marx and Simmel) have repeatedly described. From the history of the gift and the money, Mauss also concludes that there does not have to be a complete difference between quantity and quality – quality can have degrees, thus it can be quantified (Mauss and Simiand, 1934). Money can be context sensitive and personal, so that societal reforms could also build on a reform of money:

> His theory that money was originally infused with social meaning is integral to the thinking behind recent attempts to "rehumanize" money through practical reform.... Mauss's work ... demonstrates how even within the most calculating environments, money is by no means as detached from mana as our predominantly economic, utilitarian mode of theorizing it has led us to expect.
>
> (Dodd, 2014, p. 34)

Also Karl Polanyi (1968) holds that money does not always have to be an anonymous, alienating, absolute means. He makes the distinction between special-purpose and general-purpose monies. This means that money can be exchanged in the non-industrial premodern world for a limited range of goods, while in modernity one can (almost) buy everything for money. Special-purpose monies are culturally embedded – for example, in kinship systems. With various special-purpose monies, different transfers can be accomplished. According to Polanyi, premodern money is ranked money. This view was further developed by Paul Bohannan (1955) in his hugely influential study on the use of money among the Tiv in Nigeria. The Tiv organised their exchanges along three hierarchical spheres, everyone had a special-purpose money. The specificity of the different monies provided for the maintenance of different social spheres. In spite of the criticism that Bohannan's study attracted (cf. Hann and Hart, 2011, p. 58ff.), it shows that money does not have to be neutral, but that there is money that is ranked and codified and does not contribute to the dissolution of social bonds. However, Polanyi and Bohannan assume that only premodern money was strongly embedded socially and culturally, thus they accept the view that modern money is abstract and without ties. With Dodd (2014, p. 286), however, one could carefully scrutinise this dichotomy. One would have to show that not only is premodern money a special-purpose money, but that all monies are. There is a diversity of monies, and modern forms of money are also always embedded culturally and socially. The value of money "comes from its social life" (ibid., p. 361).

We can assume that there was never pure or ideal money. In addition, the uses of money are highly variable. People make completely different use of money, and it is always culturally embedded. In sociology, this view has been strongly advocated in recent decades, particularly by Viviana A. Zelizer (2012). Because people make different use of money, they transform it and adapt it to their aims. In this sense, all monies are specified and differentiated – just as Polanyi describes for special-purpose money. In various studies about the use of money – such as by prostitutes, life insurance for children, or the distribution of family income for different spheres and purposes (for example, in the earmarking of money) – Zelizer has made clear that social practices modify money. Thus, money is employed in everyday use for payments, which are sometimes framed as compensation, in other contexts as entitlement, and in still others as a gift (cf. Zelizer, 1996). Compared with Marx and Simmel, one can gather from her studies the thesis that money does not transform all qualities into quantities, but that money can also serve specific non-monetary values and qualities. To a large extent, however, Zelizer shies away from the normative consequences of her empirical and analytical insights – she deems a strong criticism of money misguided (but see Zelizer, 2005; also Steiner, 2009) – whereas Keith Hart draws further normative conclusions.

In his studies on the importance of money, the anthropologist Keith Hart explicitly joins company with Mauss and Polanyi, and in recent years has participated in socio-political reform debates. For him, the great dichotomy in the money debate – "market vs. state money" is unsound (cf. Hart, 1986). On the state side of coins (heads), political hierarchy and authority express themselves in money – the other side of a coin (tails) shows that money is shaped by market processes of exchange. Thereby, it functions as a commodity. However, there is a third possibility to create money – which has largely been ignored in conventional debates – namely by communities. Especially the Internet has created real opportunities for this in recent years: people are trying to design the production and possible uses of money themselves and counteract phenomena associated with money, such as alienation and detachment. They consciously focus on the resource of trust, which is fundamentally necessary for money. We have reconstructed trust (see above) as a passive perception category, whose active action side is in the risk of giving. Money is also fundamentally dependent on the background mechanism of the gift. If the users of money see how they stand with different (e.g. national, regional, or global Internet-based) currency in exchange with diverse groups of people, it becomes clear how our local ways of life are associated with completely different situations elsewhere. However, if the "social life of money" is made ostensibly invisible because of the alleged excessive complexities, the binding effect of money also as a means of social (and not just economic) exchange is lost. In principle, there is also a reasonable chance that with the use of money people could understand themselves as members of one world; then namely when one can see that money not only selectively links buyers and sellers, but that a community always stands behind it, which recognises the use of money and trusts it (cf. Hart, 2013).

Money already serves as a possibility to capture the various connections to others in the form of debtor and creditor relations – it is a means of collective memory (cf. Hart, 2005). Hart's political concept includes, however, that a national or supranational currency (like the euro) is not sufficient to realise people's different exchange needs. He makes the case for currency pluralism, with different ranges and priorities of the various monies. These considerations can build on a long tradition, but could never be discursively and practically dominant. Robert Owen's labour exchange and Pierre-Joseph Proudhon's exchange banks would be called early precursors to the reform of the monetary system, as Silvio Gesell's idea of free money represents a key innovation in the twentieth century. And since the 1980s and 1990s, we can see a veritable global boom in alternative currencies. Local Exchange Trading Systems (LETS), for example, represent a complementary currency on a non-monetary basis. Goods and services are exchanged here based on supply and demand with the help of a virtual unit of account. This virtual money functions as a means of exchange and is meant to develop primarily communitising functions. Regional currencies (Degens, 2013, p. 23ff) usually have a greater regional dissemination than LETS and Time Banks, and are also increasingly used in the formal economy. Thereby, regional currencies are linked to the respective national currency, whereby conversion fees are intended to prevent a drain. Regional money is therefore covered by the legal tender. The aim of this money is the strengthening and revitalisation of the regional economy, in particular by regionally producing and trading daily consumer goods. This is achieved through a higher velocity of money, which, in turn, is due to a negative interest rate. The Chiemgauer, the highest-grossing regional currency in Germany, is subject to a storage fee of 0.002% per day or 8% annually. With such a demurrage, the store of value function is severely limited. This corresponds to the underlying idea of Silvio Gesell, that not all functions of money are equally realisable: if money is hoarded, it is removed from circulation and can only inadequately fulfil its function as a medium of exchange. Positive interest rates create incentives to withhold money and to increase its value.

Actually the gift is always already an implicit component of money, even the abstract, impersonal money of modernity. Ultimately, all the calculations of risks and probabilities by banks, businesses, economists and investors are burdened with great uncertainty – everyone also knows that and has to primarily show confidence in money. If they do not, a currency collapses in no time at all. Thus the following is pivotal: "The escape from uncertainty is provisional" (Ganssmann, 2012, p. 134). Jens Beckert (2013a, b) goes so far as to assert that economic activity is constitutively dependent on fictions. Fictions deal with an uncertain future, as if the expected events were already reality, even though we know that these future events are in principle unpredictable. Thus economic subjects act as we have described for the gift, which also simulates a reality in a risky way in order to allow it to become real. One has to trust in a currency, meaning that one is "betting" that everyone is ready in the future to exchange a piece of paper for a different value. The expected reality depends on others recognising and ratifying the concept of reality. The value of a currency is based on the trust that people give the currency. And this gift, which everyone performs, illustrates the magical power of money. This also becomes clear in the phenomenon of credit: the creditor actively trusts that the loan will be repaid – one gives credit in the belief of repayment. Violations of such collective expectations are then apparent in crashes, bursting financial bubbles, and panics – as Mauss also already emphasised (cf. Mauss and Simiand, 1934). With these remarks, it should have become clear that the gift finds entrance into the system of money, not only in premodern, but also in modern societies – of course, in different measures, and in the accentuation of completely different aspects of the gift.

Conclusion

The chapter has posed the question whether or not the logic of the gift is limited to the small area of personal relationships or face-to-face interactions. We showed that the gift is – in principle – present everywhere, that it is not confined to microsociological situations. This thesis depends on a flat ontology of the social and built on the idea that institutions often function as interdependence breakers of the logic of the gift. The gift depends on seeing where mediated "thin" interaction situations allow the logic of the gift only incompletely and where organisations and institutions also hedge the power of the gift with their role expectations as interdependence breakers. The example of the interorganisational networks showed that this is never fully done. Furthermore, institutions as macrophenomena are also produced in concrete situations – either by situations extending temporally and spatially through effect chains, or by invoking macrophenomena in concrete situations and thereby creating them performatively.

Moreover, it has been shown that the gift constitutes a background mechanism, a symbolic medium of exchange, that enables interaction within institutional orders and across institutional borders. Even money, the universal means of exchange, has not fully decoupled from the gift. Gifts are thus reconstructed as a ubiquitous background mechanism, which enables social order in the rear of language – namely at both the micro- and the macrolevel. The non-equivalence of the gift (Caillé, 2000), which also always carries elements of the giver's identity and a strong affective valuation in itself (Mauss speaks of *mana*), is the condition of possibility also of money, equivalent exchange and instrumentality.

Social order must be actively fabricated by the gift in order for it to become real. Risky advance services (there is always the risk of rejection or non-reciprocation) normally accompany all interactions and represent the condition of the possibility of cooperation. The gift as a background mechanism for cooperation itself has no clear normative foundation, cannot be forced or secured by self-interest. This mechanism is only weakly institutionalised. Gifts enable manifold and flexible interactions, but these cannot be provided with guarantees and certainties. Gifts are omnipresent, allow interactions and are at the same time extremely fragile.

References

Adloff, F. 2016. *Gifts of Cooperation, Mauss and Pragmatism*. London: Routledge. DOI: 10.4324/9781315692982

Beckert, J. 2013a. Imagined Futures. Fictional Expectations in the Economy. *Theory and Society*. **42**, pp. 219–240. DOI: 10.1007/s11186-013-9191-2

Beckert, J. 2013b. Capitalism as a System of Expectations: Toward a Sociological Microfoundation of Political Economy. *Politics & Society*. **41(**3), pp. 323–350. DOI: 10.1177/0032329213493750

Bellah, R. 2005. Durkheim and Ritual. In: Alexander, J. C. and Smith, P. Eds. *The Cambridge Companion to Durkheim*. Cambridge: Cambridge University Press, pp. 183–210. DOI: 10.1017/CCOL9780521806725.008

Blau, P. 1964. *Exchange and Power in Social Life*. New York: Wiley. DOI: 10.2307/2574842

Bohannan, P. 1955. Some Principles of Exchange and Investment Among the Tiv of Central Nigeria. *American Anthropologist*. **57**, pp. 60–70. DOI: 10.1525/aa.1955.57.1.02a00080

Caillé, A. 2000. *Anthropologie du don*. Paris: Desclée de Brouwer.

Caillé, A. 2019. *Extensions du domaine du don. Demander – Donner – Recevoir – Rendre*. Arles: Actes Sud.

Cicourel, A. V. 1981. Notes on the Integration of Micro- and Macro-Levels of Analysis. In: Knorr-Cetina, K. and Cicourel, A. V. Eds. *Advances in Social Theory and Methodology. Toward an Integration of Micro- and Macro-Sociologies*. Boston, MA: Routledge & Kegan Paul, pp. 51–80.

Collins, R. 1981. Micro-Translation as a Theory-Building Strategy. In: Knorr-Cetina, K. and Cicourel, A. V. Eds. *Advances in Social Theory and Methodology. Toward an Integration of Micro- and Macro-Sociologies*. Boston, MA: Routledge & Kegan Paul, pp. 81–108.

Coulter, J. 2001. Human Practices and the Observability of the "Macro-Social." In: Schatzki, T. R., Knorr Cetina, K. and von Savigny, E. Eds. *The Practice Turn in Contemporary Theory*. London: Routledge, pp. 37–49.

Degens, P. 2013. Alternative Geldkonzepte—ein Literaturbericht. *MPIfG Discussion Paper*, No. 13/1.

Dodd, N. 2014. *The Social Life of Money*. Princeton, NJ: Princeton University Press. DOI: 10.2307/j.ctt6wq0p6

Durkheim, É. 2008[1912]. *The Elementary Forms of Religious Life*. Oxford: Oxford University Press.

Ganssmann, H. 2012. *Doing Money. Elementary Monetary Theory from a Sociological Standpoint*. Milton Park: Routledge. DOI: 10.4324/9780203804469

Garfinkel, H. 1963. A Conception of, and Experiments with, "Trust" as a Condition of Stable Concerted Actions. In: Harvey, O. J. Ed. *Motivation and Social Interaction: Cognitive Approaches*. New York: Ronald Press, pp. 187–238.

Garfinkel, H. 1967. *Studies in Ethnomethodology*. Englewood Cliffs, NJ: Prentice-Hall. DOI: 10.2307/2574750

Giddens, A. 1990. *The Consequences of Modernity*. Oxford: Polity Press.

Graeber, D. 2010. Communism. In: Hart, K., Laville, J. K. and Cattani, A. D. Eds. *The Human Economy*. Cambridge: Polity Press, pp. 199–210.

Graeber, D. 2011. *Debt: The First 5,000 Years*. New York: Melville.

Granovetter, M. 1985. Economic Action and Social Structure: The Problem of Embeddedness. *American Journal of Sociology*. **91**, pp. 481–510. DOI: 10.1086/228311

Granovetter, M. 2017. *Society and Economy. Framework and Principles*. Cambridge, MA: Harvard University Press.

Habermas, J. 1987. *Theory of Communicative Action*. Two Volumes. Boston, MA: Beacon Press.

Habermas, J. 1996. *Between Facts and Norms: Contributions to a Discourse Theory of Law and Democracy*. Cambridge, MA: MIT Press.

Habermas, J. 2012. *Nachmetaphysisches Denken II. Aufsätze und Repliken*. Berlin: Suhrkamp.

Hann, C. and Hart, K. 2011. *Economic Anthropology. History, Ethnography, Critique*. Cambridge: Polity.

Hart, K. 1986. Heads or Tails? Two Sides of the Coin. *Man, New Series*. **21**(4), pp. 637–656. DOI: 10.2307/2802901

Hart, K. 2005. Notes towards an Anthropology of Money. *Kritikos*. **2**, June 2005, no pagination.

Hart, K. 2013. *Prospects for the Anthropology of Money and Finance*. Download from the "The Memory Bank." [Accessed 7 January 2014]. Available from: www.thememorybank.co.uk

Hirschauer, S. 2014. Intersituativität. Teleinteraktionen und Koaktivitäten jenseits von Mikro und Makro. *Zeitschrift für Soziologie*. Sonderheft: *Interaktion, Organisation und Gesellschaft*, pp. 109–133.

Hodson, R. 1991. The Active Worker: Compliance and Autonomy at the Workplace. *Journal of Contemporary Ethnography.* **20**(1), pp. 47–78. DOI: 10.1177/089124191020001003

Klemm, M. 2015. *Sozialität zwischen sprachlicher Kommunikation und performativer Praxis.* Post-doctoral Thesis, University of Erlangen-Nuremberg.

Knorr-Cetina, K. 1981. Introduction: The Micro-Sociological Challenge of Macro-Sociology. In: Karin Knorr-Cetina, K. and Cicourel, A. V. Eds. *Advances in Social Theory and Methodology: Toward an Integration of Micro- and Macro-Sociologies.* Boston, MA: Routledge & Kegan Paul, pp. 1–47.

Knorr-Cetina, K. 2009. The Synthetic Situation: Interactionism for a Global World. *Symbolic Interaction.* **32**(1), pp. 61–87. DOI: 10.1525/si.2009.32.1.61

Kühl, S. 2014. *Ganz normale Organisationen. Zur Soziologie des Holocaust.* Berlin: Suhrkamp.

Latour, B. 2005. *Reassembling the Social: An Introduction to Actor-Network-Theory.* Oxford: Oxford University Press.

Lessenich, S. 2019. *Living Well at Others' Expense. The Hidden Costs of Western Prosperity.* Cambridge: Polity Press.

Luhmann, N. 1964. *Funktionen und Folgen formaler Organisation.* Berlin: Duncker & Humblot.

Luhmann, N. 1995. *Social Systems.* Stanford, CA: Stanford University Press.

Luhmann, N. 2013. *Theory of Society.* Two Volumes. Stanford, CA: Stanford University Press.

Mauss, M. 1969[1914]. Les origines de la notion de monnaie. In: *Œuvres II, Représentations collectives et diversité des civilisations.* Paris: Les éditions de Minuit, pp. 106–112.

Mauss, M. 1990[1925]. *The Gift.* New York and London: Norton.

Mauss, M. and Hubert, H. 1981[1899]. *Sacrifice: Its Nature and Functions.* Chicago, IL: Chicago University Press.

Mauss, M. and Simiand, F. 1934. La monnaie, réalité sociale. *Les Annales Sociologique,* série D, fascicule 1, pp. 58–86.

Messner, D., Guarín, A. and Haun, D. 2013. The Behavioural Dimensions of International Cooperation. *Global Cooperation Research Papers.* Vol. 1. Duisburg: Centre for Global Cooperation Research.

Mouzelis, N. 1992. The Interaction Order and the Micro-Macro Distinction. *Sociological Theory.* **10**(1), pp. 122–128. DOI: 10.2307/202026

Parsons, T. 1969. *Politics and Social Structure.* New York: The Free Press.

Parsons, T. 1975. Social Structure and the Symbolic Media of Exchange. In: Blau, P. M. Ed. *Approaches to the Study of Social Structure.* New York: Free Press, pp. 94–120.

Polanyi, K. 1968. The Semantics of Money-Uses. In: Dalton, G. Ed. *Primitive, Archaic, and Modern Economies: Essays of Karl Polanyi.* Boston, MA: Beacon Press, pp. 175–203.

Polanyi, K. 2001[1944]. *The Great Transformation. The Political and Economic Origins of Our Times.* Boston, MA: Beacon Press.

Rawls, A. W. 1987. The Interaction Order Sui Generis: Goffman's Contribution to Social Theory. *Sociological Theory.* **5**, pp. 136–149. DOI: 10.2307/201935

Schatzki, T. 2015. Spaces of Practices and of Large Social Phenomena. *EspacesTemps.net, Travaux.* **24**, March 2015, no pagination.

Simmel, G. 1991. Money in Modern Culture. *Theory, Culture & Society.* **8**, pp. 17–31. DOI: 10.1177/026327691008003002

Simmel, G. 2004. *The Philosophy of Money.* London: Routledge.

Steiner, P. 2009. Who is Right About the Modern Economy: Polanyi, Zelizer, or Both? *Theory and Society*. **38**, pp. 97–110. DOI: 10.1007/s11186-008-9072-2

Uzzi, B. 1997. Social Structure and Competition in Interfirm Networks: The Paradox of Embeddedness. *Administrative Science Quarterly*. **42(**1), pp. 35–67. DOI: 10.2307/2393808

Uzzi, B. 1999. Embeddedness in the Making of Financial Capital: How Social Relations and Networks Benefit Firms Seeking Financing. *American Sociological Review*. **64**, pp. 481–505. DOI: 10.2307/2657252

Wenzel, H. 2001. *Die Abenteuer der Kommunikation*. Weilerswist: Velbrück.

Zelizer, V. A. 1996. Payments and Social Ties. *Sociological Forum*. **11**(3), pp. 481–495.

Zelizer, V. A. 2005. Circuits within Capitalism. In: Nee, V. and Swedberg, R. Eds. *The Economic Sociology of Capitalism*. Princeton, NJ: Princeton University Press, pp. 289–322.

Zelizer, V. A. 2012. How I Became a Relational Economic Sociologist and What Does That Mean? *Politics & Society*. **40(**2), pp. 145–174. DOI: 10.1177/0032329212441591

3 Beneficence, reciprocity and institutions in Smith

Benoît Walraevens

Introduction

Adam Smith has long been seen among economists as someone who held that men are rational beings who always act out of self-interest.[1] Yet, even if we generously assume that these claims are only related to the *Wealth of Nations*,[2] they do not do justice to the richness and complexity of Smith's thought.[3] It is true that in this book Smith famously wrote that "It is not from the benevolence of the butcher, the brewer, or the baker, that we expect our dinner, but from their regard to their own interest" (*WN,* I.ii.2, p. 27). What Smith wants to underline here is, first, that in "commercial societies" in which the division of labour is "thoroughly established" and everyone becomes "in some measure a merchant" (*WN,* I.iv.1, p. 37), man needs the cooperation of a multitude of other people to satisfy his own needs (*WN,* I.ii.2, p. 26). So in often impersonal, anonymous market exchanges we rely on others' self-interest to obtain from others "the far greater part of those good offices we stand in need of" (ibid.). But note that what is implied here is that the exchange of goods and services among individuals generally unknown to each other, at least requires of them to understand and take into account *other people*'s interests (*WN,* I.ii.2, p. 26; Bhanu Mehta, 2006, Fleischacker, 2011). We need to put ourselves into others' place and to restrain our natural, selfish passions to satisfy them if we want to satisfy ourselves (Walraevens, 2014). Going further, Darwall argued that Smith's view of exchange presupposes a reciprocal recognition of men as equals (2004, p. 133). And Smith never claimed that human nature is merely selfish, nor that our lives should be reduced to the self-interested commerce of impersonal market exchange. Quite the contrary.

Indeed, the very first lines of Smith's other great work, his *Theory of Moral Sentiments*,[4] a book now rediscovered in both philosophy (Sen, 2009) and economics (Smith and Wilson, 2019), leave no doubt about his intention to criticise the selfish view of human nature of Hobbes and Mandeville:

> How selfish soever man may be supposed, there are evidently some principles in his nature, which interest him in the fortune of others, and

> render their happiness necessary to him, though he derives nothing from it except the pleasure of seeing it.
>
> (*TMS*, I.i.1.1, p. 9)

This chapter aims to study Smith's analysis of these unselfish, other-regarding motivations and actions, the "passive feelings" and "active principles" which prompt men to help and benefit other people. Unsurprisingly, Smith's ideas on altruism have not attracted the same attention than his views of self-interest.[5] However, as we will try to show, Smith's works offer a rich and unique view of beneficence, gift-giving and reciprocity, and of the influence of institutions upon them. According to Smith and Wilson (2019), Smith's views on beneficence (and justice) may even provide a true alternative to existing models in economics, the social preferences' models built upon traditional hypothesis of rationality and utility maximisation of agents, offering better predictions and explanations of experimental results than the latter. If Smith has been said to be at the origin of the negation of the gift and altruism in modern economics (Marchionatti and Cedrini, 2017), it seems to be due to a lack of knowledge or to a misunderstanding of his works, and especially of his *TMS*.

The chapter is organised as follows. The first section will present Smith's moral theory of the virtue of "beneficence". We will underline the fundamental place of beneficence in Smith's view of the character of the wise and virtuous man and the characteristics of his theory of beneficence, built upon the Stoics' concept of *oikeiosis,* while criticising their vision of cosmopolitanism. The second section will focus on positive reciprocity, or "reciprocal beneficence", arising from sentiments of gratitude towards our benefactors. Smith provides us with both a positive and normative account of reciprocity, identifying what should be a proper reward for those who benefited us, or others, with his concept of the impartial spectator. The third and last section will be devoted to the place of beneficence at the social level, first, and then to the influence of institutions on the meaning and practices of beneficence for Smith. As to the former, we will highlight how Smith explains the formation and evolution of social norms of benevolence, kindness and generosity and why, for him, relations of reciprocal beneficence or mutual kindness are essential to the happiness of society. As to the latter, we will study Smith's scattered references to specific practices of gift-giving and reciprocity in his works, dealing with different types or "stages" of societies, from "savage" societies of hunters-gatherers to the modern commercial, "civilized" societies. Finally, we will also explain why Smith thinks that the state should avoid as much as possible to legally enforce some "duties" of beneficence.

Smith's theory of virtue and beneficence

This section aims to outline Smith's views on beneficence and their origins. Before doing that, it is necessary, first, to understand the place of beneficence within Smith's theory of virtue. At the beginning of Part VII of *TMS,* Smith writes that every treatise on morality should answer two questions, the first one, on which we will focus here, being: "Wherein does virtue consist?", or what "constitutes the excellent and praise-worthy character, the character which is the natural object of esteem, honour, and approbation" (*TMS,* VII.i.2, p. 265). Part VII of *TMS,* the last of the book, can be considered as a short history of moral philosophy (Biziou, 2016) of which Smith's theory would be an apogee (*TMS,* VII.i.1, p. 265). The first characteristic of his moral theory is that it is an "eclectic" (Hanley, 2009) or "pluralist" (McCloskey, 2008) theory, combining elements of different theories and traditions, with Epicurean, Stoic and Christian influences. Smith thus rejects the idea that virtue could be reduced to either propriety (Plato, Aristotle, Shaftesbury), prudence (Epicure) or disinterested benevolence (Hutcheson) *alone.* Those who insisted on one of these aspects have given only partial answers to the question of the character of virtue.

The second characteristic of Smith's moral theory is that it belongs to the tradition of "virtue ethics" (Hanley, 2009; McCloskey, 2008), in the sense that it tries to define the virtues of character which are conducive to happiness. This is most visible in Part VI of *TMS,* which was new to the sixth and last edition of the book, published in 1790, a few months before Smith's death. It is thus noteworthy that Smith developed his views on virtue, and especially on beneficence, over time. On his own admission, Part VI was meant to be "a practical system of morality" for his readers (*Corr,* p. 287). For Smith, men are moved by their passions, which are neither virtuous nor vicious *per se,* independently of their "causes". He identifies two kinds of passions: the passions of the body and the passions of the imagination. The latter are subdivided into three classes: the selfish, the social and the unsocial passions. To each of them is associated a specific, cardinal virtue: prudence to the selfish passions (ambition, vanity, pride, greed), beneficence to the social passions (kindness, generosity, charity) and justice to the unsocial passions (anger and resentment). Prudence defines how people can virtuously affect and promote their own happiness. The prudent man acts out of his real, enlightened self-interest. Against Hutcheson (1725, p. 102), Smith thus finds important to highlight and prove that "self-regarding" motivations and actions can also be virtuous (*TMS,* VII.ii.3.16, p. 304). Justice and beneficence, by contrast, focus on how we can affect, positively and negatively, other people's happiness, that is how our conduct can benefit or hurt them (*TMS,* VI.ii. intro, p. 218). Beneficence will teach us how to do good, while justice will dictate us how not to do evil. Smith adds a fourth "cardinal" virtue of character: self-command, a kind of "meta-virtue", indispensable to the practice of every other virtue (*TMS,* VI.iii.11, p. 241).

Prudence, justice and beneficence are the result of the agent's self-command towards, respectively, his selfish, unsocial and social passions. We act virtuously or with "perfect propriety" for Smith when we restrain the intensity of our passion(s) so that every well-informed and impartial spectator can "sympathize" with us and thus approves of our conduct. Beneficence is an essential part of the character of the perfectly virtuous man who always acts according to the prescriptions of the impartial spectator and sees himself as "but one of the multitude" (*TMS,* VI.ii.2.2, p. 228; II.ii.2.1, p. 83). Besides, Smith claims that what "constitutes the perfection of virtue" is "to feel much for others and little for ourselves", to "restrain our selfish, and to indulge our benevolent affections" (*TMS,* I.i.5.5, p. 25). For him, beneficence is the highest or noblest virtue of character, the most admirable and praiseworthy of all, as is confirmed by his depiction of the "wise and virtuous man", introduced in the section on "universal benevolence", or cosmopolitanism (*TMS,* VI.iii.3, pp. 235–236). Beneficence is the apex of human nature.

Moreover, other-regarding affections, principles and actions are natural to man for Smith, as they were for Hutcheson (1725, pp. 112, 148) and for Hume (*THN,* 3.2.2.5, p. 313; 3.3.3).[6] Indeed, "Nature ... exhorts mankind to acts of beneficence, by the pleasing consciousness of deserved reward" (*TMS,* II.ii.3.4, p. 86) and by rendering "every man the peculiar object of kindness, to the persons to whom he himself has been kind" (*TMS,* VI.ii.1.19, p. 225). Note here that Smith made of "bene*ficence*" (actually doing good), a virtue of Christian inspiration, rather than mere "bene*volence*" (mere good willing) one of his cardinal virtues. For him, "man was made for action, and to promote by the exertion of his faculties such changes in the external circumstances both of himself and others, as may seem favourable to the happiness of all" (*TMS,* II.iii.3.3, p. 106). Wishing well for others, or mere benevolence is not enough to be virtuous (*TMS,* II.iii.3.3, p. 106) because virtue is not based only on intentions and motivations. We must *actually* promote the happiness of others to deserve full praise, gratitude and reward, as we shall see. The third point we want to make is that beneficence for Smith "is always free", so that it cannot be extorted by force because "the mere want of beneficence tends to do no real positive evil" (*TMS,* II.ii.1.3, p. 78). While Marcel Mauss (2012[1923–1924]) famously argued that there is a triple obligation to give, to receive and to give back, for Smith it seems that we never have any obligation to give, nor to give back, at least at first sight.

Thus Smith here nuances his point, distinguishing two forms of beneficence: the generosity of the benefactor, who makes the "initial" gift, and the "reciprocal beneficence" or "counter-gift" of the recipient of the gift towards his benefactor out of "gratitude". The former is for Smith the noblest form of beneficence. We will focus on the latter in the next section. It is important to mention now that for Smith even the "want of gratitude...cannot be punished". Indeed, it would be "still more improper" to oblige someone to recompense his benefactor "than is his neglecting to perform it". Yet of "all the duties of beneficence, those which gratitude recommends to us approach nearest to what is called a perfect and complete obligation" (*TMS*, II.ii.1.3, p. 79). Whereas what "charity" and "generosity" would prompt us to do "is still more free, and can still less be extorted by force than the duties of gratitude" (*TMS*, II.ii.1.3, p. 79). Smith's theory of altruism thus allows an implicit critique of the modern, "altercentric" view of altruism supported by Robert Frank in economics in which "altruism does not differ from strict rules of justice" with "moral dictums" and "obligatory commitments", which do not pay much attention to particular circumstances and persons involved (Khalil, 2001, pp. 431–432).

Smith then concludes that "we talk of the debt of gratitude, not of charity, or generosity" (*TMS*, II.ii.1.3, p. 79). So, if there is no *strict* obligation to give, it seems like reciprocating gifts or help is close to a "moral" obligation or "moral norm" (Gouldner, 1960). Smith's view of beneficence seems to be in line with Testart's definition of the gift as a transfer not demanded by anything or anyone and with no demanded counterpart (Athane, 2011; Testart, 2007). For Smith a truly beneficent man can reasonably *expect* a return because he knows that he *deserves* it from the point of view of an impartial spectator (*TMS,* II.ii.1.3, p. 78) but he cannot *demand* it. The only difference between Smith and Testart being that for the former intentions and motivations *matter* for defining gratitude and reciprocal beneficence while the latter's definition of the gift is neutral towards the intentions of the giver, as Hobbes' definition was (Athane, 2011, p. 203).

Indeed, Smith tries to explain the motivations or causes of beneficence. An action is truly beneficent or virtuous if it improves someone else's well-being and, most importantly, if it is done out of "proper" motives, that is, unselfish, disinterested motives like kindness, generosity, charity, or sympathy. But Smith, whose goal in *TMS* is first and foremost to describe human nature and social interactions as they are, rather than as they should be, is aware that seemingly generous acts can be made out of improper, egoistic motives like showing our domination and impose on others or giving to get a return (*TMS,* III.5.1, p. 162; *TMS,* II.i.3.1, pp. 71–72). As a consequence, while Smith goes against Mandeville in showing that truly beneficent acts exist, he concedes him that beneficence sometimes *can* be the veil of selfishness. All the more so, it seems, when one considers the pleasures that benefactors themselves get or reasonably expect from their other-regarding conduct. As we mentioned earlier, first, acts of beneficence naturally go along with "the pleasing consciousness of deserved reward" (*TMS,* II.ii.3.4, p. 86). Two distinct pleasures are thus derived from being beneficent: a pleasure of self-approbation (*TMS*, II.ii.2.4, p. 85) not unlike what economists call a "warm-glow" effect (Andreoni, 1990), and a pleasure in observing the pleasure we have given to someone through our kind action, the pleasure of sympathy (unless our recipient is ungrateful).[7] But Smith is not arguing here that benefactors try to maximise their utility or pleasure in giving, or that they are, in fact, egoistic when they do. As Kolm (2008, pp. 78–79, 140) noticed, Smith states that the "value" of counter-gifts by direct and indirect reciprocators will significantly exceed the "cost" of our initial gift (*TMS,* VI.ii.1.19, p. 225). But it does not mean that for Smith giving could be self-interested. If we give in order to be given back, i.e. if we exhibit selfish, "improper" motives, we will be less reciprocated (or not reciprocated at all), because gratitude will be diminished or non-existent. Likewise, giving only in order to get social praise and fame, or acting out of "vanity" as Mandeville underlined, is not truly beneficent and virtuous. "Selfish" giving would be inefficient and self-defeating for Smith. We thus agree with Khalil (2001, p. 430) in thinking that Smith's theory of altruism answers both to Mandeville's and to its modern economic counterpart, Axelrod's "egoistic" model of altruism based on self-interested, reciprocal cooperation.

Smith's theory of beneficence also tries to explain who is naturally recommended to our beneficence. His answer is deeply indebted to the Stoics' *oikeiosis* theory, as can be found in Cicero's *De Officiis* (Biziou et al., 2003, p. 305; Forman-Barzilai, 2010, pp. 121–122). It is based on the idea of concentric circles, our affections and good offices being centred on the self and then weakening when social and spatial distance increases. The core of Stoic moral perfectionism is to break these circles of intimacy to become a citizen of the world, reaching cosmopolitanism. Smith underlines that beneficence, like sympathy on which it is founded, decreases with distance and that the intensity of our beneficence is linked to the knowledge we have of people (our familiarity or "intimacy" with them; see Nieli, 1986) and relatedly to the real impact we can have on their happiness, as Hume had claimed. So, Smith begins his chapter on "the Order in which Individuals are recommended by Nature to our own care and attention" with self-care, that is, with the Stoics' principle of self-love according to which man "is first and principally recommended to his own care" because he is "fitter and abler to take care of himself than any other person", feeling his own "pleasures" and "pains" more sensibly than them (*TMS,* VI.ii.1.1, p. 219). Then the circle extends and our "warmest affections" and good offices are directed towards the members of our own family, because they are the persons with whom we usually live and thus are more "habituated to sympathize with", so that "they are naturally the persons upon whose happiness or misery [our] conduct must have the greatest influence" (*TMS,* VI.ii.1.2, p. 219). Beneficence inside families is not linked to "blood ties" or to genetical proximity. Then our circle of beneficence extends to include our friends and acquaintances with whom we often interact and thus that we know well. Our "good offices" are directed towards people who have a "connection with ourselves" and/or those who benefited us in the past, but also "those who are distinguished by their extraordinary situation … the rich and the powerful, the poor and the wretched" (*TMS,* VI.ii.1.20, p. 225).[8] So Smith does not present self-love and benevolence as necessarily contradictory principles of human nature. Rather for him there is a kind of natural continuum between our self-regarding and other-regarding principles of action. The third step of beneficence appears when it extends to our society or state. Public spirit or patriotism, based on the "love of our country", is nothing but this extended beneficence towards our nation because "the state or sovereignty in which we have been born and educated, and under the protection of which we continue to live, is, in ordinary cases, the greatest society upon whose happiness or misery, our good or bad conduct can have much influence" (*TMS,* VI.ii.2.2, p. 227). The fourth, ultimate step is reached with "universal benevolence", the Stoic principle of cosmopolitanism in which man sees himself as a citizen of the world, ready to sacrifice his interest and that of his society or country even for distant strangers, out of his "love of humanity" (*TMS,* VI.ii.3). Yet, Smith departs from the Stoics, arguing that cosmopolitanism is beyond the reach of our imperfect human species and is just good for gods (Forman-Barzilai, 2010, chap 4). While our "goodwill is circumscribed by no boundary", our "effectual good offices can very seldom be extended to any wider society than that of our own country". For Smith it is thus unlikely that we could feel much generous sentiments towards people we don't know, see or are acquainted with, nor can we know how to effectively improve their well-being. And it is good that it is so because:

> ... the care of the universal happiness of all rational and sensible beings, is the business of God, not of man. To man is allotted a much humbler department, but one much suitable to the weakness of his powers, and to the narrowness of his comprehension; the care of his own happiness, of that of his family, his friends, his country...
>
> (*TMS,* VI.ii.3.6, p. 237)

Smith wants to underline the "superiority of practical action to mere cosmopolitan sentiment or good feeling" (Hanley, 2013, p. 228). For him beneficence and gift-giving are mainly to be found in private, intimate, personal relationships, that is, in the "domestic" sphere.

Gratitude, reciprocal beneficence and the happiness of society

As we shall see presently, Smith's views on positive reciprocity or reciprocal beneficence are rich and innovative, providing an alternative to social preferences models based on rationality and utility maximisation (see Bolton and Oekenfels, 2000; Falk and Fischbacher, 2006; Fehr and Schmidt, 1999). Indeed, Smith offers a non-utilitarian, emotions-based moral theory of reciprocity, having no equivalent in economics (Walraevens, forthcoming). Along these lines, Smith and Wilson (2019) convincingly showed that it can provide testable and actually better predictions of people's choices in experiments, while *truly* explaining reciprocity and its causes rather than merely providing *ex post* rationalisations of people's observed behaviour. Smith's model of positive reciprocity is based on man's natural passion of gratitude[9] and on his fundamental desires of praise (getting the sympathy and approbation of others) and praiseworthiness (getting the sympathy and approbation of the impartial spectator), that is, on man's nature as a social and ethical being judging of the propriety and merit of others' actions and of his own. We begin this section with Smith's *descriptive* account of positive reciprocity and then analyse his *normative* account, defining what should be a *proper* "reward" for beneficent acts.

First of all, for Smith positive reciprocity, returning good for good received, is "natural" to man. Indeed, "of all the persons … whom nature points out for our peculiar beneficence, there are none to whom it seems more properly directed than to those whose beneficence we have ourselves already experienced" (*TMS,* VI.ii.1.19, p. 225). In other words, for Smith "kindness is the parent of kindness" (*TMS,* VI.ii.1.19, p. 225). His analysis of positive reciprocity is based on the passion of "gratitude", which prompts us to "reward" our benefactors (*TMS,* II.i.1.4, p. 68). Gratitude is caused by everything that makes us feel some pleasure and comes from "sensitive" beings because the satisfaction of gratitude consists in "retaliating those sensations upon what gave occasion to them" (*TMS,* II.iii.1.3, p. 94). Receiving a gift creates a feeling of "debt", of which we will not be unloaded until we have "recompensed" our benefactor (*TMS,* II.i.1.5, p. 68), as Gouldner later remarked too (1960, p. 174). When there are multiple benefactors, people tend to think that their gratitude is "divided among the different persons who contributed to their pleasure", so that "a smaller share seems due to anyone" (*TMS,* II.iii.2.2, p. 98). Smith later argues that, actually, returning the pleasure we had is neither the sole nor the true end of reciprocal beneficence:

> what gratitude chiefly desires, is not only to make the benefactor feel pleasure in his turn, but to make him conscious that he meets with this reward on account of his past conduct, to make him pleased with that conduct, and to satisfy him that the person upon whom he bestowed his good offices was not unworthy of them.
>
> (*TMS,* II.iii.1.4, p. 95)

Reciprocity is a very specific type of exchange, a deeply *moral* and *personal* relationship in which people are seen as end in themselves, not as means to satisfy ourselves. We thus disagree with Hanley and Tegos according to which positive reciprocity in Smith is "self-regarding" (Hanley, 2009, p. 180) or solely "founded on enlightened *amour-propre*" and "interested rationality" (Tegos, 2018, p. 159). As Smith writes, we are happy to find someone whose sentiments are in agreement with our own, someone who transcends his natural preference for himself and sees himself as an impartial spectator would do, as "one but in the multitude in no respect better than any other" (*TMS,* II.ii.2.1, p. 83). Our experiences of reciprocity foster our sense of the fundamental moral equality of men and our "humanity", this extreme sensibility and concern for others' sentiments and happiness. Our benefactor values us as we value ourselves, he "distinguishes us from the rest of mankind" (*TMS,* II.iii.1.4, p. 95) and makes us feel loved and esteemed. So it is to "maintain in him these agreeable and flattering sentiments" that we return his favours (*TMS,* II.iii.1.4, p. 95).

Smith indicates, though, that reciprocity can come from external, uninvolved spectators, what Kolm (2008, p. 5) called the "Descartes effect" because it was first noticed by the French philosopher in his work on the passions of the soul. There are always three points of view of any given situation: the viewpoint of the agent, that of the affected party and that of unaffected spectator(s) (Harpham, 2010). But why is it that unaffected, external spectators will exert some reciprocity? Smith's explanation is based on his analysis of the faculty of "sympathy". In the case of beneficent actions, an external, uninvolved spectator will feel what Smith calls a "redoubled sympathy" (*TMS,* I.ii.4.1, p. 38), approving of and sympathising with both the kindness of the benefactor and the gratitude of the beneficiary (*TMS,* I.ii.4.1, p. 39; *TMS,* II.i.2.4, p. 70). The necessary condition for the natural gratitude of the spectator to emerge and for reciprocity to take place is that the individual approves of the motives behind the generous act (*TMS,* II.i.3.1, p. 71). Importantly, the gratitude of the spectator is necessarily less intense than the "original" passion of the agent, since it is only a "copy" of it in the imagination of the spectator. So that we can reasonably expect less significant "rewards" from uninvolved spectators. But it is quite easy to sympathise with all the benevolent affections, Smith argues (*TMS,* I.ii.4.1, p. 39), and by way of consequence, it should not be uncommon to see indirect reciprocity (*TMS,* VI.ii.1.19, p. 225). However, there is always the possibility that we face some "ingratitude" with regard to our beneficence. Ingratitude happens when we do not "recompense" our benefactor, especially when we have it in our power and he "needs our assistance" (*TMS,* II.ii.1.3, p. 78). It will excite "dislike and disapprobation" from people and from the impartial spectator for the "selfishness of the motives" of the ungrateful person (*TMS,* II.ii.1.3, p. 78). So, again, even though beneficence is always free and cannot be extorted by force, the strong desire we have for praise and praiseworthiness and our symmetric aversion for blame and blameworthiness are powerful incentives to compel us to reward our benefactors. To use a distinction made by Bourdieu and Testart (Athane, 2011, pp. 160, 220), the *obligation* to reciprocate gifts and benefits for Smith is a "moral" rather than an "economic" or "juridical" obligation. We turn now to Smith's normative view of reciprocal beneficence. It has to do with the "moral" or "refined" sentiments of gratitude (Elster, 2011; Harpham, 2010) and with the "proper" reward for gifts and favours. For Smith, the norm of reciprocity is founded on the impartial spectator's point of view, which is the equivalent in our imagination of a fully informed uninvolved observer. We need to distance ourselves from our "natural" station and feelings of gratitude to restrain the intensity of our passion so that every impartial spectator can sympathise with it (*TMS,* II.i.5.7, p. 76). But what are the criteria upon which the impartial spectator will judge of the propriety and justice of rewards, and thus of reciprocity? The judgement of the impartial spectator on the "merit" of actions, and thus on reciprocity, is mainly based on three elements. First, it depends on the *consequences* of the action on our well-being, whether it caused us some pleasure. Hence this simple rule that the more pleasure we had, the more gratitude we will feel for our benefactor and the greater our reward will be. If the agent failed to help or serve us, gratitude will strongly diminish (or vanish). Second, the impartial spectator will assess the propriety of the *motives* or *intentions* of our benefactor, to see whether he approves them (*TMS,* II.iii.1.6, p. 96). If egoistic reasons are discovered behind the beneficence or gratitude of someone, such as giving in order to receive in return or to impose on others and show our superiority, only "little gratitude seems due" in such cases (*TMS,* III.5.1, p. 162; *TMS,* II.i.3.1, pp. 71–72). Likewise, only "a very small return" seems due in case of "foolish" or "profuse generosity" (*TMS,* II.i.3.2, p. 72). And satisfying gratitude out of the "cold sense of duty" is only a second best for the proper and just gratitude of the impartial spectator (*TMS,* III.5.1, p. 162). Third, identifying proper returns for acts of beneficence and mischief requires taking into account the *intentionality* of these actions. If we have been involuntary benefited, we will naturally feel less gratitude (*TMS,* II.iii.1.6, p. 96). Note that Smith is aware of the issue of information asymmetry between givers and receivers. In an ideal world we should judge of the merit and demerit of actions on intentions alone. But men's motivations for acting are not always easily discernible. That is why Nature, in its wisdom, made us judge of the merit of an action also and mostly on its consequences, which are more visible and straightforward.

These three criteria (outcomes, motivations and intentionality[10]) are associated by Smith with a traditional rule of reciprocity based on the "equality" between the gift and the counter-gift. In his words, to "make a return of equal, and if possible of superior value to the services we have received, would seem to be a pretty plain rule, and one which admitted of scarce any exceptions" (*TMS,* III.6.9, p. 174).[11]

It seems to be a precise and quite common rule but we immediately ask: equality of what and for whom? Many interpretations of this rule are possible, as Elster nicely shows (2009, pp. 149–150).[12] And Smith is well aware of the ambiguities and indeterminacy of this so-called "rule" of equal or higher value in reciprocity (*TMS,* III.6.9, p. 174), which clearly distinguishes the latter from economic exchange. He uses different examples to illustrate his point, one of them being particularly noteworthy:

> if your friend lent you money in your distress, ought you to lend him money in his? How much ought you to lend him? When ought you to lend him? Now, or to-morrow, or next month? And for how long a time?
> (*TMS,* III.6.9, p. 174)

For Smith, it is obvious that "no general rule can be laid down, by which a precise answer can, in all cases, be given to any of these questions" (*TMS,* III.6.9, p. 174). The impartial spectator always takes into account the specificities of each case. His recommendations are highly context-dependent, taking into account the "character" of the persons and their personal "circumstances", so that

> you may be perfectly grateful, and justly refuse to lend him a halfpenny: and, on the contrary, you may be willing to lend [...] him ten times the sum which he lent you, and yet justly be accused of the blackest ingratitude.
>
> (*TMS,* III.6.9, p. 174)

Beneficence, social rules and institutions

As we have just seen, the impartial spectator's point of view is necessary to define what a perfectly proper reciprocity is in a specific context involving two individuals. But this effort of distancing from our natural point of view is out of reach for most of us, Smith claims. Only the wise and the virtuous always follow their "inner voice". Most people are prone to self-deceit, this "fatal weakness of mankind", which makes us unable to judge ourselves with impartiality (*TMS,* III.4.8, p. 158). Yet, Nature has offered us a "remedy": the "sense of duty", by which we adhere to general rules of morality we have formed from "our continual observations upon the conduct of others", allowing us to act with "tolerable decency" (*TMS,* III.4.7, 158; III.5.1, p. 163). Smith presents a proto-evolutionary view of morality. The general rules of morality are conventions, emerging from the "concurring sentiments of mankind" (*TMS,* III.4.11, p. 160). We memorise our experiences of approbation and disapprobation as both agent and spectator and infer general rules of conduct from them, which we strive to follow in order to maximise our chances of social approval. For example, "the man who has received great benefits from another person, may, by the natural coldness of his temper, feel but a very small degree of the sentiment of gratitude" (*TMS,* III.5.1, p. 162) and "though his heart therefore is not warmed with any grateful affection, he will strive to act as if it was, and will endeavour to pay all those regards and attentions to his patron which the liveliest gratitude could suggest" (*TMS,* III.5.1, p. 162). Most importantly, "he will carefully embrace every opportunity of making a proper return for past services" and this "without any selfish intention of obtaining new favours" or "any design of imposing upon his benefactor or the public" (*TMS,* III.5.1, p. 162). The real motive of his action may be his "reverence for the established rule of duty", that is, to act according to "the law of gratitude" (*TMS,* III.5.1, p. 162). So we go against Elster (2011) who claimed that Smith never mentioned that gratitude could be "enforced by social norms".

But Smith makes clear that this "cold" sense of duty is only a second best, clearly inferior to truly affective, grateful reciprocity (*TMS,* III.6.4, p. 172). Moreover, Smith identifies a crucial difference between the rules of justice and those of beneficence. The former are "precise, accurate and indispensable" while the latter always remain "loose, vague and indeterminate" (*TMS,*

III.6.11, pp. 175–176). In other words, "there are no rules by the knowledge of which we can infallibly be taught to act upon all occasions with … proper beneficence" (ibid., p. 176). And among the rules of social virtues, those concerning "noble" beneficence, the rules of "generosity", "kindness" or "hospitality" are "still more vague and indeterminate" than the "duties of gratitude" (*TMS,* III.6.9, p. 174). These points help explain Smith's distrust towards the enforcement of duties of beneficence by the state: the natural looseness, indeterminacy and context-dependence of what the impartial spectator prescribes us to do to be beneficent conflicts with the necessarily general laws that the state could define to impose duties of beneficence. Moreover, obliging people to be beneficent would go against the intrinsic freedom attached to acts of beneficence, and thus would corrupt them. Beneficence must be voluntary to arouse gratitude. So, even though he acknowledges that the "civil magistrate … may prescribe rules [which] command mutual good offices to a certain degree" and thus prescribe some "duties of beneficence" (from parents to their children), as is the case "in all civilized nations", he warns us that of all the duties of legislators it is the one "which requires the greatest delicacy and reserve to execute with propriety and judgment" (*TMS,* II.ii.1.8, p. 81). Pushing it too far would be destructive of citizens' liberty (*TMS,* II.ii.1.8, p. 81). In the end, relations of beneficence and reciprocity are not essential to the *existence* of society, whose "pillar" is justice, but they are essential to its *flourishing* and *happiness* (*TMS,* II.ii.3.1–3, pp. 85–86). Paying taxes is neither a gift towards the state nor a beneficent act in Smith's sense since it is a "demanded" transfer (Testart, 2007) or a "juridical obligation". In Smith's words, it is *not* left to the "freedom of our own wills" and it *can* be "extorted by force". Thus Smith would certainly agree with Godbout and Caillé (1992) for whom beneficence and gift-giving belong to the universe of the "domestic sphere" of personal relationships, rather than to the sphere of the market and the sphere of the state.[13]

Now, one remaining question to answer is the influence of institutions on the meaning and practices of beneficence in society. To explain it, we will study some concrete examples taken from Smith's work. The first one we consider is the decline of family bonds among civilised nations, the natural consequence of which being less beneficence among family members (*TMS,* VI.ii1.13, p. 223). This is caused by the fact that in "commercial societies" the "authority of the law is always perfectly sufficient to protect the meanest man in the state", so "the descendants of the same family, having no such motive for keeping together, naturally separate and disperse, as interest or inclination may direct" and "soon cease to be of importance to one another", losing "all care to one another" (*TMS,* VI.ii.1.13, p. 223). Even though Smith does not explicitly say so, work mobility is another cause of this phenomenon. Another striking example of the influence of the economic environment on social relationships is the development of "friendships" among "colleagues in office" and "partners in trade" who "call one another brothers" and "frequently feel towards another as if they really were so" (*TMS,* VI.ii.1.15, pp. 223–224). Even though this form of "utilitarian" friendship in which "their good agreement is an advantage to all" is clearly inferior for Smith to the "true" friendship of men of virtue, people seem to feel real sentiments and attachments towards one another because of their "habitual sympathy" and so we can infer that they are likely to provide reciprocal services or mutual "good offices" out of other-regarding principles.

In the *LJ* and *WN,* Smith uses a "four stages theory" of human history to explain the foundation, emergence and history of law and government, against prevailing social contract theories. There, Smith refers to numerous practices of gifts and beneficence in different societies and times. One of them is the custom of making "gifts" to judges in societies of hunter-gatherers and shepherds, because "they will never enter on the consideration of a cause without a gratuity" (*LJ (A),* iv.16, p. 206; *LJ(B),* 307, pp. 529–530; *WN,* V.i.b.13, p. 715). For example, "no one can have access to the Mogul unless he have a present in his hand, and so in all other rude and barbarous nations" (*LJ (A),* iv.16, p. 206). In this type of societies, there is neither a publicly funded government nor institutions of justice because private property, and conflicts over it, is still limited. The magistrate is often the chief of the tribe (and their general in time of war), exercising all powers by himself and maintaining everyone under his dependence (*WN,* V.i.b.7, p. 712). And he accepts his role of judge "without any reward" (*LJ(B),* 307, pp. 529–530). Therefore, one could think that the gifts he receives are a form of payment or salary for his charge and in way they are so. But it seems to be more complex than that because despite having no "reward", the magistrate "was fully satisfied with the eminence of his station" (*LJ(B),* 307, pp. 529–530). So the gifts made seem to be some symbols of recognition of the dependence of people upon him (*LJ(A),* iv.32, p. 212). Importantly, this relationship has the features of a reciprocity relationship. Indeed, these "presents" must be "voluntary" and it "cannot be prevented while one is willing to give and another to receive" (*LJ(B),* 307, pp. 529–530). But of course Smith understood the "bad effect" of this practice, namely, the corruption and partiality of judges towards those who made the greatest gifts (*LJ(B),* 307, pp. 529–530; *WN,* V.i.b.14, p. 716).[14] These practices stopped once judges were appointed fixed salaries paid from taxes collected on the citizens in order to afford the increasing expenses of the sovereign, especially to defend his nation (*WN,* V.i.b.17, p. 718). Another practice of "gift-giving" linked to the lack of proper institutions of justice (unable to enforce "punishments") in savage societies, that Smith mentions (using sources like Charlevoix and Lafitau), is the custom to make "presents" to expiate a crime, "appease the friends of the slain" and obtain forgiveness (*LJ(A),* ii.96–7, pp. 106–107; *LJ(A),* ii.99, p. 108).

But maybe the most interesting example of the influence of institutions on practices of beneficence in Smith's works is his analysis of the "hospitality" and "charity" of land owners and clergymen in feudal societies. In this type of societies, based on agriculture, the rich proprietor, "having nothing for which he can exchange the greater part of the produce of his lands which is over and above the maintenance of the cultivators, consumes the whole in rustick hospitality at home" (*WN,* III.iv.5, p. 413). So that he maintains a multitude of "retainers" and other people who live in complete dependence towards him and "must obey him", like "soldiers must obey the prince who pays them" (*WN,* III.iv.5, p. 413; see also III.iv.11, p. 419). The gift of hospitality from the landlords and clergymen was a means to establish their power and authority over people (*WN,* V.i.g.22, p. 802). In other words, it is the economic backwardness of these societies, the lack of spending opportunities, or means of gratifying their "vanity" which explains the hospitality and charity of the clergy and nobility towards the poor. Smith then explains that the power of both classes was destroyed by the "gradual improvements of arts, manufactures, and commerce", that is, with the advent of commercial societies which furnished them with "something for which they could exchange the whole surplus of their lands … without sharing it either with tenants and retainers", in other words: luxury goods (*WN,* III.iv.10, p. 418; V.i.g.25, p. 803). And then their charity and hospitality immediately vanished (*WN,* III.iv.10, p. 418; V.i.g.25, p. 803), with the positive though unintended side-effect that people were freed from their dependence upon them. The same goes for the clergy whose charity and hospitality gradually declined once they discovered how to spend their revenues upon themselves (*WN,* V.i.g.25, pp. 803–804). In commercial societies, beneficence is more "left to the freedom of our own wills" (*TMS,* II.ii.1.5, p. 79) but hospitality, the gift to receive (Godbout, 2019), could disappear, as Montesquieu claimed (Caillé et al., 2019, p. 10). The rise of what the latter called the "spirit of commerce" associated with the principles of "frugality" and "oeconomy" goes against the "generosity" and "good fellowship" of hospitality, Smith argues (*TMS,* V.2.13, p. 209).

Conclusion

Smith is usually seen among economists and social scientists as someone who focused exclusively on man's propensity for the economic exchange of goods and services, that is, on the self-interested commerce among strangers typical of market societies. But as we tried to show here, Smith carefully studied and conceptualised other forms of exchanges or "transfers" between people. More precisely, he offers a rich analysis of gift-giving and reciprocity which is quite unique among economists and of which we can find some resonance in contemporary works on the gift by sociologists and anthropologists. Charity, generosity and gratitude are natural principles of human nature for Smith, though they are mainly to be found in the domestic sphere of private, intimate, personal relationships. And Smith undoubtedly understood that the meaning and practices of gift-giving and reciprocity vary over time and space with the evolution of economic, social and political institutions. Smith was first and foremost a moral philosopher whose goal was to refute the selfish view of human nature offered by Hobbes, Mandeville and the Augustinians. We conclude that among economists, Smith should be seen as an important thinker of the gift and altruism.

Notes

1 This view was best encapsulated by Stigler's famous claim that "The *Wealth of Nations* is a stupendous palace erected upon the granite of self-interest" (1971, p. 265). Note that Smith makes a very sparse use of "self-interest" in his works, often preferring "self-love".

2 Then *WN*.

3 On this and other abuses of Smith in economics, see Sen (2011). Bhanu Mehta even claims that "*The Wealth of Nations* is a virtual catalogue of the passions and rival motivations that impede the pursuit of self-interest" (2006, p. 253). Relatedly, I won't discuss the "Adam Smith Problem" because, as many Smith scholars, I don't believe that there is any "Problem" at all of compatibility between the vision of human nature in *WN* and *TMS*, or between self-love and sympathy or benevolence, as I show later.

4 Then *TMS*.

5 Notable exceptions are Khalil (2001), Hanley (2009), Harpham (2010) and Elster (2011), whose works we will discuss later.

6 It does not mean that for him human nature is always or mainly benevolent. Smith speaks of the "feeble spark of benevolence that Nature has lighted up in the human heart" (*TMS*, III.3.4, p. 137), like Hume talked of man's "limited" or "confin'd generosity of man" (*THN*, 3.3.3.2, p. 384; 3.2.2.18, p. 318).

7 Praiseworthiness is, for Smith, of higher value than and can be enjoyed independently from social praise (*TMS*, III.2.5, pp. 115–116). Moreover, the pleasure of social approbation is of little value when it is not coupled with the pleasure of self-approbation (*TMS*, III.2.4, pp. 114–115).

8 This idea of beneficence towards "extraordinary situations", and especially towards the rich and powerful, is peculiar to Smith (Biziou et al., 2003, p. 313, note 3; Tegos, 2018, p. 162).

9 Smith's views on gratitude (and beneficence) owe much to his reading of Seneca's *De Beneficiis* and Cicero's *De Officiis* (Elster, 2010; Harpham, 2010; Tegos, 2018, pp. 154–159).

10 Most economic models of reciprocity focus either on outcomes (Fehr and Schmidt, 1999; Bolton and Ockenfels, 2000) or on perceived intentions (Rabin, 1993; Falk et al., 2003; Dufwenberg and Kirchsteiger, 2004). One notable exception is Falk and Fischbacher (2006) which takes into account both intentions (or "intentionality" here) and outcomes. Interestingly, this model was then used and refined by Stanca et al. (2009) to include motivations in order to create experiments testing the importance of the latter on reciprocity.

11 The common superior value of the counter-gift over the initial gift was analysed by anthropologists like Maunier, who called this the "*augment*" (Athane, 2011, pp. 121–123).

12 If we suppose that *A* makes a gift to *B* and *B* wants to return it, the rule could mean that:

   i the value of the gift for *A* should be equal to the value of the counter-gift for *B*
   ii the value of the gift for A should be equal to the value of the counter-gift for A
   iii the value of the gift for *B* should be equal to the value of the counter-gift for *B*
   iv the value of the gift for *B* should be equal to the value of the counter-gift for *A*.

13 On the complex relationship between the gift and welfare states, see Silvestri (2020).

14 See also (*LJ(B)*, 307, p. 530; *WN*, V.i.b.16, pp. 717–718). Note that it is in line with Smith's idea that gratitude and reciprocity increase with the value of the gift.

References

Andreoni, J. 1990. Impure Altruism and Donations to Public Goods: A Theory of Warm-Glow Giving. *The Economic Journal*. **100**(401), pp. 464–477. DOI: 10.2307/2234133

Athane, F. 2011. *Pour une histoire naturelle du don*. Paris: PUF.

Berry, C. 2012. Adam Smith's Science of Human Nature. *History of Political Economy*. **44**(3), pp. 471–492. DOI: 10.1215/00182702-1717257

Berry, C. 2013. *The Idea of Commercial Society in the Scottish Enlightenment*. Edinburgh: Edinburgh University Press.

Bhanu Mehta, P. 2006. Self-Interest and Other Interests. In: Haakonssen, K. Ed. *The Cambridge Companion to Adam Smith*. Cambridge: Cambridge University Press, pp. 246–269. DOI: 10.1017/CCOL0521770599.010

Biziou, M. 2016. Adam Smith and the History of Philosophy. In: Hanley, R. Ed. *Adam Smith. His Life, Thought and Legacy*. Princeton, NJ: Princeton University Press, pp. 422–442.

Bizou, M., Gautier, C. and Pradeau, J. F. 2003. *Théorie des Sentiments Moraux,* traduction, introduction et notes. Paris: PUF Quadrige.

Bolton, G. and Ockenfels, A. 2000. ERC: A Theory of Equity, Reciprocity and Competition. *American Economic Review*. **90**(1), pp. 166–193. DOI: 10.1257/aer.90.1.166

Caillé, A., Chanial, P., Gauthier, F. and Robertson, F. 2019. Le don d'hospitalité. Quand recevoir c'est donner. *Revue du Mauss*. **53**, pp. 5–26. DOI: 10.3917/rdm.053.0005

Darwall, S. 2004. Equal Dignity in Adam Smith. *Adam Smith Review*. **1**, pp. 129–34.

Dufwenberg, M. and Kirchsteiger, G. 2004. A Theory of Sequential Reciprocity. *Games and Economic Behavior*. **47**(2), pp. 268–298. DOI: 10.1016/j.geb.2003.06.003

Elster, J. 2009. *Le désintéressement. Traité critique de l'homme économique I*. Paris: Seuil.

Elster, J. 2011. Reciprocity in Seneca and Smith. *Adam Smith Review*. **6**, pp. 152–171.

Falk, A. and Fischbacher, U. 2006. A Theory of Reciprocity. *Games and Economic Behavior*. **54**, pp. 293–315. DOI: 10.1016/j.geb.2005.03.001

Fehr, E. and Schmidt, K. 1999. A Theory of Fairness, Competition and Co-operation. *The Quarterly Journal of Economics*. **114**(3), pp. 817–868. DOI: 10.1162/003355399556151

Fleischacker, S. 2004. *On Adam Smith's Wealth of Nations. A Philosophical Companion*. Princeton, NJ: Princeton University Press.

Fleischacker, S. 2011. Equal Dignity in Adam Smith. *Adam Smith Review*. **1**, pp. 129–134.

Forman-Barzilai, F. 2010. *Adam Smith and the Circles of Sympathy. Cosmopolitanism and Moral Theory*. Cambridge: Cambridge University Press. DOI: 10.1017/CBO9780511676352

Godbout, J. 2019. Recevoir c'est donner. *Revue du Mauss*. **53**, pp. 159–174. DOI: 10.3917/rdm.053.0159

Godbout, J. and Caillé, A. 1992. *L'esprit du don*. Paris: La Découverte.

Gouldner, A. 1960. The Norm of Reciprocity: A Preliminary Statement. *American Sociological Review*. **25**(2), pp. 161–178. DOI: 10.2307/2092623

Hanley, R. 2009. *Adam Smith and the Character of Virtue*. Cambridge: Cambridge University Press.

Hanley, R. 2013. Adam Smith and Virtue. In: Berry, C., Paganelli, M. and Smith, C. Eds. *The Oxford Handbook of Adam Smith*. Oxford: Oxford University Press.

Harpham, E. J. 2010. Adam Smith's Lost World of Gratitude. In: Ginsberg, B. and Mink, G. Eds. *Political Science as Public Philosophy. Essays in Honor of J. Lowi.* London: Norton and Company, pp. 345–363.

Heath, E. 2013. Adam Smith and Self-Interest. In: Berry, C., Paganelli, M. and Smith, C. Eds. *The Oxford Handbook of Adam Smith.* Oxford: Oxford University Press, pp. 241–264.

Hume, D. 2000[1739–1740]. *A Treatise of Hume Nature.* In: Norton, D. and Norton, M. Eds. Oxford: Oxford University Press.

Hutcheson, F. 2008[1725]. *An Inquiry into the Original of Our Ideas of Beauty and Virtue.* In: Haakonssen, K. and Leidhold, W. Eds. Indianapolis, IN: Liberty Fund.

Khalil, E. 2001. Adam Smith and Three Theories of Altruism. *Recherches économiques de Louvain.* **67**(4), pp. 421–435. DOI: 10.3917/rel.674.0421

Kolm, S. C. 2008. *Reciprocity.* Cambridge: Cambridge University Press.

Marchionatti, R. and Cedrini, M. 2017. *Economics as Social Science. Economics Imperialism and the Challenge of Interdisciplinarity.* New York: Routledge.

Marouby, C. 2004. *L'économie de la nature. Essai sur Adam Smith et l'anthropologie de la croissance.* Paris: Seuil.

Mauss, M. 2012[1923–1924]. *Essai sur le don.* Paris: PUF.

McCloskey, D. 2008. Adam Smith, the Last of the Former Virtue Ethicists. *History of Political Economy.* **40**(1), pp. 43–71. DOI: 10.1215/00182702-2007-046

Meek, R. 1976. *Social Science and the Ignoble Savage.* Cambridge: Cambridge University Press.

Nieli, R. 1986. Sphere of Intimacy and the Adam Smith Problem. *Journal of the History of Ideas.* **47**(4), pp. 611–624. DOI: 10.2307/2709721

Okan, E. 2017. How Did It All Begin? Adam Smith on the Early and Rude State of Society and the Age of Hunters. *European Journal of the History of Economic Thought.* **24**(6), pp. 1247–1276. DOI: 10.1080/09672567.2017.1381134

Paganelli, M. 2018. Adam Smith on the Future of Experimental Evolution and Economics. *Journal of Bioeconomics,* **20**, pp. 23–28. DOI: 10.1007/s10818-017-9265-8

Pauchant, T. 2017. Adam Smith's Four Stages Theory of Socio-Cultural Evolution: New Insights from His 1749 Lecture. *Adam Smith Review.* **9**, pp. 49–74.

Rabin, M. 1993. Incorporating Fairness into Game Theory and Economics. *American Economic Review.* **83**(5), pp. 1281–1302.

Sen, A. 2009. *The Idea of Justice.* Harvard: Harvard University Press.

Sen, A. 2011. Uses and Abuses of Adam Smith. *History of Political Economy.* **43**(2), pp. 257–271. DOI: 10.1215/00182702-1257388

Silvestri, P. 2019. The All Too Human Welfare State: Freedom Between Gift and Corruption. *Teoria e critica della regolazione sociale.* **2**, pp. 123–145. DOI: 10.7413/19705476007

Smith, A. 1981[1776]. *An Inquiry into the Nature and Causes of the Wealth of Nations.* In: Campbell, R. and Skinner, A. Eds. Indianapolis, IN: Liberty Fund.

Smith, A. 1982[1759–1790]. *The Theory of Moral Sentiments.* In: Raphael, D. and Macfie, A. Eds. Indianapolis, IN: Liberty Fund.

Smith, A. 1982[1762–1766]. *Lectures on Jurisprudence.* In: Meek, R., Raphael, D. and Stein, P. Eds. Indianapolis, IN: Liberty Fund.

Smith, A. 1987. *Correspondence of Adam Smith.* In: Mossner, E. and Ross, I. Eds. Indianapolis, IN: Liberty Fund.

Smith, V. and Wilson, B. 2019. *Humanomics. Moral Sentiments and the Wealth of Nations for the Twenty-First Century.* Cambridge: Cambridge University Press.

Stanca, L., Bruni, L. and Corazzini, L. 2009. Testing Theories of Reciprocity: Do Motivations Matter. *Journal of Economic Behavior and Organization.* **71**(2), pp. 233–245.

Tegos, S. 2018.Libéralité et moeurs des 'rangs moyens' chez Adam Smith. In: Le Jallé, E. and McIntosh-Varjabedian, F. Eds. *Liberal, Libéralité, Libéralisme. Histoire et Enjeux Philosophiques, Culturels, et Littéraires.* Paris: Honoré Champion, pp. 147–166.

Testart, A. 2007. *Critiques du don. Etudes sur la circulation non marchande.* Paris: Syllepse.

Vanterpool, R. 1988. Hume on the "Duty" of Benevolence. *Hume Studies.* **XIV**(1), pp. 93–110. DOI: 10.1353/hms.2011.0493

Walraevens, B. forthcoming. Reciprocity in Adam Smith. *Oeconomia-History, Philosophy, Methodology.*

Walraevens, B. 2014. Vertus et justice du marché chez Adam Smith. *Revue Economique.* **65**(2), pp. 419–438. DOI: 10.3917/reco.652.0419

4 The gift as total social fact

From Mauss to money

Diego Viana

Introduction

This chapter explores the Maussian approach to the gift in order to raise a hypothesis concerning market economies/societies, money in particular. The gift is usually understood, in economics and social science, from its form as an act or interaction that differs from exchange in that an equivalent return is not presupposed. The object given is often contrasted to the commodity, though not necessarily. For example, when Waldfogel (1993) argues against Christmas gifts, the argument is based on an understanding of the given good as a utility-satisfying commodity. On the other hand, for the economics of donations, such as Arrow (1972), this is not the case.

Though the concept of gift, understood in this sense, has traditionally been treated as the basis of an economic structure (gift economies) opposed to market economies based on exchange, this strict opposition has been shown to be exaggerated. Akerlof (1982) suggests that labour relations necessarily transcend the simple buying and selling of work, while the opposition between gift and commodity is dubious (Lanna, 2014). The strict distinction between gift-giving and exchanging leads to misunderstanding how different forms of interaction and behaviour are extreme cases of a continuum, and stems from a strictly horizontal reading of social relations. As a reader of Polanyi will recognise, such interactions occur within an institutional framework that cannot be derived from them, and where the division of activities between those performed as gifts and those performed as trading is drawn.

But there is yet another meaning of the gift, which connects the two already brought up, and is therefore indispensable for understanding the outreach of the notion of *gift*. This chapter explores the third meaning through the work of Marcel Mauss. Mauss's *Essai sur le Don* (*The Gift*), published in 1925, became a landmark in economic anthropology. It was taken up by Lévi-Strauss (1987), Sahlins (1972), Hart (1986), Graeber (2011), Caillé (2007). Philosophers adopted Maussian concepts like *mana*, *potlatch* and *hau*, in order to think all that exceeds market transactions. Economics has paid less attention to Maussian insights, with notable exception like Mirowski (1987) and recently Egbert (2018).

The core of Mauss's contribution lies in the *total social fact*, which describes ceremonies of gift-giving not only as a time for transferring goods or performing feasts, but the moment when the institutional framework of a social configuration is both created and reasserted. The crucial term in this understanding will be shown to be *creation*: not only the structure of gift-giving expresses the relations within a given social configuration, in these moments the gifts are vectors of the birth and rebirth of these relations, insofar as they are *meaningful* and can orient the activities of the entire cycle of social activity.

The total social fact is usually envisioned as an amalgam of social domains, making it a prospective interface between social sciences. The concept not only raises relevant questions to sociology, anthropology, law, economics, etc., it also suggests ways to connect questions concerning power and circulation, sovereignty and society. This leads Caillé (2007) to state that the Maussian gift is a new, dynamic paradigm for social sciences at large. For Caillé, the central component of the gift is the creation of obligations.

In this chapter, the total social fact is viewed from the sociogenic angle. The cases Mauss analyses are usually gift-giving ceremonies, but their intrinsic sense lies not in the circulating gifts, but on how this circulation consists in a society giving itself its core institutions. Any social configuration must assert itself through this "original" gift, which is only "original" in retrospect: it is the act through which the collective presents itself with its beliefs, its reasons to be what it is, its relation to its past, its sense of the sacred, its future, and all that regards transcendence.

This approach applies the total social fact to market economies, assuming they are no exception to the rule. Following authors like Aglietta, Orléan, Théret and others associated under the name "monetary institutionalism",[1] I explore the hypothesis that market economies/societies realise their total social facts through money and finance. Monetary institutionalism sprang in France from the Regulation School in the 1980s. Regulationists kept a dialogue with Anglo-Saxon institutionalism and counted five main institutional structures that organise market economies: the market, wage-labour, competition, the international economy and the monetary system (Brenner and Glick, 1991). Beginning in the early 1980s with the work of Aglietta and Orléan (1982), this last institution attained a central position, giving birth to a new current of thought.

The last section of this chapter attempts to take the monetary institutionalists' hypothesis even further. Though these authors recognise in money a crucial institution for the interaction between the economic and other social spheres, they do not break apart from the understanding that money is generated within market transactions, by the market itself or by the State. But as we shall see, though concretely money can be issued by markets once they both (money and markets) exist, ontologically money can only be fully grasped in its social, political and institutional role once it is thought as expressing something that precedes market relations and performs an important role in shaping them. Even if, given the existence of markets, the relations incarnated in money can take the shape of a commodity and thus seem to emerge from it, this does not mean that the ontogenesis of money should be traced to the commodity or to market interactions in general.

The question of money creation is at the centre of the problem, and is addressed through Werner's (2014) experiment on how banks create money. Yet by stating that banks create new money when it issues a sum through a loan, only part of the story is told. Even if one loan, individually, is an act of money creation, it can only achieve general recognition through the connection this bank has to the financial system. As issuance, the process of money creation by banks is also an instance of the self-generation and self-reproduction of the monetary system as a whole, i.e. of the "general" creation, or institution, of money. Yet money creation is an operation by which a certain social configuration gives itself a set of values, which entails that the individual instance of money creation (issuing through loans) restates the institution in the same way as the total social fact, as ceremony, restates the myth. The chapter explores this hypothesis.

Credit is clearly not a gift, if by gift one means only the first sense of the term, as a transfer with the expectation of precise reciprocation. But there is a catch: if the bank is not alienating anything of its own when it grants a client a line of credit, then the kind of relation involved is not simply the traditional market transaction. Commenting on Baudelaire and Mauss, Derrida writes that the gift is paradoxical because though it implies altruism and the transfer of a possession (I give what I have to someone who will then have it), any gift creates a bond of some kind which is always in excess of the transfer itself (Derrida, 1991, p. 119). Credit creation, on the other hand, not being a gift proper, involves the same kind of overflow and excess. But this excess, which one would usually associate to a gift, is decisive for money to be money, as otherwise it would only satisfy a particular need or utility and would not carry with it the social senses of obligation and value it effectively carries.

Consequently, any theory that derives money from the market relations in general or from a commodity in particular will bypass a constitutive aspect of money, which reveals itself in its inception. The models considered to be most solid in economics, i.e. Walrasian general equilibrium models, up to the dynamic stochastic general equilibrium (DSGE) models, are known for their difficulty in incorporating money. In 1981, Frank Hahn writes that "[t]he most serious challenge that the existence of money poses to the theorist is this: the best developed model of the economy cannot find room for it" (Hahn, 1981, p. 1). As recently as 1993, Martin Hellwig still states that "we do not, as yet, have a suitable theoretical framework for studying the functioning of a monetary system" (Hellwig, 1993, p. 215). After the crash in 2008, the dimmed role attributed to money in macroeconomic models was pointed out as a major failure and gave rise to a renewed interest in Modern Money Theory (Mitchell et al., 2019).

The reason is that all these models cling to the idea that market interactions, including monetary exchanges, can be understood purely, among actors exchanging commodities. Money can hence appear as merely a commodity (in financial terms, an asset), and there is no particular reason for holding money rather than spending it in exchange for a palpable commodity. But if money arises from credit and money creation is a gift (bringing into existence), then money plays a crucial role among economic institutions and should be interpreted accordingly.

In the first section, three ways of understanding the gift are reviewed. Section "Gift and grant" explores the gift as a transaction, supported by Boulding's (1981) theory of grants, where this sense of the term "gift" is very clearly stated. Section "Gift economies" describes gift economies, as opposed to market economies and as a concept in themselves. Section "Coming into existence" is dedicated to the ontogenetic concept of gift, i.e. the gift as "bringing into existence". The second section discusses the total social fact (section "Total social fact"). Section "The paradigmatic gift" discusses Caillé's suggestion that Mauss's gift is a paradigm for social sciences, and section "Total social fact and trust" relates it to other concepts in social sciences useful for discussing money and market economies/societies. The third section is dedicated to the total social fact in market economies. In section "Money and markets", the question of monetary crises and obligations is addressed. The next section describes Werner's experiment with money creation and relates it to Aglietta and Orléans's theory of the triadic monetary system. Section "Double creation" explores the implication of the arguments developed so far.

Typology

Gift and grant

The first and most general meaning of the term "gift" is the one we find, clearly stated, in Boulding's *Preface to Grant Economics* (1981). A gift in this sense is an instance of grant, where an individual transfers a good to another without the imposition of conditions for a counter-transfer. Robberies or taxes (tributes) are grants originated from threats. Gifts are defined as transfers originating from the link between the giver and the well-being of the receiver, or *love*, which Boulding names an "integrative system" (Dolfsma and Kesting, 2013, p. 39). Clientelistic systems employ such gifts and grants widely.[2]

Here reciprocity is possible, but not necessary. It occurs when two individuals grant each other goods of similar values unconditionally. Trade involves conditionality: goods are transferred in view of the return they may bring. For Boulding, trade may have emerged from reciprocal grants (e.g. the "Indian gift"; Parry, 1986), indicating a possible continuity between different forms of transfers. In all, an economy can be viewed as the sum of exchanges and grants, including government grants, private grants, family grants, etc.

As an unconditional transfer, this sense of the term only describes interactions within economies as they are given, with their institutional framework in place. It is thus more a phenomenology of gifts in the modern economy than an investigation of the nature of gift-giving. The logic at work is the same that underlies economic thought in general: methodological individualism (Boudon, 1979), where the starting point for any explanation of social phenomena is individual behaviour. Within this framework, the gift is explained by its atomistic appearance, not the structures it presupposes. This is why grants and particularly gifts appear as compensating inefficiencies of exchange.

This is also the epistemological background when Offer (1997) writes that non-market exchange and gifts "persist in modern times" (p. 450), and "gifting may be, if not always 'efficient' in the formal sense, at least a viable alternative to the market system" (*idem*). There is a place for gifts in market economies, for Offer, when information does not circulate quicker through prices than through other forms of communication. This is the case in personal relations, and the standard case is the household, where interactions are predominantly non-transactional.

The gift cannot be explained with an atomistic framework. Boulding points to the gift's overflowing from individualism. The book is subtitled "economy of love and fear", and shows that grants and gifts are a source of power and mark of hierarchy: by giving, one side of the interaction expresses their higher status; returning a gift re-establishes the horizontality (Dolfsma and Kesting, 2013, p. 415). There is complementarity between grants and exchange, but, from the economist's perspective, these power relations remain secondary to the objective transfer of goods.

Gift economies

Following the individualistic definition of *gift*, one would interpret gift economies as systems where the exchange of equivalents is absent *de facto*, but virtually given, since the formal conditions for its emergence are present: individuals, goods, interactions. With this strict framework, gift economies would be interpreted as "primitive" systems, where distribution or reciprocity predominates because markets are underdeveloped. This is often the case when economists write about non-Western forms of distribution, as in Dalton's (1965) critique of W.E. Armstrong, concerning the Rossel islanders' system of compensatory objects.

Yet contemporary initiatives aimed at creating non-capitalist ways of life often evoke the notion of gift economy, as an alternative to market-based systems, such as Eisenstein (2010) or Vaughan (1997). Online file-sharing communities and open-source initiatives also claim to reinstate forms of gift economies (Skågeby, 2010; Zeytlin, 2003). These perspectives share the shift in focus from individual, self-interested interaction to community-based thinking, where generosity is prized. The authors often evoke non-Western societies as examples of gift economies to inspire their initiatives, quoting from Sahlin's (1972) argument that "primitive" societies live in relative comfort, contrary to the rooted Hobbesian belief that life outside the Western framework is "brutish and short". These authors assume a radical opposition between "commodity" and "gift".

But it is misleading to oppose gift economies to market economies, as if one could simply choose between them. First, gift economies can hardly be grasped simply as economies – not that market societies can. Since Malinowski and Mauss, the study of these societies reveals that ceremonial gift-giving has a social import binding several aspects of collective life, from the political to the religious, the aesthetic and economic. In the Melanesian *kula*, Malinowski and Mauss show that a form of exchange (*gimwali*) is intricately tied to the gift system: exchange is not the *antipode* of the gift.

The tradition founded on Mauss is based on the realisation that a particular gift belongs to a system wherein not only reciprocity is a component, but *acquires sense*. For Mauss, the particular gift materialises a series of obligations: giving, accepting and returning, thus organising a cycle of interactions. The organised cycle is the framework wherein collective life appears as social order, which is why the gift eludes any atomistic interpretation. The gift is institutional as the basis of a system of relations, whereby behaviours become predictable. Relations of trust *and distrust* acquire form: there are socially justified manners to trust or distrust someone. This is how there are *gift economies*, as distribution and production systems organised around ritualised acts of giving.

This concept of gift fits poorly into individualism. A grant in the economic sense "dies out", like bilateral exchange. Boulding evokes the power relations implicated in these operations, but they remain subsidiary: they are not the core of gift-giving and lose much of their structural import in the epistemological framework of mainstream economics. Contrarily, the *particular* gift in gift economies is only the manifestation of underlying obligations, which are usually indirect, creating circuits at least triangular (Leach, 1961; Lévi-Strauss, 1987; Sahlins, 1972). The establishment of obligations (alliances, rivalries, reciprocity) is as much reason for the gift as distributing goods.

The obligations are also disproportional. They should not be cancelled, unless a group wants to cease relations with another. This is necessary for a gift economy; otherwise, the obligations might constitute an economic exchange. The disproportion is a form of indeterminacy, generating an openness to be filled by concrete manifestations of activities and behaviours. Lastly, any equilibrium is *exceptional* and occasional. Thinking collective phenomena through the gift has the advantage of doing away with equilibrium. Gift ceremonies exist to relaunch a disequilibrium, keeping relations among individuals and groups indefinitely metastable.[3]

What stands out is that, with these ceremonies, societies *give themselves* their structure of meaning and activity. Gift economies, with their structures of trust and obligations, do not float in the air, as it might seem from how the proponents of new gift economies describe them. They are founded and refounded through a periodic event – which Mauss names "total social fact" and is the subject of section "Mauss". In this sense, the term *gift* designates a *fundamental* institution, instituting the *system* of institutions where interactions occur. But before we can define more clearly the total social fact as it appears in Mauss's text, it is necessary to examine the third sense of the term "gift", which is central to the concept of total social fact. As we shall see, the distinctive character of the total social fact is that at each turn it elaborates the foundations on which it stands, as if the configuration of social life had to be lifted by its bootstraps: the set and system of myths and events that it evokes – even the construal of historical events – not only lives, but comes to life in the re-enactment, which is also at the same time an enactment. This is why the total social fact expresses the third and most decisive sense of the gift: that of bringing into existence.

Coming into existence

The third sense is crucial to the social, political, economic and institutional implications of gift-giving. A fecund attempt to connect the senses of the *gift* was made by the poet Lewis Hyde in the book *The Gift* (1983), where he examines the anthropological tradition surrounding the gift in light of an indelible character of donation present in art. Talented artists are *gifted* in the sense of a creativity that cannot be generated, only perfected, by exercise. To keep this gift undeveloped is a morally reproachable waste. This is one of the interpretations of the "parable of the talents" in the Gospels: one's abilities are divine gifts; it is sinful to lay them to waste. Hyde underscores the gift's *creative* aspect in relation to artistic creation. This sense involves the notion of *bringing into existence*, but beyond the individual exercise of one's capacities. Herodotus wrote that Egypt was a gift of the Nile, not because the river planned to create a civilisation, but because it overflowed with life by its sheer natural power. In several mythologies, crucial forms of human technicity are gifts from divine figures, like Prometheus.

The *gift* contains the idea that a certain configuration of reality, social and even cosmic, must be instituted, not as an evolution from a prior state, but an overflow of something *transcending* it. Gift-giving ceremonies are usually celebrations of the act by which life was given to a community, like Christmas or Pesach. These ceremonies are decisive for the community, as its relation to a realm of meaning beyond it hinges on the correct performance of the re-enactment. The meaning of its daily life and institutions flows from this event. But while these ceremonies take support in the relation to the transcendent, it is *the ceremony itself* that affirms the transcendent and gives it concreteness: an immanent act produces its own transcendent justification. As we shall see, this is a central tenet of Mauss's concept of "total social fact".

When the monetary institutionalists rely on the "life debt" (*dette de vie*) to explain the foundational feature of money, they are trying to account for the aspect of the gift as "bringing into existence", which will be shown to be inextricable from the concept of money in section "Double creation". The life debt is a notion borrowed from Malamoud's (1989) reading of the Vedas and expresses the understanding that the ancestors, the gods, the land, have given individuals and communities not only their lives, but also the conditions for life to continue. Like Münchhausen's ability to lift himself from a mire by pulling his own hair, the collective institutes its forms of living, meaning and acting: it bootstraps its world. Hence the idea of a "life debt": not an indebtedness for life, but the expression of how the simple fact of *being alive* is owed to something – or someone; to acknowledge a "life debt" is to assert a fundamental connection to something wider than oneself, something that transcends the immediately perceived world we live in, i.e. a realm of entities that precede and outlast the community as it stands.

Properly speaking, these entities never formulate a demand for compensation. More importantly, no actual compensation is possible for the gift of life, not even life itself: dying is no way to return given life; no equivalence exists between bringing into existence and taking existence away. Nonetheless, it would be sinful and disastrous to bypass the compensations, as this would break the link to transcendence, the ultimate link to life. With the *life debt*, what is stated is the bond to the entire community (Aglietta and Orléan, 2002); once the life debt is recognised, the individual's activity is *conditioned* by the obligation to act according to how their universe was organised. The affirmation of transcendence is also, paradoxical as it may seem, the affirmation of immanence; and the validity of the relation to the transcendent is demonstrated by everyday life: survival, thriving, fertility, peace.

The recourse to the life debt has been criticised for its excessive reliance in an Indo-European framework. For Breton (2000), the concept of life debt is perfectly valid for Vedic India, but hardly so for Melanesia, where what is stressed is "the cosmological need to relaunch the regenerative movement of the society" (p. 1366). Indeed, in this chapter, the cosmological relaunch of the society is at the core of the problem of the gift – and of money. Nevertheless, the important question is why these theoreticians evoke the life debt in their explanation of money. It is because it helps to account for one of the main problems in understanding money: confidence in its value in time, for periods longer than a generation, as money has no particular use value and will only be held and accepted it there is a reasonable certainty that it will remain valuable in the future.

For example, in general equilibrium microeconomics, the attempt to describe the ontogenesis of money with methodological individualism and bilateral contracts faces serious difficulties, especially when money is seen as neutral, as Aglietta and Orléan (2002, p. 104) stress: money cannot be understood as a contract between two individuals. An attempt to solve this difficulty is found in models that apply notions like Samuelson's "overlapping generations" (*cf.* Weil, 1987); the strategy is to introduce a chronologic dimension, under the form of a dependence between generations. This dependence takes shape when generations can trust each other through the acceptance of a good as money.

But, as Aglietta (2016, p. 78) states, there is nothing contractual about this confidence in money; the model steps out of itself. Weil writes that "holding this money to provide for old-age consumption requires confidence and trust as, in the absence of a benevolent government, no one can guarantee to the young that the next generation will agree to exchange goods for money" (1987, p. 2). Monetary institutionalism resorts to the "life debt" theory in order to account for the confidence and faith that transcend a present generation, by stating that the ontogenesis of money cannot be attributed to bilateral contracts, which includes market relations. As we shall see, in Laum's (2019) wake, they attempt to theorise a religious origin of money, translated into secular terms through the concept of *sovereignty*. This issue will reappear in section "Double creation".

Mauss

Total social fact

The *total social fact* is presented at the end of Mauss's *Gift*. The concept describes certain occasions, within the calendar of a society, that have the purpose of *founding* and *reasserting* the sense of interactions in a society – i.e. what people concretely consider they are doing when they interact socially – and by extension its institutions. Let us examine how these occasions present themselves and what role the gift, in its three senses, plays in them.

First, Mauss insists in the "dynamic or physiologic" (Mauss, 2010, p. 102) perspective in analysing societies; he is not interested in structures, but in the exercise of rules and myths. Second, Mauss states that each society he discusses has a *particular moment*, involving the whole collective or its most important institutions and individuals, which is "the living aspect, the fleeting moment when society, or men, become sentimentally aware of themselves and their situation in relation to others" (*idem*). For Mauss, studying the total social fact is "urgent" and "fruitful", as "[f]acts that relate to the general functioning of society are likely to be more universal than the various institutions, or various themes that relate to these institutions" (*idem*).

The most well-known among the ceremonies Mauss evokes are the Kwakiutl *potlatch* and the Melanesian *kula*, both gift-giving ceremonies with agonistic import, wherein members of the upper classes define their relative positions of power and prestige, while reasserting their ascendancy over the lower ranks. Mauss describes a situation in which the meeting of clans leads either to complete trust or complete distrust; these communities "*seldom* meet together", and must reassert their state of friendship or war at every turn. In doing so, they establish a common ground of meaning and common rules for activities.

Thus in the "particular" and "fleeting" moment of the total social fact, the gift in the first sense (the transfer of an object, usually a sacred object) is the vector of the gift in the third sense ("bringing into existence"), within the general context of the gift in the second sense (a system of non-equivalent transfers of goods). All these senses can be found separately in other moments of a society and in any society, as we have seen in section "Typology". For example, in our own world there are grants (first sense, including government transfers), gift activism (second sense, as in the projects cited in section "Gift economies") and re-enactment ceremonies (third sense, as in public holidays). There is very little connection between them, but they are all part of our social life.

In sum, the total social fact can be defined as the process that generates the framework in which activities within a society are performed. Thus, at any other point in the calendar, the connection between individuals takes place according to the positions they occupy and the access they have to symbolic power. All this stems from the role they play in relation to the total social fact. These arrangements are unstable: sense can be broken; the instituted social domain can crumble. Mauss writes that "[i]t is by opposing reason to feeling, by pitting the will to peace against sudden outbursts of insanity (…) that peoples succeed in substituting alliance, gifts, and trade for war, isolation and stagnation" (p. 105); incidentally, this passage comes after Mauss gives an example of the reverse process: relations of friendship among groups turning into war because of a misplaced word. Nonetheless, the encounters determine the mood for the interval between them: either "alliance, gifts, and trade" or "war, isolation and stagnation". If the institutional framework is not reaffirmed at the right moment, all is lost until a set of meanings is re-established.

Mauss's essay could have remained strictly a study of societies "unlike our own", in his terms, if he hadn't suggested a certain universality of the total social fact. His strategy to reach universality is to overcome the analysis of structures as they are given at a certain point in the development of a society, which would be merely compared to the structures of other societies. Mauss seeks to question how these structures arise, what is necessary for communities to establish and keep a particular way of living, given that any such arrangement is contingent and unstable. In the next topic, this idea of "universality" is examined in further detail.

The paradigmatic gift

Alain Caillé, a founder of the M.A.U.S.S. group (anti-utilitarian movement in social sciences), sees in Mauss the possibility to criticise both methodological poles of social sciences, the aforementioned methodological individualism and that which Caillé names "social holism", consisting in thinking society with large aggregates. In Caillé's terms, these are respectively the first and second paradigms of social science (Caillé, 2007, pp. 13–18). The gift would be the "third paradigm", with a relational character (*idem*, p. 12). For Caillé, the essential component of the gift is the *obligation*. That the gift is a transfer is secondary in relation to the establishment of something beyond it and that it does not precisely determine. The form of the obligation is also secondary to there being an obligation. Mauss's triple obligation – giving, accepting, returning – is for Caillé the expression of general obligation.

This is the underlying problem in Lévi-Strauss's *Introduction* (1987) to Mauss. He criticises his predecessor for overlooking how these obligations are only the phenomenal aspect of a deeper structure, which is reciprocity. Lévi-Strauss's structuralism is rooted on the idea that the phenomenal forms of interaction, and rules like the prohibition of incest, generate a circulatory exchange system, even if it takes the form of gifts. The crucial point is that gift-giving ceremonies are the place and time when, periodically, the sense of the obligations, and consequently the circuits of relations, receive their determinate form, and are reaffirmed or modified. This is one reason why they fuse several domains of collective life: juridical, aesthetic, economic, religious. The core of Mauss's contribution is to direct the investigations towards the *ontogenesis* of structured collective life.

Caillé proceeds by stating that what makes the gift a third, relational paradigm for social science is that this excess of indeterminacy, which gets determined in periodical operations, is a necessary condition for any social formation. It must therefore also be present in market economies, where interactions rely heavily on calculation and interest. Following this reasoning, the interactions themselves are surface phenomena, bound together by the essential, though often implicit, operations whereby obligations are opened and given form.

The question is: what is the operation of ontogenesis in a market economy/society? It is important to stress the ambivalence in these events, creating the undetermined excess through which the social emerges and subsists. The exchange of equivalence in market economies seems to lack such ambiguity; when individuals exchange goods, they supposedly obtain utility and are satisfied. They part ways with nothing hanging between them. The interaction seems to die out.

Total social fact and trust

Still it seems impossible to explain anything in collective existence based solely on interaction as exchange of equivalence; not even the economy. When Hobbes opposes natural law and the human ability to "perform covenants", the latter can only be satisfactorily isolated from the former by positing the overarching figure of the Leviathan (Skinner, 2008). A similar strategy is present in Mises (1996), who wishes to explain the economy as derived from the pure interaction of individuals, but needs an external figure (namely the State) to take care of the legal system, assuring that contracts will be respected, which is precisely the most central and indispensable position. Orléan (1994) shows that any intertemporal trust game needs to evoke an external actor; it could be the justice system or the community as a whole (reputation). The attempt to found trust on an actor *within* the game, as in models with "hired hitmen", introduces the question of the trust in this new actor, thus commencing an infinite regression.

Since Adam Smith, the notion of *trust* or *confidence* operates the link between individual interactions and the duration of collective existence. But it is not simple to establish trust. Repeated interactions over time (trusting someone because they have behaved well in the past or because one expects further interaction) do not suffice, especially in complex economies where great sums and great power are at stake. In the vocabulary of monetary institutionalism, trust in bilateral transactions is dubbed *methodical*, stemming from routine and the previous knowledge of effective procedures (Aglietta and Orléan, 2002, p. 104).

But even market economies cannot function only with methodical trust, as systems become large and face changing circumstances and crises, where alliances and peace turn into distrust and isolation. Théret (2008) distinguishes two other forms of trust: hierarchic and ethic. Hierarchic trust relates to regulation, i.e. institutions: law, custom, authority. But the most intriguing form of trust is the *ethic*, which binds the two other forms and justifies them. Ethic trust relates to a certain belief in the universality of the social configuration, the *world*, where the interactions, their meaning and legitimacy, occur. Ethic trust is not aimed at anyone in particular, but at the whole collective. Théret and the other monetary institutionalists do not establish the link, but it is clear that their concept of *ethic trust* is an attempt to incorporate the total social fact. Ethic trust, which grounds methodical and hierarchic trust, must be instituted, and work inside the "sentimental consciousness" of all.

The total social fact can be a channel for understanding the problem of trust in a new light. This concept helps to examine *how* the relations of trust and their limitations are established and asserted, what are the concretely established causes for trusting and ceasing to trust. The other side of trust is the fear and violence of broken relations. Mauss believed that market economies also rely on the generation of obligations, through an excess, ambiguity, indeterminateness and a logic of gift. The affective import of the social relation was vivid in his thought, with the threat of violence and the perspective of alliances at the core of his problem. Writing between the two world wars, witnessing the rise of fascism and the crumbling of the liberal state, Mauss, a non-Marxist socialist, was trying to conceive forms of social solidarity suited for market economies/societies, as would materialise in the welfare state. He tries to think beyond the "methodical trust" of market relations. His questions attain the realm of "ethic trust", in a time of "ethic distrust".

One of his main purposes in writing the essay was to argue for the establishment of a public pension system, saying that workers give more of themselves than they receive in wages. Lanna (2014) raises the question of whether the concept of surplus-value can be interpreted as an involuntary gift, which might seem to be Mauss's intention in speaking of an excess in production over remuneration. But Mauss's take surpasses the direct capital-labour relation, referring to the entire nation: work generates prosperity, stability, social bonds, transforms landscapes and cityscapes, etc. If private vices lead to public benefits, it is thanks to this outgrowth, the excess of gifts as "bringing into existence".

This is one way in which the principle Mauss discovers in the gift can be identified in market economies/societies. It cannot be grasped only with the first sense of the term. The worker does not "give" his work without expectation of something in return; even the idea that the excess in production over remuneration (surplus-value) is a forced gift does not reach the entire scope of the problem, though it does fit into Boulding's category of non-intentional grant. To understand what is operating, one must recover the sense of the gift as bringing into existence something different than itself. It is only through this wider sense of the concept of gift that the narrower sense (a transfer of goods) is revealed to carry over trust and take part in structuring the field of social relations.

Money

Money and markets

This last section is the most speculative. In it, I adopt the monetary institutionalists' stance in order to suggest that in market economies the dynamic of the total social fact is fulfilled by monetary operations. As an institution, the monetary system performs all the characteristics of the total social fact. The obligations in a market economy are manifold; besides the capital/labour relation, there is also the debtor/creditor relation, the seller/buyer relation, and other subsidiary forms: among sectors, within firms, between the State and the private sector. All these relations share a particular sense as components of a market economy; the obligations they entail are connected. They all involve payments, calculations, and they form a single, cohesive system. They should thus spring and be renewed through similar operations, if we are to look for the total social fact in market economies.

One of the central questions in the study of money is how it is possible that such a thing exists. Historically, the question has been formulated thus: why is a particular good valued beyond its use? Why is a conventional token central in social life? Once the analysis steps out of the presuppositions of methodological individualism, the problem acquires a different shade, as the nature of goods as commodities and individuals as maximising agents ceases to be self-evident. A question arises: *what is the ontogenesis of these categories*? And the problem of the total social fact appears: somehow, the actors of a market economy/society must become "sentimentally aware of themselves". The affective character of the problem can only be clarified by questioning money and its institutional framework.

The last great financial crisis led to a renewed interest in banking, finance and money among economists. Mainstream economics is known to attach little importance to money as a concept, often treating it as a peculiar commodity (Hicks, 1989). It is also known for conceiving banks as intermediaries for real investment. Only crises arouse interest in monetary studies, as in the Great Depression: Irving Fisher took to writing about money in the 1930s, and the period's greatest intellectual legacy was probably Keynesianism.

The link between economic crises and the interest in money is not casual, according to the monetary institutionalists. In crises, the power disputes surrounding money come to the fore, revealing the foundational aspect of this institution and its related institutions: banks and financial firms; central banks and government treasuries. Moreover, Théret (2008) argues that crises can be monetary *in nature*, not just of production and demand ("the real economy"), but moments when the operativity of the social configuration is in crisis. Monetary crises are thus political because they are financial, and financial because they are political, meaning that the institution of money operates the interface of the realms of finance and politics, the organisation of the economy and the shaping of power relations.

One way to penetrate the problem is through the opaque relation money and finance keep with the gift. They relate poorly to the first sense. Money can be used for granting, but this occurs in philanthropy, government programmes and non-profit organisations, hardly in finance. They relate only laterally to the second sense; though banking and finance operations may be analogous to the total social fact, bringing about obligations and activities that surpass the transactions, they are not based on gift-giving, but on conditioned contracts of debt, credit and the priced exchange of assets.

We are left with the third sense: *coming into existence*. Here we find something unique to the monetary economy, beyond the spill-over noticed by Mandeville, Smith or Mauss: the creation of money itself, the (ceremonial?) operations permitting and legitimating the emergence of a nearly sacred object of exchange and dispute. The clearest occurrence of this sense of the *gift* in monetary operations is that money can simply be made to exist, as long as there are sufficiently powerful and legitimate agents decreeing that money *is*. When proponents of the gold standard decry the horrors of "fiat money", they aim at precisely this aspect of the matter; but they overlook the fact that even for gold, the transformation into money is a transubstantiation, an act of custom, law or, as in monetary institutionalism, *sovereignty*.

Keynes's comparison of gold to "the moon" and paper money to "green cheese" (2013, p. 235) expresses how strange this phenomenon is for the economist. That people should want "the moon" is as much an expression of money's sociogenic instituting as the assertion that they would accept cheese instead. One cannot objectively "have" the moon any more than gold is "by nature" money. That a publicly controlled central bank is likened to a cheese factory is the counterpart, not the degradation, of gold being likened to the moon.

The framework of the gift, as a system of operations whereby behaviours and interactions are determined, by means of a series of obligations, explains why financial and monetary crises reveal some of the underlying structures of the contemporary market economy. There is much in the market economy that is reminiscent of Mauss's total social fact, specifically in money.

The monetary system is the backbone of a structure of obligations, that the transactions manifest concretely – loans, bonds, futures, derivatives, insurance. From a strictly financial point of view, all these elements of the system share the same moving principle, which is time; they correspond to manifest forms of uncertainty regarding the future – as the uncertainty becomes *manifest* through the efforts to counteract and reduce it. Money and the monetary system are this manifestation, as in Keynes's definition of money as a "link between the present and the future" (Keynes, 2013, p. 262).

Yet the "changing views about the future" are not all there is to the transcendence that money incarnates. Money is no less a link between the private and the public, the individual and the collective, than it is a link between present and future. And from a perspective that, besides the economic and financial, attempts to incorporate the social and political, these links are equally important. Like the ceremonies in Mauss, financial contracts are systematic forms of establishing bonds, agonistic in essence, expressing rivalries within the highest ranks of society, and spilling over towards the link with the lower ranks (this is where the capital-labour relation appears, conditioned by relations *within* capital). As in ceremonies like the *kula* (that also spills over to a system of interactions), finance operates and gives form to both alliance and conflict. Times of peace, alliance and trade veil these operations, as the structures wherein interactions and activities take place seem solid. In these moments, one can theorise the economy disregarding money. This is why periods of crisis favour the emergence of theories of money, banking and finance. They are times of conflict, when each actor seeks to guarantee their own position and take advantage of other actors' woes. They are occasions when hierarchy and authority come to the fore.

Comparing finance to Mauss's total social fact is more than an exercise in analogy. The point is to question how a certain social formation gives itself its structure of sense, activity and behaviour. In Polanyi's (1977) terms, in modern societies the economy is *disembedded* from the social framework, to the extent that society finds itself embedded in the economy – which ultimately turns out to be embedded in finance.

If Mauss is correct that the total social fact is universal, one must examine the process whereby this configuration is generated and reinforced, including the categorisation of labour, land and money as fictitious commodities. An important part of the monetary institutionalists' trajectory consists in attempting to theorise this process. Aglietta and Orléan write that "money engenders economic subjects because it is radically different from them. With monetary mediation, subjects relate to that which isn't them, the *social as institution*" (2002, p. 19); and a theory of money must "recognize in this mysterious thing the process of socialization *par excellence* in trading societies" (*idem*, p. 18).

A difficulty one faces in the transposition of the gift and the total social fact into the modern economy and money lies in their visibly historical character. It is not shocking to state that gift-giving ceremonies re-enact foundational moments that are only enacted in the re-enactment itself. But it is counter-intuitive to make the same claim for monetary systems that are formally instituted by law and whose decisive moments are well documented.

But the response to this challenge has two main components. The first is historical. The history of money and finance since the Middle Ages reveals that the developments of monetary forms and systems, as well as the creation of financial instruments, come about as responses to challenges of metastable economies and societies. For Amato and Fantacci (2013), the distinctive character of this process is the passage to an anonymous kind of finance (i.e. among people who do not necessarily meet or know each other) and from monetary multiplicity to a near monetary unicity (at least within national borders, but with a strong hegemony even in the world market). The seemingly foundational moments, such as the Medieval fairs where bills of exchange first appear (*cf.* Aglietta, 2016), the establishment of the Bank of England (*cf.* Ingham, 2004), the Bretton Woods conference, and the formal institution of each currency, are better understood as turning points or quantum leaps than as foundations. They are episodes where the multiple dimensions of money are brought together, in an undecided and metastable state, in order to form a determinate and stable system.

The second component comes not from the history of money, but from the history of the *concept* of money in economics. Traditionally, mainstream economic theory thought the ontogenesis of money as an emergence from bilateral exchange transactions, i.e. the direct exchange of goods (barter), as a means to reduce transaction costs and expand liquidity. There is a noteworthy twist in the theories of money as originating from barter (or goods in general), which is interesting for the purposes of this chapter. The two most famous descriptions of the market origin of money are arguably Menger's (2009) and Knapp's (2013). These are also two opposing theories of the nature of money: the first defines money as the "privileged" commodity used for mediating trade, to which the law and state will only later attach an institutional grounding, whereas the latter defines the passage from "privileged commodity" to money as the sovereign act of law, from a State who can determine what it will accept for taxation. But the two theories coincide in that a category shift is necessary for something to be recognised as money. For Knapp, it is the *charta*, an act of jurisprudence. For Menger, it is the acceleration of transactions with that good, which becomes *infinitely* liquid (*Absatzfähig*, which also translates as saleable), and later becomes regulated by law. By becoming *infinitely saleable*, a good is ejected from the realm of positive, individuated commodities. It then becomes money. In both cases, it is necessary for the good to be *extracted* from the regular functioning of the markets whence it originates.

The task is to do without this moment of extraction by abandoning the commodity-origin of money altogether. One step in this direction is the "money as debt" tradition of Grierson (1977), Ingham (2004), Minsky (1986) and others. But it remains necessary to further develop the link between exchange operations and the system of obligations where they occur, and which ultimately justifies them. The autonomous individual known as *homo oeconomicus* is an actor in a structure of sense where this kind of behaviour (interested, atomistic, maximising) is meaningful. Monetary institutionalists argue that the link is operated by money. But *how* the system is generated and maintained can only be grasped by understanding the gift-as-creation import of money.

Werner's test

The gift-as-ontogenesis aspect of money can be illustrated through an experiment held by the economist Richard Werner (2014). According to Werner, the two main theories of banking are the "financial intermediary" theory and the "fractional reserve" theory. In the first, banks only distribute money (printed by the state or a commodity like gold). In the second, banks create money through the multiplying factor, by lending a multiple of the deposits they hold. In this sense, banks do not actually *create* money; they expand it. A third theory goes further: banks *create* money by adding amounts to their balance, i.e. making a loan. This is the "credit-creation theory" of banking. Elements of this theory are found in Wicksell, Schumpeter and Macleod. It is based on the idea that money is credit, not a commodity.

According to Werner, the credit-creation theory lost influence with the emergence of the fractional reserve theory, where individual banks do not create money, but the banking system does. The reason (Samuelson and Nordhaus, 1995) is that each bank's loan is another's deposit, creating a credit chain that multiplies the volume of money. The fractional reserve theory assumes a loan is made from the deposits a bank obtains, and is compatible with a commodity theory of money. The current hegemonic view is the financial intermediary theory: "[b]anks have been dropped from economic models, and finance models have not suggested that bank action has significant macroeconomic effects. The questions of where money comes from and how the money supply is created and allocated have remained unaddressed" (p. 12).

Werner is a proponent of the credit-creation theory and attempts an empirical demonstration by taking a loan from a bank and examining the internal accounting. And as he expected, a loan is made without withdrawing from another part of the balance sheet. Furthermore, deposits appear in a bank's balance sheet as loans: "the bank treats customer deposits as loans to the bank, recorded under the rubric 'claims by customers', who in turn receive as record of their loans to the bank (called 'deposits') what is known as their 'account statement'" (pp. 14–15).

Money creation by banks is no miracle. When an amount comes into existence, it does so through the inscription of a loan – an obligation. Once a bank affirms the existence of a deposit and expands its balance sheet, it engages in a circuit of obligations no less than the depositor. The bank owes the borrower, because their deposit is a liability: when the borrower makes an outside transaction, the bank *must* make the transfer. And the borrower owes the bank, they *must* pay back the loan and interest.

The cycle is, in turn, linked to the monetary system as a whole, where one finds not only the private institutions, but also a clearing house, a Central Bank, a public Treasury. These institutions are responsible among other things for intervening when the math ceases to add up: when there are defaults, bank runs, illiquidity. They are also the institutions that officially determine the rules that guide the financial system – though this definition is in practice not established independently of the private actors, particularly the bigger ones. The polarity between central institutions and a variety of other actors is relevant to the understanding of how money gives life to the third sense of the gift, as we shall see in section "Double creation".

This process is consistent with Aglietta and Orléan's (1982) theory of the tryptic monetary system. The "homogenous system" is represented by the sovereign power (e.g. central bank) issuing the currency, i.e. determining how assets are denominated; the "fractioned system" designates private actors who provide financing and funding, thus creating assets and ultimately the money supply. The "hierarchic system" describes the tense relation between these two poles, thus completing the triadic description of a monetary system. For Aglietta and Orléan, the monetary system consists in the deployment of two opposing tendencies, one towards centralisation (the currency, named A after *argent*) and the other towards dispersion (private credit, named V). Total dispersion leads to hyperinflation and total centralism leads to a credit crunch and depression.

From the perspective of this chapter, what matters in this description is that all movement within this system is ruled by the "reimbursement norm" or N_0. Credit and money can be created almost infinitely, as long as in the end there are no radical changes to what was projected and creditors are sure to get back what they advanced. Debtors wish to extend the possibilities of further private credit, while creditors want to make sure their loans will return without losses (as with high inflation). These poles represent different forms of value, as the central and private (hegemonic and fractional) represent powers.

Money creation is oriented by the obligation to pay, associated with the desire of gain. There is hardly a gift in this system (in the first sense), but the concrete form of the economic system, as it relies on financial actors for funding, is determined by means of this complex structure organising the "bringing into existence" of money. The system's agonistic character is visible in the divergent interests of creditors and debtors, causing pressure on the central authority and private actors. The functional moments provide alliance, peace and trade, when life can carry on without a thought about money. But crises expose the underlying conflicts and indeterminateness.

Double creation

It is insufficient to state that governments determine the currency, but generate a small part of the money supply, whereas banks create money *de facto*, but rely on a currency determined by the government. Aglietta and Orléan show that the openness and indeterminacy typical of the gift is present in market economies through this double form of "bringing into existence" which is money creation. On the one hand, there is the formal institution of a currency, establishing and enacting its own emission rules, and subject to an effort of control. On the other, there is the potential of a wild creation of loans, deposits, assets that can be monetised (M_N), derivatives. Market economies operate in the space between Keynes's moon and green cheese, or Aglietta and Orléan's homogenous and fragmentary systems. The constant movement between the poles is the concrete enactment of the monetary economy, in a way formally dissimilar to gift-giving ceremonies but dynamically reminiscent of the events Mauss analyses, particularly in their agonistic character.

Except for the formal presence of objects given, all other aspects are present: dispute, the formation and breaking of alliances (and contracts), periodicity, references to a transcending temporality (Esposito, 2011). Ethnographic studies of financial markets underscore these aspects (Hertz, 1998; Ho, 2009). Eichengreen (1996) stresses the importance of coordinating capacities for the international capital markets to function correctly; the coordination between central authorities worked fairly well until 1914; in the interwar period, conflict reigned, generating crises that led to fascism. A sounding reference is Varoufakis's (2011) choice of name for the international capital recycling mechanism after 1945: the "global Minotaur". In resorting to a mythological figure, Varoufakis expresses not only the character of the US-led financial system after 1971, when "[t]he hegemon, for the first time in world history, strengthened its hegemony by wilfully enlarging its deficits" (p. 18), but also points to the transcendent character of global finance as an institution, resonating with Maussian images – indeed, the US public deficit would make a privileged object of study from the prism of the gift as "bringing into existence".

Making money *come into existence* is an exercise of sovereignty, in the forms of power or prestige. Sovereignty does not designate specifically the legitimacy of the State, but the nodes where power and prestige are concentrated (Aglietta and Orléan, 2002). A non-negligible part of the exercise of sovereignty consists in *refraining* from bringing about further amounts of money. The effort to keep the value of money reasonably constant is an ascetic exercise that expresses sovereignty. This was viewed as one of the gold standard's greatest strengths and has reappeared in modified forms. The monetarist task of expanding the monetary base at 2%, the Eurozone's Maastricht criteria and the imperative of an independent central bank are institutional strategies to guarantee that money is not created without restraint, making it lose value by becoming *vulgar*.

Another part of the exercise of sovereignty consists in knowing when to *promote* the wild creation of monetary assets, through private banks or a cheese factory. This is what happened whenever the gold standard was suspended, as in wartimes (Eichengreen, 1996). It is also the imperative behind quantitative easing. A good example comes from Mario Draghi, whose performative act of declaring that the euro would be saved whatever it took, and it would be enough, was the quintessential act of sovereignty.[4]

These contradictory exercises of sovereignty correspond to the two poles of Aglietta and Orléan's triad: the contraction of the reimbursement norm and its expansion. Such movements are the actual and effective management of the system, through negotiation of the conflicting interests of creditors and debtors. Each measure is an act of power seeking to promote alliance, peace and trade, rather than war and isolation.

The question that remains open concerns the link between the sovereign act of instituting a monetary form, as the centrepiece of a monetary system, and the multiple acts of credit creation that constitute the regular functioning of the monetary system. The answer is twofold. First, as in the case of Maussian ceremonies, the validity of the system must be expressed and consequently restated throughout the period in which it functions, so that its relations will remain metastable and it can absorb the antagonisms and the uncertainty into money, which is what manifests them *a praesenti*. This is the process we have followed with Werner's experiment and that is shaken in times of crisis, demanding a relaunch of the "fleeting instant" of the total social fact.

Second, it is only through the sequence and repetition of monetary operations that the system as an institution (as instituted) can properly *be*. The image of a founding moment after which a system remains stable is established *a posteriori*, even if one can pinpoint decisive moments in monetary history, such as the creation of the Bank of England, the *Reichsmark* after the German hyperinflation (1923), the Bretton Woods conference, or Richard Nixon's 1971 speech whereby the gold standard was abandoned. These are all points in time that mark serious transformations in the development of money; they are relevant instances of the total social fact and indeed have a rather ceremonial appearance, resembling the narratives of myths that one finds in ceremonies like those described by Mauss, Malinowski, Sahlins and many others. But they are outstanding cases that create discontinuities in a continuum under the form of periodicity. Their constant, day-to-day restatement takes place in the operations of finance, as we have seen with the aid of Werner's experiment.

Conclusions

Mauss's total social fact helps to understand the importance of Werner's experiment in credit as money creation because it allows for a shift in focus, from the object of money to the creation itself, just as Mauss's analysis of ceremonies like the *kula* (where he insists in using the term money against the criticism of his peers) shifts the focus from the gifts themselves (in the first sense of the term) to the convergence of meanings taking place at the moment of gift-giving. This means that when a credit relation creates money and thus validates the existence of the bootstrapped monetary system (third sense of the term gift), what matters most is not that it has reproduced an amount of something valuable, but that it has established an obligation (second sense) valid until repayment, thus restating the validity of the monetary system of relations as a whole. This is what sets the economic actors in movement and consequently, the economy as a coordinated, meaningful whole.[5]

It is no wonder that the monetary institutionalists, seeking to place money at the centre of economic life, resort to non-Western gifting objects (Servet, 2012) to argue that the meaning of money surpasses commerce by far, being capable of founding institutional frameworks. Mauss himself evokes the origin of money during a discussion of the *kula*, with his "Note of principle" (Mauss, 1990, pp. 126–129). The circulating objects share with money the power to engage people affectively and mobilise them to action. They are gifts and must be so; otherwise they would not fulfil their institutional role.

Market economies/societies are no less founded on total social facts than gift economies, even though gift-giving is secondary to bilateral contracts and exchange. An important consequence of viewing market economies from this standpoint is that one ceases to place *exchange* at its centre. If market economies/societies are founded on total social facts, they are not founded on individual exchange, which is one among many forms of interaction determined by the self-given institutional framework. They are founded on the power to create institutions.

What we learn from Mauss, Werner, Aglietta and Orléan is that a monetary transaction, though it may seem to be based on equivalence and exactitude, in reality is always in excess of itself. In other words, it is always situated at some point of a system of trust and confidence, with an agonistic dispute of values at its centre. Money exists primarily for this dispute, which involves political relations, legal institutions and everything that makes up the total social fact; it is only secondarily destined to mediate bilateral transfers of goods. The dispute is the moment when the obligations are created, and, in the case of a monetary economy, when money is created as a carrier of the obligation, of trust and distrust. The exceeding charge of social and political import in money may be invisible most of the time while an economy functions. But, as we have seen, it shows up during crises, which is also the time when the regular, asset-based explanations of money go under.

Notes

1 Though the researchers work on the subject of money and institutions, with a loose connection, for over 30 years, their extra-official name was adopted in 2016, for the *Institutionnalisme monétaire francophone* conference in Lyon.

2 No wonder, then, that Buarque de Hollanda (2016) stresses the importance of affective ties in clientelism and patrimonialism, coining the term "cordial man" to designate the logic of domination and exploitation in Brazil. Such systems rely heavily on both threats and love between patron and client.

3 Metastability designates a thermodynamic state where the potentials exceed stability and will begin a process of change as soon as a signal is received. It is applied to social phenomena by Gilbert Simondon (2005, p. 26).

4 Draghi's speech can be watched here: https://www.youtube.com/watch?v=hMBI50FXDps

5 By revealing how the obligation, the commitment and in sum the total social fact are at the root of the ontogenesis of money, we seem to be vindicating views such as Georges Bataille's (1949) analysis of the Marshall plan as an enormous gift. Indeed, by lending money at a loss, the United States brought to life a system of economic activities that might otherwise have remained dormant for many decades.

References

Aglietta, M. 2016. *La Monnaie entre Dettes et Souveraineté.* Paris: Odile Jacob.

Aglietta, M. and Orléan, A. 1982. *La violence de la monnaie.* Paris: Presses Universitaires de France.

Aglietta, M. and Orléan, A. 2002. *La Monnaie entre Violence et Confiance.* Paris: Odile Jacob.

Akerlof, G. 1982. Labor Contracts as Partial Gift Exchange. *Quarterly Journal of Economics.* **97**(4), pp. 543–569. DOI: 10.2307/1885099

Akin, A. and Robbins, J. Eds. 1999. *Money and Modernity: State and Local Currencies in Melanesia.* Pittsburgh: University of Pittsburgh Press.

Amato, M. and Fantacci, L. 2013. *The End of Finance.* Cambridge: Polity.

Arrow, K. 1972. Gifts and Exchanges. *Philosophy and Public Affairs.* **1**(4), pp. 343–362. DOI: 10.2307/2265097

Bataille, G. 1949. *La Part Maudite. Précédé de: la Notion de Dépense.* Paris: Minuit.

Boudon, R. 1979. *La Logique du Social. Introduction à l'Analyse Sociologique.* Paris: Hachette.

Boulding, K. 1981. *A Preface to Grants Economics: The Economy of Love and Fear.* New York: Praeger.

Brenner, R. and Glick, M. 1991. The Regulation Approach: Theory and History. *New Left Review.* **188**, pp. 45–119.

Breton, S. 2000. Le monde de la dette. *Annales. Histoire, Sciences Sociales.* **55**(6), pp. 1361–1366. DOI: 10.3406/ahess.2000.279921

Buarque de Hollanda, S. 2016. *Raízes do Brasil.* São Paulo: Companhia das Letras.

Caillé, A. 2007. *Anthropologie du Don.* Paris: La Découverte.

Dalton, G. 1965. Primitive Money. *American Anthropologist.* **67**(1), pp. 44–65. DOI: 10.1525/aa.1965.67.1.02a00040

Derrida, J. 1991. *Donner le Temps, 1: La Fausse Monnaie.* Paris: Galilée.

Dolfsma, W. and Kesting, S. 2013. *Interdisciplinary Economics: Boulding's Engagement in the Sciences.* New York: Routledge. DOI: 10.4324/9780203520215

Egbert, H. 2018. Marcel Mauss and Economic Theories: The Institution of Money. MPRA Paper N. 85522.

Eichengreen, B. 1996. *Globalizing Capital: A History of the International Monetary System.* Princeton, NJ: Princeton University Press. DOI: 10.2307/j.ctt7pfmc

Eisenstein, C. 2010. *Sacred Economics: Money, Gift, and Society in the Age of Transition.* Available from: http://sacred-economics.com/wp-content/uploads/2012/01/sacred-economics-book-text.pdf

Esposito, E. 2011. *The Future of Futures. The Time of Money in Financing and Society.* Cheltenham: Edward Elgar. DOI: 10.4337/9781849809115

Graeber, D. 2011. *Debt: The First 5000 Years.* New York: Melville House.

Grierson, P. 1977. *The Origins of Money.* London: Althone.

Hahn, F. 1981. *Money and Inflation.* Cambridge, MA: MIT Press.

Hart, K. 1986. Heads or Tails? Two Sides of the Coin. *Man.* **21**(4), pp. 637–656. DOI: 10.2307/2802901

Hellwig, M. 1993. The Challenge of Monetary Theory. *European Economic Review.* **37**(2–3), pp. 215–242. DOI: 10.1016/0014–2921(93)90014-2

Hertz, E. 1998. *The Trading Crowd. An Ethnography of the Shanghai Stock Market.* Cambridge: Cambridge University Press.

Hicks, J. 1989. *A Market Theory of Money.* Oxford: Oxford University Press. DOI: 10.1093/0198287240.001.0001

Ho, K. 2009. *Liquidated: An Ethnography of Wall Street.* Durham, NC: Duke University Press. DOI: 10.1215/9780822391371

Hyde, L. 1983. *The Gift: Creativity and the Artist in the Modern World.* New York: Vintage.

Ingham, G. 2004. *The Nature of Money.* Cambridge: Polity.

Keynes, J. M. 2013. *The General Theory of Employment, Interest and Money.* Cambridge: Cambridge University Press.

Knapp, G. 2013. *The State Theory of Money.* Eastford, CT: Martino Fine Books.

Lanna, M. 2014. Além das coisas; o elogio da alienabilidade de Marcel Mauss. *Revista de Antropologia da UFSCAR.* **6**(2), pp. 34–56.

Laum, B. 2019. *Heiliges Geld. Eine historische Untersuchung über den sakralen Ursprung des Geldes.* Berlin: Matthes & Seitz.

Leach, E. R. 1961. *Rethinking Anthropology.* London: Athlone Press.

Lévi-Strauss, C. 1987. *Introduction to the Work of Marcel Mauss.* London and New York: Routledge.

Liep, J. 2009. *Papuan Plutocracy: Ranked Exchange on Rossel Island.* Aarhus: Aarhus University Press.

Malamoud, C. 1989. La théologie de la dette dans le brahmanisme. In: Malamoud, C. Ed. *Cuire le monde: Rite et pensée dans l'Inde ancienne.* Paris: La Découverte, pp. 115–136.

Maurer, B. 2002. Repressed Futures: Financial Derivatives' Theological Unconscious. *Economy and Society.* **31**(1), pp. 15–36. DOI: 10.1080/03085140120109231

Mauss, M. 1990. *The Gift.* London and New York: Routledge.

Menger, C. 2009. *On the Origins of Money.* Auburn: Ludwig von Mises Institute.

Minsky, H. 1986. *Stabilizing an Unstable Economy.* New York: McGraw-Hill.

Mirowski, P. 1987. The Philosophical Bases of Institutionalist Economics. *Journal of Economic Issues.* **21**(3), pp. 1001–1038. DOI: 10.1080/00213624.1987.11504695

Mises, L. 1996. *Human Action: A Treatise on Economics.* New York: FEE.

Mitchell, W., Randall Wray, L. and Watts, M. 2019. *Macroeconomics.* London: Macmillan.

Offer, A. 1997. Between the Gift and the Market: The Economy of Regard. *Economic History Review.* **3**, pp. 450–476. DOI: 10.1111/1468-0289.00064

Orléan, A. 1994. Sur le rôle respectif de la confiance et de l'intérêt dans la constitution de l'ordre marchand. *Revue du MAUSS.* **4**(2), pp. 17–36.

Parry, J. 1986. The Gift, the Indian Gift and the "Indian Gift." *Man.* **23**, pp. 353–372. DOI: 10.1080/02757206.2017.1375489

Parry, J. and Bloch, M. Eds. 1989. *Money and the Morality of Exchange*. Cambridge: Cambridge University Press. DOI: 10.1017/CBO9780511621659

Polanyi, K. 1977. *The Livelihood of Man*. London: Academic Press.

Sahlins, M. 1972. *Stone Age Economics*. London and New York: Routledge.

Samuelson, P. and Nordhaus, W. 1995. *Economics*. New York: McGraw-Hill.

Servet, J. M. 2012. *Les Monnaies du Lien*. Lyon: Presses Universitaires de Lyon.

Simmel, G. 1978. *The Philosophy of Money*. London and New York: Routledge.

Simondon, G. 2005. *L'Individuation à la Lumière des Notions de Forme et d'Information*. Grenoble: Millon.

Skågeby, J. 2010. Gift-giving as a Conceptual Framework: Framing Social Behavior in Online Networks. *Journal of Information Technology*. **25**(2), pp. 170–177. DOI: 10.1057/jit.2010.5

Skinner, Q. 2008. Hobbes and Republican Liberty. Cambridge: Cambridge University Press.

Théret, B. (dir.) 2007. *La Monnaie Dévoilée par ses Crises*. Paris: Éditions de l'EHESS.

Théret, B. 2008. Os três estados da moeda. Abordagem interdisciplinar do fato monetário. *Economia e Sociedade*. **17**(1), pp. 1–28. DOI: 10.1590/S0104-06182008000100001.

Varoufakis, Y. 2011. *The Global Minotaur*. London: Zed Books.

Vaughan, G. 1997. *For-Giving. A Feminist Criticism of Exchange*. Available from: http://gift-economy.com/wordpress/wp-content/uploads/2013/05/forgiving_english.pdf

Waldfogel, J. 1993. The Deadweight Loss of Christmas. *The American Economic Review*. **83**(5), pp. 1328–1336.

Weil, P. 1987. Confidence and the Real Value of Money in an Overlapping Generations Economy. *The Quarterly Journal of Economics*. **102**(1), pp. 1–22. DOI: 10.2307/1884677

Werner, R. 2014. Can Banks Individually Create Money Out of Nothing? The Theories and the Empirical Evidence. *International Review of Financial Analysis*. **38**, pp. 1–19. DOI: 10.1016/j.irfa.2014.07.015

Zeytlin, D. 2003. Gift Economies in the Development of Open Source Software: Anthropological Reflections. *Research Policy*. **32**(7), pp. 1287–1291. DOI: 10.1016/S0048-7333(03)00053-2

Part II

Applied, empirical or experimental case studies

5 Lab scientists' innovativeness

A case study of networks and favour exchange

Wilfred Dolfsma and Rene van der Eijk

Introduction

Innovation is important for firms to strengthen or even maintain their position in a competitive market economy (Ancona and Caldwell, 1987; Daneels, 2002; Despande et al., 1993; Dougherty, 1992; Peters and Waterman, 1982; Tidd, 2000; Wigg, 1997). Developing new goods and services involves recombining and then further developing existing knowledge, as Schumpeter suggests. Useful new knowledge arises from research in labs attached to large companies (Autio et al., 2004; Nelson, 1959). Even though the discussion among economists about the Schumpeterian question, whether small or large firms will contribute most to innovativeness, is still undecided (Dolfsma and Van der Panne, 2014), it seems obvious that large firms and the labs they support significantly contribute to innovation. Understanding what makes the employees in these labs more innovative is important.

What, then, explains the innovative contribution of lab scientists? While there have been a number of studies on this topic (Allen and Cohen, 1969; Bouty, 2000; Cross and Cummings, 2004), much is still to be learned. Research has been either of a quantitative kind analysing the *structure* of the networks of individuals involved in innovation, or it has been of a qualitative kind emphasising the importance of trust and social capital or the *nature* of relations (cf. Wallin and Von Krogh, 2010). Structural embeddedness is clear from how well someone is connected in the network; relational embeddedness is clear from how often someone gives advice and help to others – how generous someone is perceived to be. Gifts we define here as unsolicited transfers of material and immaterial goods between two individuals. Social exchange theory argues that in (knowledge) gift exchange between individuals a subjective balance of giving and reciprocating will be there, over time rather than at any point in time, for a relation to continue (Ekeh, 1974; Cropanzano and Mitchell, 2005; Van der Eijk et al., 2009). In between a gift and a return-gift, the giver holds what Coleman (1988, p. 108) has called a "credit slip". The claim to a return favour is not a formal one, however. Gifts exchange is subject to social norms and institutions. Social institutions about what is considered an appropriate gift, when a recipient is expected to return a gift, how valuable gift and return-gift should be, and how one is expected to give, receive and reciprocate can differ between social settings and be specific to a more or less "local" community (Van der Eijk et al., 2009).

While taking a network perspective as well (cf. Aalbers et al., 2014; Brass, 1984; Dolfsma and Van der Eijk, 2016; Mehra et al., 2001), we include both the nature and the structure of relations between lab scientists to determine what explains their innovativeness. We focus on lab-internal relations rather than take into account the relations that lab scientists maintain with the outside.[1] Distinguishing between structural and relational embeddedness (structural position of an individual, and nature of the relations the individual is engaged in) we find that structure of relations is conducive to individual lab scientist innovativeness, but, most significantly, that nature of the contacts positively moderates this effect (rather than have a direct effect itself).

The Matthew effect: *structure* and *nature* of relations

Both in fundamental and in more applied research, developing new knowledge depends on close collaboration between individuals exchanging relevant compatible knowledge. Robert Merton (1968, 1988) has indicated that both the *structural* position in a network of relations that scientists are in and the *nature* of the relations they entertain explain the innovative contribution of researchers. Merton claimed that individual scientists who maintain many contacts as well as known to offer active and generous support to the contacts maintained perform better. Peripherally positioned individuals seek to establish and maintain relations with such central players by involving them in projects expecting them to contribute less than their equal part. The more peripherally positioned scientists would, however, be reciprocated by the more central player albeit likely the reciprocal gift is of less worth. Merton referred to this phenomenon as the Matthew Effect, drawing on a reference to the Bible.

In his account, Merton was not specific, conceptually nor empirically, about what would explain this Matthew Effect – *structure* of the contacts in a network, the *nature* of the contacts or the interaction between these. Merton confounded what is nowadays referred to separately as two different types of embeddedness that are analysed in parallel literatures: structural vs. relational embeddedness (Rodan and Galunic, 2004). Indeed, the two aspects – structure and nature of relations – of the Matthew effect merge according to Merton as "charisma becomes institutionalized" (Merton, 1968, p. 60; cf. Granovetter, 1992), making it difficult to disentangle them empirically especially in qualitative research. We conceptually distinguish, and empirically test, the separate and combined (moderated) contribution of each of these two different ways in which individuals can be embedded.

Cooperation among scientists is indispensable to develop new knowledge. The division of labour in knowledge creation has progressed substantially, while the nature of knowledge development is highly cumulative in many areas (cf. Ensign, 2009; March and Simon, 1958; Mokyr, 2002; Nelson, 1959; Scotschmer, 1991; Tortortiello, 2015; Wuchty et al., 2007). Although collaboration is required or even the norm (Merton, 1968), departures from the norm occur (Haas and Park, 2010), and patterns of cooperation and knowledge sharing can differ for individuals even within a single community. Merton (1968, p. 57) observes that in practice "eminent scientists get disproportionately great credit for their contributions to science while relatively unknown scientists tend to get disproportionately little credit for comparable contributions" (cf. Haas and Park, 2010). Merton refers to the Matthew effect for an explanation: scientists who are better connected provide more support and help to others and are (thus) more innovative (cf. Oetl, 2012). Merton draws on social exchange theory, a theory about interaction and exchange in the social realm which claims that social relations exist and persist as and when a continued exchange of valuables is maintained (Cropanzano and Mitchell, 2005). What is exchanged is not necessarily of equal value at any moment in time, in case of gift exchange preferably it is not (cf. Van der Eijk et al., 2009).

Merton is not clear about the extent to which the structure of relations that individuals such as (lab) scientists may be involved in, on the one hand, or, on the other hand the nature of relations, contributes to the Matthew Effect. While Merton and others have ostensibly focused more on the structural element of the location of an academic in a social network (cf. Lincoln, 1982; Nadler and Tushman, 1988; Salanick, 1995), a scholar such as Bouty (2000) has, for instance, emphasised the nature of relations by pointing to how the favours reciprocated between scientists helps the scientists involved in it perform better (cf. Ensign, 2009; Van der Eijk et al., 2009).

While the kind of research focusing on social networks is more amenable for quantitative research (Borgatti and Halgin, 2011; Zaheer and Soda, 2009), research focusing on favour (gift) exchange has been largely qualitative. Literature on the role of trust and social capital in general and in relation to knowledge transfer and innovation in particular has similarly been largely of a qualitative kind (cf. Bouty, 2000; Hechsher and Adler, 2006). The literature on favour exchange has emerged from anthropology, where an emphasis on use of the qualitative methods aiming for "thick description" (Ensign, 2009; Geertz, 1973; Van der Eijk et al., 2009) is pervasive. Drawing on social exchange theory in general, and the theoretical contributions from the literature on social networks and favour exchange in particular, we are able to employ quantitative methods of analysis here and are thus, importantly, able to determine the extents to which the two types of embeddedness, separate and jointly, explain innovativeness of individual lab scientists. We use two alternative measures for our dependent variables: the more subjective measure of Idea Performance as measured by immediate superiors, and the more objective Patent Performance measure. This research framework is presented in Figure 5.1.

Direct effect: structure of relations (centrality in network). The position a researcher holds in a network of knowledge exchange relations

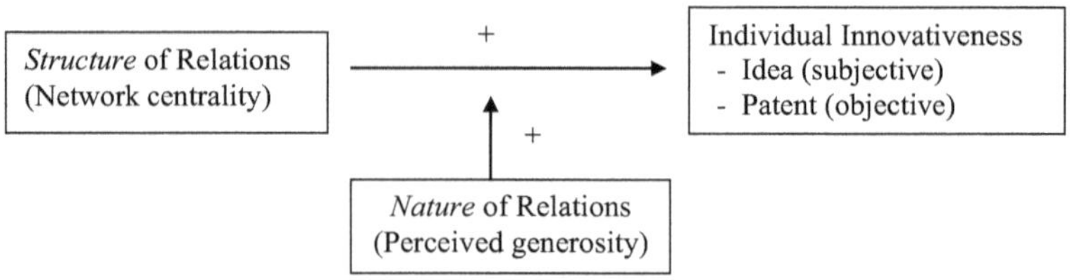

Figure 5.1 Conceptual framework.

determines the innovativeness of her contributions. Social network literature assumes that "network structure [is seen] as a substitute for trust" (Moran, 2005, p. 1136). Centrality, as the most important indicator of position in a network, is found to be a strong predictor of an individual's contribution to innovation (Aalbers et al., 2013; Ibarra, 1993; Provan et al., 2007). Centrally located researchers in networks are more likely to have (access to) relevant knowledge that is relevant in a particular domain than researchers in the fringes (Sparrowe et al., 2001; Wasserman and Faust, 1994). Centrally positioned researchers receive more information and insights from more alters (Borgatti and Halgin, 2011; Brass, 1984; Zaheer and Soda, 2009). Centrally positioned individuals can leverage this for their own benefit (Burt, 1992), and are thus in a position to be more creative themselves as well (Burt, 2004; Ohly et al., 2010; Sparrowe et al., 2001). Individuals centrally located in a network tend to perform well, in part, as social exchange theory suggests, because they receive disproportionately more than they themselves objectively give in return (cf. Van der Eijk et al., 2009). What centrally positioned individuals give in return, however, is perceived as of high quality. Being centrally positioned as a lab scientist will make sure that those contacts one maintains that involve social exchange of favours will help you access more, more reliable and more valuable knowledge. While the contribution of centrally located scientists may be relatively small in objective terms, they are likely to have developed meta-skills relevant for doing research that allows them to avert research dead-ends, think creatively about possible solutions, and, in case of fundamental science in which scientists of research labs can also be involved (Blank, 1991; Roach and Sauermann, 2010; Sauermann and Stephan, 2010), navigate the publication or patent application process more effectively (cf. Dietz et al., 2000; Merton, 1968, p. 61). The number of contacts an individual holds also helps in evaluating ideas according to the standards valid in a larger social or company-specific context (Binnewies et al., 2007; Ohly et al., 2010).

H1: Researchers centrally located in the network structure of a research lab will contribute more to innovation, both in an objective and in a subjective sense.

Moderator: nature of relation (Perceived generosity). Social Exchange Theory claims that individuals, who are known to be generous, for instance, in providing and returning advice and support (knowledge gifts), are individuals whom one would like to collaborate with (cf. Cropanzano and Mitchell, 2005). In science, favours can take the form of involving someone in a research project (when others could be approached as well), inviting someone as a keynote (when others might deliver an equally good presentation), citing someone (when other work could be cited as well). In a research lab attached to a private organisation, favours can take the form of helping someone setting up or even doing an experiment the person does not have the facilities or resources for themselves, giving unsolicited advice or including someone on a patent application where the person could perhaps be not included too. Gifts in the setting of a research lab can also be advice advocacy for someone's internal project proposal. Gifts and return-gifts are unsolicited and cannot be contractually enforced. A mixed bag of motives is involved in gift-giving, including that of self-interest (Van der Eijk et al., 2009). Considerations of immediate self-interest may not prevail in interactions in networks where knowledge and advise is exchanged (e.g. Ensign, 2009, especially Chapter 5). Gift exchange, however, can include self-interested calculation, which is exactly why, contrary to expectations economists would have, rare and valuable knowledge is actually commonly shared and easily obtainable provided that "assurances … [return favors] will follow" (Ensign, 2009, p. 106). When someone is involved in exchange of gifts, this has been found to be beneficial for the parties involved.

Favour or gift exchange is found to play a significant role in explaining both the contribution that scientists make to the innovativeness of their firm and the extent to which a firm is successful at innovation (Bouty, 2000; see also Ensign, 2009). There is substantial indication that the self-reinforcing process can lead to a situation in which some scientists receive more than the quality of their work warrants (Tol, 2009). Establishing a structural relation with a centrally positioned individual can be initiated by giving a gift. When the centrally located individual accepts, this enhances the position of the giver. The return-gift by the centrally located individual then objectively of lower value, but the public nature of the act enhances the position of the give because the return-gift can be of high value subjectively but potentially also by the mere fact of the give receiving a gift from a centrally placed giver.

Centrally located individuals may be expected to invest fewer efforts, or sometimes much less efforts, into a joint project than others invest for a similar recognition and reward (cf. Ouchi, 1980; Uzzi, 1998; Van der Eijk et al., 2009). Those gifts (knowledge favours) are of two kinds. The first is praise and status-related offerings such as citations to their work (patents), invitations to join an editorial board or committee of experts or invitations as a keynote speaker. While this is not necessarily knowledge-related (Agnew et al., 1994), it does enhance a reputation and fortifies a central position in a network. The other kind of gifts is the offering of joining a particular project of knowledge creation. Scientists might be offered to share in the benefits of a research effort even when less than proportional time and effort might have been invested in the project by them (Kijkuit and Van den Ende, 2010). The mostly anthropological and largely qualitative literature on gift exchange has shown that central or powerful individuals indeed not just receive many gifts, but are likely to give less in return in objective terms (Bodeman, 1988; Buunk et al., 1993; Ensign, 2009; Goffman, 1971). In subjective terms, however, an individual scientist in the periphery is likely to perceive the return-gift from the central player as valuable.

A "self-confirming process" (Merton, 1968, p. 62) may start with an apparently random event to enhance the reputation of a scientist to increasingly benefit from the Matthew Effect (cf. Dolfsma and Leydesdorff, 2009). In line with what Merton suggests, scientists who are or happen to be more centrally positioned are likely to receive more gifts than those in the fringes (cf. Reagans and McEvily, 2003). Asymmetric relationships are to be expected between prominent and less prominent network actors: "[p]rominent leaders are the object of extensive relations from followers, while the latter are the objects of few relations" (Knoke and Burt, 1983, p. 199).

A relationship where knowledge favours are exchanged will not start with the exchange of sensitive information but may evolve over time to a point where such information is actually exchanged (Bouty, 2000; Van der Eijk et al., 2009). Giving of knowledge favours between individuals can be risky. Knowledge may spill over to others preventing a focal actor from receiving the credit for newly developed knowledge gifted to someone who could use it. Nevertheless, as those involved in the voluntary, non-contractual knowledge favour exchange are likely to exchange only with others that they have come to trust, and that have something to offer in return at a later stage. Failing to reciprocate may jeopardise the position of the givee, not just with respect to the giver but because of one's reputation in the larger community (Cropanzano and Mitchell, 2005; Ensign, 2009; Van der Eijk et al., 2009).

Because of the possible risks involved in knowledge favour exchange, we argue that the two conceptually distinct aspects of embeddedness – structure and nature of relations – reinforce one another. Perceived generosity will not directly impact an individual's innovativeness, contrary to what Merton suggests implicitly (1968, 1988): when someone (A) who gives advice and is seen by B to be generous (nature of relation) will not benefit from this view if there is no prior structural relation between A and B. We argue for a moderation of the structure of a relation by the nature of a relation. Individuals, centrally positioned and who are perceived as generous since they are involved in knowledge favour exchange are thus likely to be more innovative. We thus hypothesise that:

H2: Individuals more involved in knowledge gift exchange will be able to leverage their central position in an innovation network (moderation) and will be more innovative in a subjective and objective sense.

Data and method

Research setting. We collected data at a Research and Development laboratory of a Dutch multinational with offices and production facilities in 49 countries around the world operational in the chemical industry. We refer to this company as company CHEM. This is a case study that relies on the analysis of both quantitative and qualitative data. We determining to what extent the nature and the structure of relations that an employee in the laboratories maintains contribute to their innovativeness. This can only be done with a case study research design. Laboratory scientists of any one lab cannot be expected to have contacts with laboratory scientist of another laboratory even of the same company. A cross-sectional research design is not feasible (cf. Krackhardt, 1990; Siggelkow, 2007).

CHEM has annual sales of over €8 billion and operates across a spectrum of activities. These activities include nutritional and pharmaceutical ingredients, performance materials and industrial chemicals. Activities at CHEM are clustered, while clusters are further subdivided into relatively autonomous business groups. Each business group is responsible for product development, manufacturing and sales. CHEM has recently shifted away from offering bulk products towards offering specialty and higher value-added products. The importance of innovation to develop cutting edge technology has become a more integral part of CHEM's strategy – a substantial percentage of resources are committed to R&D.

A network questionnaire, tailored for the specific setting, was administered to a total of 195 laboratory researchers and managers, with the support of management. The survey was distributed electronically through intra company mail from the office of the R&D manager to signal the company's support and avoiding possible technical IT problems by hosting the data outside of CHEM. All senior researchers and project managers in the laboratory were targeted. Laboratory assistants were excluded as these just perform tests at the direction of researchers and managers. As a result of this procedure, a clear network boundary was identified (Krackhardt, 1990). After three weeks, 95% of the surveys were returned. Personalised reminders increased the response rate to 97% – the high response rate that social network analysis requires (Aalbers and Dolfsma, 2015; Scott, 1991; Wasserman and Faust, 1994). We managed to address first-level (respondent) non-response and second-level (item in questionnaire) non-response. Using the data collected, we obtained a complete view of the network of individuals involved in knowledge development. The literature suggests a number of variables to measure favour exchange and networks. We used a name generator question to collect relational (dyadic level data) and relationship characteristics network data (e.g. Marsden, 1990, 2004). The group of individual responded shared 1111 ties among them; six individuals were connected to nobody.[2]

Dependent variable. *Idea Performance.* To measure individual innovation performance managers were asked to rate the researcher's creativity over the last six months, drawing from company records ["To what extent is this person particularly creative: someone to come up with novel and useful ideas, using a 1–5 scale, from weak to outstanding"] (Rodan and Galunic, 2004). Managers were asked to assess behaviours rather than attitudes, for a specific period (cf. Tsui, 1984). Measurement of individual innovativeness requires supervisor (or peer) assessment, but the method is found to yield reliable results (cf. Amabile, 1996; Avery and Murphy, 1998; Moran, 2005). Interviews with senior managers at the organisation indicated that line management were the most appropriate individuals to evaluate researchers' innovation performance. Line managers are directly involved with them and are formally responsible for rating them as well. Subjective innovation performance assessment varies considerably across the 195-person lab in the data (Appendix): managers can and do differentiate between the innovative contribution that individual lab scientists made. The extent to which line managers' evaluation is subject to social pressures or the inclination to avoid conflict seems limited.

In order to complement our individual level data we sought an alternative way of measuring individual innovativeness, we include *Patent Performance* or the number of patents a laboratory researcher was (co-) granted (Bertin and Wyatt, 1988; Narin et al., 1987). Being involved in patent applications and having one's name included on a patent that is granted can have a significant impact on his career (Dietz et al., 2000).

It is, however, important to realise that patenting can be stimulated to varying degrees and in different ways in different scientific domains and even firms. Financial incentives for individual researchers to apply for a patent can play a minor role (Sauermann et al., 2010). As the number of patents applied for cumulates, tenure needs to be included in the analysis as a control variable. Comparing the results from the analyses for these two performance measures as dependent variables allows us to both tease out some noteworthy differences and determine how robust our findings are. It is remarkable to observe that the Idea Performance measure is statistically unrelated to the Patent Performance measure (see Appendix for descriptive statistics).

Independent variable. *Degree Centrality* provides an indication of the network structure of an individual actor, indicating how prominent the individual is in the network (Scott, 1991; Wasserman and Faust, 1994). We use In-degree Centrality, the number of times an individual is mentioned by alters, since it does not rely on self-reporting and thus is more reliable (Sparrowe et al., 2001). We did not require that the contact corroborate the tie – asymmetric relationships, in which ties are not reciprocated, may be expected between prominent and less prominent network actors (Knoke and Burt, 1983). Centrally located individuals may fail to mention all alters they in actual fact do relate to, but this potential problem is limited by employing the roster method and combining a survey with interviews (Aalbers and Dolfsma, 2015; Marsden, 1990, 2004). Each respondent was asked to list his or her key contacts, ["Over the past six months are there any work related contacts from whom you regularly sought (research related) information and advice to enhance your effectiveness as a researcher? Who are your most valued work contacts?"].

Moderator variable. To determine the frequency of *Favor Exchange* an individual laboratory scientist or manager is involved in we adopted an item by Flynn (2003). Respondents could indicate how often they exchanged favours with each network relation they mentioned. ["Please rate the frequency with which you exchange favors with regard to the innovation development process with this person"]. We use this data as interval data by coding according to the number of exchange days [yearly = 1, quarterly = 4, monthly = 12, etc.]. We calculated an overall measure of engagement in favour exchange for each respondent by taking the average of the reported ratings provided by the alters an individual was connected with.

Control variables. A number of variables are included as control variables because they could affect the extent to which an individual is (seen to be) innovative in the setting studied (Dolfsma and Van der Eijk, 2016). *Gender* of the respondent was gathered using the survey instrument (dummy variable: female =1, male =0). Newcomers interact and perform in a different way compared with those who are already socialised into an organisation (Gundry, 1993). Duration of a person's tenure rather than age is used since company-specific experience and contacts are relevant. *Tenure* in the organisation was measured in years employed at CHEM. As this treats individuals who have had a career prior to joining CHEM similar to engineers who may just have graduated, we included *Age* of the respondent as well, measured in year. *Department Size* as well as *Business Unit* were included as control variables as networking and exchange opportunities can differ if the size of an immediate group of laboratory scientists in an actor's environment varies (Tortoriello, 2015) – the laboratory studied at CHEM was subdivided into two Business Units and these are further divided into departments. CHEM has 12 departments in total in this laboratory. Someone working in a larger group can more easily access and exchange knowledge with others even if the groups are part of the same company. Larger groups allow for more specialised knowledge to be developed. Company records allowed us to assign department and business unit membership. While department and business unit membership indicate the ease with which knowledge possessed by others is available formally, a laboratory scientist's innovativeness might be affected by their *physical proximity* to others (Monge et al., 1985). We introduce a dummy for *physical proximity*, measured as the co-location of designated work-spaces on the same floor in the same building, to control for this. Finally, centrality in a network can, but need not, be related to ego's formal position in the organisation's hierarchy (Knoke and Burt, 1983). We thus control for *Seniority*, data for which was drawn from company personnel records distinguishing three hierarchal levels and converted into a dummy variable [0= scientist, 1 = senior scientist, 2= manager].

Estimation. Descriptive statistics (Appendix) do not indicate that the data require the use of more complex and less straightforwardly interpretable statistical regression methods than OLS. The highest VIF score in any of the models is 1.569, which indicates that multicollinearity is no concern.

Results

Results of the hierarchical OLS regression analyses to determine the extent to which network structure and favour exchange variables affect individual lab scientist innovativeness are presented in Table 5.1. Each model has two versions, analysing innovativeness both in subjective (Idea Performance) and in objective (Patent Performance) terms. In presenting hierarchical regression models we aim to indicate just how the two elements in Merton's account of what explains an individual lab scientist's innovativeness contribute, by first adding to the base models the variable knowledge Favor Exchange. In our hierarchical regression modelling we then add the structural element of network centrality. Finally, we add the moderation of central positioning in an innovation network (structure of the relation) by the extent to which someone is perceived as generous (nature of the relation).

Across the different models in Table 5.1,[3] being perceived as generous in itself does *not* make individuals more innovative – not in subjective and neither in objective terms. This is a finding not in line with what Merton argued. Being centrally positioned, however, does indeed produce a substantial and highly significant positive effect on individual innovativeness. This clearly is in line with Merton's prediction, and with much recent literature. We thus conclude that hypothesis 1 needs to be seen as confirmed, both for individual lab scientists' objective and subjective innovativeness.

In line with what hypothesis 2 suggests, an individual who is perceived as generous is able to leverage her position in the network so as to become more innovative. Here, however, the effect for the objective measure for individual lab scientists' innovative is positive and significant, but the same is not true for subjective innovativeness. We, thus, conclude that we cannot unequivocally support hypothesis 2.

Discussion

In his seminal article, sociologist of science Robert Merton conflated what may be referred to as relational and structural embeddedness (see Rodan and Galunic, 2004). Merton argued implicitly that recognition and other gifts accrued to those scientists who were structurally well positioned, and who were also engaged in the exchange of knowledge favours and perceived as generous. In actual fact, he did not distinguish clearly between the two. In contrast to Merton, recent literature has distinguished between these two ways in which individuals can be embedded to the extent that the literature has developed in quite distinct directions: structure of contacts is analysed and discussed in very different ways and in very different lines of thought than nature of relations (Rodan and Galunic, 2004).

Table 5.1 Idea and Patent Performance of R&D Lab Researchers

DV:	*Patent Perf*	*Idea Perf*	*Patent Perf*	*Idea Perf*	*Patent Perf*	*Idea Perf*	*Patent Perf*	*Idea Perf*	*Patent Perf*	*Idea Perf*
Controls										
Tenure	0.109	−0.214***	0.105	−0.219***	0.106	−0.218***	0.105	−0.223***	0.093	−0.218***
Gender	−0.159**	−0.207***	−0.151**	−0.247***	−0.146*	−0.192***	−0.147*	−0.194***	−0.172**	−0.185***
Dept. size	0.044	−0.148*	0.057	−0.136*	0.061	−0.124	0.062	−0.12	0.048	−0.116
Business unit	−0.014	−0.064	−0.003	−0.059	−0.069	−0.132*	−0.07	−0.133*	−0.074	−0.132*
Physical proximity	−0.094	−0.129*	−0.087	−0.089	−0.11	−0.148**	−0.109	−0.145**	−0.126*	−0.139**
Seniority: sr. scientist	0.204***	0.215***	0.223***	0.184**	0.17**	0.169**	0.17**	0.169**	0.166**	0.171**
Seniority: management	0.193**	0.169**	0.194**	0.134*	0.129	0.084	0.129	0.083	0.11	0.089
IVs										
Perceived generosity			−0.014	−0.036			−0.011	−0.029	0.005	−0.034
Centrality					0.173**	0.225***	0.173**	0.224***	**0.18****	**0.222*****
Moderation										
Generosity * Centrality									**0.159****	−0.054
R^2	0.119	0.172	0.119	0.159	0.141	0.207	0.141	0.208	0.164	0.211
Adj. R^2	0.084	0.138	0.081	0.123	0.101	0.171	0.096	0.167	0.116	0.165
F.	3.402	5.179	3.589	4.401	3.577	5.693	3.164	5.055	3.404	4.6

Standardised coefficients; * $p \leq 0.10$; ** $p \leq 0.05$; *** $p \leq 0.01$

In this chapter, we have brought these two literatures together. We provide insights, showing how relational and structural embeddedness are different yet related with each other, empirically as well as conceptually. We have done so in a way that allows us to explore the relative contributions of each of the two factors, separate and in combination. Being centrally positioned in the innovation network (of a laboratory) does make individual scientists more innovative. This is in line with what Merton suggested, and in line with much of recent literature in social network analysis. Contrary to what Merton suggested, and contrary also to more recent qualitative work in anthropology, being perceived as generous only helps an individual lab scientist to be more innovative if someone also has a very favourable position in the structure of a network. Only centrally positioned individuals can expect the perception of them as generous to additionally benefit their individual innovativeness. Peripherally positioned individuals may not expect to experience this effect. This suggests that the value of what is exchanged is influenced by the position of the individuals involved in the exchange. Depending on the source, highly valuable knowledge may not be recognised as such, or, alternatively, knowledge of low quality may be unduly overvalued. More research is required to determine which individual characteristics (cf. Aalbers et al., 2013) and network features exactly might further impact this finding of how the perception of what is exchanged is influenced by who is involved in the actual exchange. The differing findings, for some independent variables, between objective and subjective individual innovativeness as dependent variable, point to some potentially interesting future lines of research. As perceived generosity only positively moderates the individual innovativeness of a centrally positioned individual in the network objective, and not subjectively: does its effect operate unconsciously? An experimental research design could shed light on this. How does distance between exchanging scientists, affecting perceptions as it does, impact the effect of perceived generosity (cf. Dolfsma and Van der Eijk, 2016)? It is clear that the nature as well as, separately, the structure of connections between individuals collaborating to exchange knowledge about innovation, for instance, in the setting of a laboratory, is unclear to themselves or their managers.

Conclusion

The extent to which a researcher is centrally positioned in a network structure and the nature of the relations entertained – in terms of someone being perceived as generous because of the knowledge gifts someone offers others – could both, according to Merton, contribute to an explanation for the innovativeness of individual lab scientists. In recent literature, these two potential contributing factors are referred to as structural and relational embeddedness of individuals (Rodan and Galunic, 2004). Whereas Merton conflated the contribution of these two, recently the literature on each has developed independently. In this chapter, we bring together these two lines of research in a quantitative study that determines if (how) the two different types of embeddedness contribute to individual innovative performance, separately and jointly. In this chapter we focus on individual innovativeness, in both an objective and a subjective sense.

In line with our theoretical argument, we find that a central network position of in individual in the knowledge transfer indeed makes actors more innovative, as they access to (research) ideas, knowledge and resources (cf. Aalbers et al., 2016; Lawler et al., 2000; Skvoretz and Lovaglia, 1995; Van den Ende and Kijkuit, 2007). Being involved in knowledge favour exchange, and thus being perceived as generous, does not make an actor more innovative per se, but does allow her to leverage his favourable network position, albeit only in an objective sense measured in terms of patent applications by an individual. Relational embeddedness, thus, positively moderates structural embeddedness – the two are certainly not independent, and, contrary to the expectations in parts of the literature, only structural embeddedness immediately impacts individual (innovation) performance.

Limitations. One important limitation for this research is that it pertains to a single firm: this study is and can only be a case study. This limitation is inherent in the kind of analysis that is required for the research question raised (Kijkuit and Van den Ende, 2007, 2010; Sparrowe et al., 2001; Reagans and McEvily, 2003). The research question involves the analysis of network data, which is data of a particular network of connected nodes. Individuals from different organisations cannot meaningfully be added to similar data for a different network – individuals from two separate organisations cannot be expected to have a contact between them. A cross-sectional research design, including data of networks from a number of organisations, conceptually makes no sense. Analysis of network data for knowledge transfer and innovation within firms is by now generally recognised, nonetheless, as offering important insights that are relevant for management too (Aalbers and Dolfsma, 2015; Borgatti and Halgin, 2011). Still, however, generalisability beyond this study cannot be suggested.

Another limitation relates to causation. Regression analysis cannot establish causation but only correlation. Because of a lack of panel data, we need to rely on the insights from theory to suggest causation. Collecting network data for a single period can already be a daunting task, given the methodological requirements involved (Aalbers and Dolfsma, 2015).

Managerial implications. Knowing which research laboratory engineer is likely to contribute to innovativeness more is an important insight for managers. Our analysis shows that it is the position in a social network of relations rather than the nature of each relation which explains innovativeness. Having a central position with many contacts is more important than actively engaging in favour exchange or being perceived as generous, contrary to what Merton implied. From the point of view of management, this is an attractive finding as intervention to change the position of a lab engineer is easier than to change the nature of his relations. Remarkable differences between what determines innovativeness in an objective sense and what determines it in a subjective sense also provide clues for management. Especially the difference for tenure is remarkable: perceived or subjective innovativeness for a lab scientist may not be grounded in objective (patent) innovative performance. Our results are thus noteworthy from an academic point of view as well as of import to managers.

Notes

1 This study is not intended as a contribution to the open innovation literature (Dahlander and Gann, 2010; Huizingh, 2011).

2 Only the 798 most frequent (daily and weekly) interactions are shown in Figure 5.1. Multi-dimensional scaling techniques are used to position "similar" nodes closer together – nodes [individuals] are similar when they mention the same alters as a contact.

3 All correlations are linear: no curvi-linear effects for in-degree centrality or gift exchange were found.

References

Aalbers, R. and Dolfsma, W. 2015. *Innovation Networks: Managing the Networked Firm.* London and New York: Routledge. DOI: 10.4324/9781315757520

Aalbers, R., Dolfsma, W. and Koppius, O. 2014. Rich Ties and Innovative Knowledge Transfer Within a Firm. *British Journal of Management.* **23**(1), pp. 96–109. DOI: 10.1111/1467–8551.12040

Aalbers, R., Dolfsma, W. and Koppius, O. 2013. Individual connectedness in innovation networks: On the role of individual motivation. *Research Policy.* **42**(3), pp. 624–634. DOI: 10.1016/j.respol.2012.10.007

Aalbers, R., Dolfsma, W. and Leenders, R. T. A. J. 2016. Vertical and Horizontal Cross-Ties. *Journal of Product Innovation Management.* **33**(2), pp. 141–153. DOI: 10.1111/jpim.12287

Agnew, N. M., Ford, K. M. and Hayes, P. J. 1994. Expertise in Context: Personally Constructed, Socially Selected, and Reality-Relevant? *International Journal of Expert Systems.* **7**(1), pp. 65–88.

Allen, T. J. and Cohen, S. I. 1969. Information Flow in Research and Development Laboratories. *Administrative Science Quarterly.* **14**, pp. 12–19. DOI: 10.2307/2391357

Amabile, T. M. 1988. A Model of Creativity and Innovation in Organizations. *Research in Organizational Behavior.* **10**, pp. 123–167.

Ancona, D. and Caldwell, D. 1987. Management Issues Facing New Product Teams in High Technology Companies. In: Lewin, D., Lipsky, D. and Sokel, D. Eds. *Advances in Industrial and Labor Relations.* Vol. 4. Greenwich, CT: JAI Press, pp. 191–221.

Arvey, R. D. and Murphy, K. R. 1998. Performance Evaluation in Work Settings. *Annual Review of Psychology.* **49**, pp. 141–168. DOI: 10.1146/annurev.psych.49.1.141

Autio, E., Hameri, A. and Vuola, O. 2004. A Framework of Industrial Knowledge Spillovers in Big-Science Centers. *Research Policy.* **33**, pp. 107–126. DOI: 10.1016/S0048–7333(03)00105-7

Belsley, D. A., Kuh, E. and Welsch, R. E. 1980. *Regression Diagnostics: Identifying Influential Data and Sources of Collinearity.* New York: John Wiley.

Bertin, G. Y. and Wyatt, S. 1988. *Multinationals and Industrial Property.* Harvester: Wheatsheaf.

Blank, R. M. 1991. The Effects of Double-blind versus Single-Blind Reviewing: Experimental Evidence from the *American Economic Review. American Economic Review.* **81**(5), pp. 1041–1067.

Bodemann, Y. M. 1988. Relations of Production and Class Rule: The Hidden Basis of Patron-Clientage. In: Wellmann, B. and Berkowitz, S. D. Eds. *Social Structures: A Network Approach.* Cambridge: Cambridge University Press, pp. 198–220.

Borgatti, S. P. and Halgin, D. S. 2011. On Network Theory. *Organization Science.* **22**(5), pp. 1168–1181. DOI: 10.1287/orsc.1100.0641

Bouty, I. 2000. Interpersonal and Interaction Influences on Informal Resource Exchanges between R&D Researchers across Organizational Boundaries. *Academy of Management Journal.* **43**(1), pp. 50–65. DOI: 10.2307/1556385

Brass, D. 1984. Being in the Right Place: A Structural Analysis of Individual Influence in an Organization. *Administrative Science Quarterly.* **29**, pp. 518–539.

Burt, R. S. 1992. *Structural Holes: The Social Structure of Competition.* Cambridge, MA: Harvard University Press.

Burt, R. S. 2004. Structural Holes and Good Ideas. *American Journal of Sociology.* **110**, pp. 442–455. DOI: 10.1086/421787

Buunk, B. P., Doosje, B. J., Jans, L. G. J. M. and Hopstaken, L. E. M. 1993. Perceived Reciprocity, Social Support, and Stress at Work: The Role of Exchange and Communal Orientation. *Journal of Personality and Social Psychology.* **65**(4), pp. 801–811. DOI: 10.1037/0022–3514.65.4.801

Cameron, A. C. and Trivedi, P. K. 1986. Econometric Models Based on Count Data: Comparisons and Applications of Some Estimators and Tests. *Journal of Applied Econometrics.* **1**, pp. 29–53. DOI: 10.1002/jae.3950010104

Coleman, J. S. 1988. Social Capital in the Creation of Human-Capital. *American Journal of Sociology.* **94**, pp. S95–S120. DOI: 10.1086/228943

Cropanzano, R. and Mitchell, M. S. 2005. Social Exchange Theory: An Interdisciplinary Review. *Journal of Management.* **31**(6), pp. 874–900. DOI: 10.1177/0149206305279602

Cross, R. and Cummings, J. N. 2004. Tie and Network Correlations of Individual Performance in Knowledge-Intensive Work. *Academy of Management Journal.* **47**(6), pp. 928–937. DOI: 10.2307/20159632

Dahlander, L. and Gann, D. M. 2010. How Open Is Innovation? *Research Policy.* **39**, pp. 699–709. DOI: 10.1016/j.respol.2010.01.013

Danneels, E. 2002. The Dynamics of Product Innovation and Firm Competences. *Strategic Management Journal.* **23**, pp. 105–1121. DOI: 10.1002/smj.275

Deshpandé, R., Farley, J. U. and Webster, J. 1993. Corporate Culture, Customer Orientation and Innovativeness in Japanese Firms: A Quadrad Analysis. *Journal of Marketing.* **57**(1), pp. 22–27. DOI: 10.2307/1252055

Dietz, J. S., Chompalov, I., Bozeman, B., O'Neil Lane, E. and Park, J. 2000. Using the Curriculum Vita to Study the Career Paths of Scientists and Engineers: An Exploratory Assessment. *Scientometrics.* **49**(3), pp. 419–442. DOI: 10.1023/A:1010537606969

Dolfsma, W. and Leydesdorff, L. 2009. Lock-in and Break-out from Technological Trajectories: Modeling and Policy Implications. *Technological Forecasting & Social Change*. **76**(7), pp. 932–941. DOI: 10.1016/j.techfore.2009.02.004

Dolfsma, W. and Van der Eijk, R. A. 2016. Distances in Organization: Innovation in an R&D Lab. *British Journal of Management*. **27**(2), pp. 271–286.

Dolfsma, W. and Van der Panne, G. 2014. Innovation, Industry Structure and Industry Dynamics: Schumpeter Mark III. *Journal of Evolutionary Economics*. **24**(4), pp. 713–736.

Dougherty, D. 2001. Re-imagining the Differentiation and Integration of Work for Sustained Product Innovation. *Organization Science*. **12**(5), pp. 612–631.

Ekeh, P. P. 1974. *Social Exchange Theory: The Two Traditions*. Cambridge, MA: Harvard University Press.

Ensign, P. C. 2009. *Knowledge Sharing among Scientists*. New York: Palgrave Macmillan.

Flynn, F. J. 2003. How Much Should I Give and How Often? The Effects of Generosity and Frequency of Favor Exchange on Social Status and Productivity. *Academy of Management Review*. **46**(5), pp. 539–553. DOI: 10.2307/30040648

Geertz, C. 1973. *The Interpretation of Cultures: Selected Essays*. New York: Basic Books.

Gneezy, U. and Rustichini, A. 2000. Pay Enough or Don't Pay at All. *Quarterly Journal of Economics*. **115**(3), pp. 791–810.

Goffman, E. 1971. *Relations in Public*. Harmondsworth: Penguin.

Granovetter, M. S. 1992. Problems of Explanations in Economic Sociology. In: Nohria, N. and Eccles, R. Eds. *Networks and Organizations: Structure, Form and Action*. Boston, MA: Harvard Business School, pp. 25–56.

Gundry, L. K. 1993. Fitting into Technical Organizations: The Socialization of Newcomer Engineers. *IEEE Transactions on Engineering Management*. **40**(4), pp. 335–345. DOI: 10.1109/17.257726

Haas, M. R. and Park, S. 2010. To Share or Not to Share? Professional Norms, Reference Groups and Information Withholding Among Life Scientists. *Organization Science*. **21**(4), pp. 873–891.

Hechscher, C. and Adler, P. S. 2006. *The Firm as a Collaborative Community*. Oxford and New York: Oxford University Press.

Huizingh, K. R. E. 2011. Open Innovation: State of the Art and Future Perspectives. *Technovation*. **31**(1), pp. 2–9. DOI: 10.1016/j.technovation.2010.10.002

Ibarra, H. 1993. Network Centrality, Power and Innovation Involvement: Determinants of Technical and Administrative Roles. *Academy of Management Journal*. **36**(3), pp. 471–501. DOI: 10.2307/256589

Kijkuit, B. and Van den Ende, J. 2007. The Organizational Life of an Idea: Integrating Social Network, Creativity and Decision-Making Perspectives. *Journal of Management Studies*. **44**(6), pp. 863–882. DOI: 10.1111/j.1467–6486.2007.00695.x

Kijkuit, B. and Van den Ende, J. 2010. With a Little Help from Our Colleagues: A Longitudinal Study of Social Networks for Innovation. *Organization Studies*. **31**(4), pp. 451–479. DOI: 10.1177/0170840609357398

Knoke, D. and Burt, R. S. 1983. Prominence. In: Burt, R. S. and Minor, M. J. Eds. *Applied Network Analysis*. Beverly Hills, CA: Sage, pp. 195–222.

Lam, A. 2005. Work Roles and Careers of R&D Scientists in Network Organizations. *Industrial Relations*. **44**(2), pp. 242–275. DOI: 10.1111/j.0019–8676.2005.00383.x

Lawler, E., Thye, S. and Yoon, J. 2000. Emotion and Group Cohesion in Productive Exchange. *American Journal of Sociology*. **106**, pp. 616–657 DOI: 10.1086/318965

Lincoln, J. 1982. Intra- (and Inter-) Organizational Networks. In: Bacharach, S. Ed. *Research in the Sociology of Organizations*. Vol. 1. Greenwich, CT: JAI Press, pp. 1–38.

March, J. G. and Simon, H. A. 1958. *Organizations*. New York: Wiley.

Marsden, P. V. 1990. Network Data and Measurement. *Annual Review of Sociology*. **16**, pp. 453–63.

Marsden, P. V. 2004. Recent Developments in Network Measurement. In: Carrington, P. J., Scott, J. and Wasserman, S. Eds. *Models and Methods in Social Network Analysis*. New York: Cambridge University Press, pp. 8–30.

Mehra, A., Kilduff, M. and Brass, D. 2001. The Social Networks of High and Low-self Monitors: Implications for Workplace Performance. *Administrative Science Quarterly*. **46**, pp. 121–146. DOI: 10.2307/2667127

Merton, R. K. 1968. The Matthew Effect in Science. *Science*. **159**, pp. 56–63.

Merton, R. K. 1988. The Matthew Effect in Science, II – Cumulative Advantage and the Symbolism of Intellectual Property. *Isis*. **79**(4), pp. 606–623. DOI: 10.1086/354848

Mokyr, J. 2002. *The Gifts of Athena – Historical Origins of the Knowledge Economy*. Princeton, NJ: Princeton University Press.

Monge, P. R., Rothman, L. W., Eisenberg, E. M., Miller, K. I. and Kirste, K. K. 1985. The Dynamics of Organizational Proximity. *Management Science*. **31**(9), pp. 1129–1141. DOI: 10.1287/mnsc.31.9.1129

Moran, P. 2005. Structural vs. Relational Embeddedness: Social Capital and Managerial Performance. *Strategic Management Journal*. **26**, pp. 1129–1151. DOI: 10.1002/smj.486

Nadler, D. and Tushman, M. 1988. *Strategic Organization Design*. Glenview, IL: Scott Foresman.

Narin, F., Noma, E. and Perry, R. 1987. Patents as Indicators of Corporate Technological Strength. *Research Policy*, **16** (2-4), pp. 143–155. DOI: 10.1016/0048-7333(87)90028-x

Nelson, R. R. 1959. The Simple Economics of Basic Scientific Research. *Journal of Political Economy*. **57**, pp. 297–306. DOI: 10.1086/258177

Oetl, A. 2012. Reconceptualizing Stars: Scientists Helpfulness and Peer Performance. *Management Science*. **58**(6), pp. 1122–1140.

Ohly, S., Kase, R. and Škerlavaj, M. 2010. Networks for Generating and Validating Ideas. *Innovation: Management, Policy and Practice*. **12**(1), pp. 50–60. DOI: 10.5172/impp.12.1.41

Ouchi, W. G. 1980. Markets, Bureaucracies, and Clans. *Administrative Science Quarterly*. **25**, pp. 129–141.

Peters, T. J. and Waterman, R. H. 1982. *In Search of Excellence*. New York: Harper and Row.

Reagans, R. and McEvily, R. 2003. Network Structure and Knowledge Transfer: The Effect of Cohesion and Range. *Administrative Science Quarterly*. **48**, pp. 240–267.

Roach, M. and Sauermann, H. 2010. A Taste for Science? PhD Scientists' Academic Orientation and Self-Selection into Research Careers in Industry. *Research Policy*. **39**, pp. 422–434.

Rodan, S. and Galunic, C. 2004. More Than Network Structure: How Knowledge Heterogeneity Influences Managerial Performance and Innovativeness. *Strategic Management Journal*. **25**, pp. 541–562. DOI: 10.1002/smj.398

Rosen, S. 1981. The Economics of Superstars. *American Economic Review*. **75**, pp. 845–858.

Salancik, G. 1995. Wanted: A Good Network Theory of Organization. *Administrative Science Quarterly*. **40**, pp. 345–349.

Sauermann, H., Cohen, W. M. and Stephan, P. E. 2010. *Complementing Merton: The Motives, Incentives, and Commercial Activities of Academic Scientists and Engineers*. Academy of Management best paper proceedings.

Sauermann, H. and Stephan, P. E. 2010. *Twins or Strangers? Differences and Similarities between Industrial and Academic Science*. NBER working paper 16113.

Scotchmer, S. 1991. Standing on the Shoulders of Giants: Cumulative Research and the Patent Law. *Journal of Economic Perspectives*. **5**(1), pp. 29–41. DOI: 10.1257/jep.5.1.29

Scott, J. 1991. *Social Network Analyses: A Handbook*. London: Sage.

Siggelkow, N. 2007. Persuasion with Case Studies. *Academy of Management Journal*. **50**, pp. 20–24. DOI: 10.2307/20159838

Skvoretz, J. and Lovaglia, M. J. 1995. Who Exchanges with Whom. *Social Psychology Quarterly*. **58**, pp. 163–177.

Sparrowe, R.T., Liden, R. C., Wayne, S. J. and Kraimer, M. L. 2001. Social Networks and the Performance of Individuals and Groups. *Academy of Management Journal*. **44**(2), pp. 316–325. DOI: 10.2307/2787040

Tidd, J. 2001. Innovation Management in Context: Environment, Organization and Performance. *International Journal of Management Reviews*. **3**(3), pp. 169–183. DOI: 10.1109/EMR.2017.7968101

Tol, R. S. J. 2009. The Matthew Effect Defined and Tested for the 100 Most Prolific Economists. *Journal of the American Society for Information Science and Technology*. **60**(2), pp. 420–426. DOI: 10.1002/asi.20968

Tortoriello, M. 2015. The Social Underpinnings of Absorptive Capacity: External Knowledge, Social Networks, and Individual Innovativeness. *Strategic Management Journal*. **36**(4), pp. 586–597. DOI: 10.1002/smj.2228

Tushman, M. L. and Scanlan, T. J. 1981. Boundary Spanning Individuals. *Academy of Management Journal*. **24**, pp. 289–305. DOI: 10.2307/255825

Uzzi, B. 1997. Social Structure and Competition in Interfirm Networks: The Paradox of Embeddedness. *Administrative Science Quarterly*. **42**, pp. 35–67. DOI: 10.2307/2393808

Van der Eijk, R. A., Dolfsma, W. and Jolink, A. 2009. On a Source of Social Capital: Gift Exchange. *Journal of Business Ethics*. **89**(3), pp. 315–329. DOI: 10.1007/s10551-008-0002-z

Wallin, M. W. and Von Krogh, G. (2010) Organizing for Open Innovation: Focus on Integration of Knowledge. *Organization Dynamics*. **39**(2), pp. 145–154. DOI: 10.1016/j.orgdyn.2010.01.010

Wasserman, S. and Faust, K. 1994. *Social Network Analysis: Methods and Applications*. New York: Cambridge University Press.

Wigg, K. M. 1997. Integrating Intellectual Capital and Knowledge Management. *Long Range Planning*. **30**(3), pp. 399–406. DOI: 10.1016/S0024–6301(97)90256-9

Wuchty, S., Jones, B. and Uzzi, B. 2007. The Increasing Dominance of Teams in the Production of Knowledge. *Science*. **316**, pp. 1036–1039.

Zaheer, A. and Soda G. 2009. Network Evolution: The Origin of Structural Holes. *Administrative Science Quarterly*. **54**, pp. 1–31.

Appendix

Descriptive statistics: means, standard deviations, correlations

		Mean	Std. Dev.	1	2	3	4	5	6	7	8	9	10
1	Tenure	15.5794	11.37251	1									
2	Gender	0.2256	0.41908	−0.293★★	1								
3	Dept. size	12.8564	5.13427	−0.133	0.08	1							
4	Bus. Unit	0.2564	0.43777	0.056	−0.064	−0.332★★	1						
5	Proximity	0.5677	0.2897	−0.048	−0.078	0.029	−0.111	1					
6	Seniority: Sr. Scientist	0.1538	0.36173	−0.021	−0.162★	0.062	−0.023	−0.035	1				
7	Seniority: Mgmnt	0.3231	0.46886	0.066	−0.006	−0.437★★	−0.104	0.022	−0.295★★	1			
8	Gift Exch.	40.3456	38.76958	−0.08	0.016	0.08	−0.106	0.022	0.051	−0.193★★	1		
9	Centrality	9.8289	7.55785	0.08	−0.147★	−0.270★★	0.310★★	0.057	0.088	0.324★★	−0.211★★	1	
10	Idea Perf.	3.4433	0.93818	−0.126	−0.217★★	−0.148★	−0.022	−0.064	0.178★	0.13	−0.134	0.267★★	1
11	Patent Perf.	1.8519	2.00777	0.155★	−0.214★★	−0.036	−0.019	−0.086	0.200★★	0.114	0.042	0.220★★	0.125

2-tailed; ★★ significant at 1%, ★ significant at 5%. A variance inflation test (VIF) was conducted to test for multi-collinearity (existence of a linear relationship between predictors), results (largest value: 3,5 for the variables Department) showed that VIF's were well within limits (Belsley et al., 1980) indicating that multi-collinearity did not bias the regression model.

6 Gift as conspicuous consumption

The case of the *Odyssey*

Paschalis A. Arvanitidis and Polyxeni Strolonga

Introduction

Thorstein Veblen (1857–1929) is acknowledged to be the founder and one of the leading figures of the Original (Old) Institutional Economics (Hodgson, 1998, 2014). Over the course of his academic life he criticised the conventional economic thought of his time, laying down the bases for the development of a new, holistic, systemic and evolutionary approach to economics. In this, proper emphasis is placed on economic change and progress rather than on static equilibrium analysis (Arvanitidis, 2014).

The *Theory of the Leisure Class* (1899/1912) (hereafter TLC) is admittedly the magnum opus among his published work. In this, Veblen analyses the formation and evolution of the socio-economic system and its institutions based on the economic behaviour of the upper-social class, named "the leisure class". Such a behaviour is characterised by "pecuniary emulation", that is, a competitive struggle for wealth accumulation and display aiming to match or surpass others, which is expressed by "conspicuous waste" of time and resources as a means of signalling wealth, status and social rank. However, such personal consumption alone is not enough; vicarious consumption is also employed in a conspicuous manner, in which presents, feasts and entertainments are offered to peers, and gifts, donations and alms are given to other people, as a means of discernible economic display. Veblen also argues that leisure-class behaviour and its "scheme of life" permeate other classes, which emulate the former in an attempt to uphold (if not, to increase) their social standing in the eyes of others, shaping in that way the social values, norms, customs and institutions of the society on the whole.

But how exactly is such a "pecuniary superiority" demonstrated? How is status-motivated behaviour actualised and pervades the whole social structure? And how do these behaviours, processes and institutions evolve and develop through time? In the TLC Veblen attempts to provide answers to all these questions outlining the driving forces and effects of the economic behaviour of the leisure class in four development stages that humanity passes: the peaceable, the predatory, the quasi-peaceable and the modern. On this account, Veblen discusses the production and consumption arrangements, the socio-economic structure and the institutions of each stage and the way these interact and evolve through time. Institutions constitute for Veblen the crystallisation of all these behaviours, relations, functions and dynamics of the society, comprising the accepted "scheme of life" of the time. In essence, institutions are prevalent, socially prescribed, habits of thought and behaviour of people who function not simply as individuals but as members of groups with specific roles in the socio-economic system[1]. On this account, examples of institutions include private ownership, patterns of taste and consumption, slavery, the dressing code and gift-giving.

The practice of gift-giving has, as scholars (e.g. Camerer, 1988; Kolm, 2000; Waller, 2007) argue, long been discussed by the discipline of anthropology and less by sociology, whereas economics, traditionally preoccupied with market exchanges, has only recently begun to explore it in depth (see, *inter alia*: Akerlof, 1982; Gerard-Varet et al., 2000; Kolm and Ythier, 2006). Certainly, a distinguished line of anthropologist has been interested in gift-giving (e.g. Malinowski, 1922; Mauss, 1954; Sahlins, 1972; Weiner, 1992), perhaps due to the importance of gift-giving rituals (e.g. "*potlatches*") in primitive societies, acknowledging it as a complex institution of ceremonial wealth display and destruction, with political, religious, kinship and economic implications (Belshaw, 1965). In these accounts, gift has strong reciprocal properties, i.e. it has to be accepted and repaid, though both the value of the reciprocal gesture and its timing are left to discretion or they are determined by custom[2]. Giving therefore, connotes obligation, in other words it is like a debt or a loan (Malinowski, 1922; Mauss, 1954; Camerer, 1988). Sociologists (e.g. Blau, 1964; Gouldner, 1960) have typically embraced and expanded the anthropologists' view that gifts convey symbolic meaning which is culturally embedded, i.e. related to social norms and values. Indeed, gifts might serve many social functions (see, Schwartz, 1967), including the development of identity, conveyance of control and subordination, expression of unfriendliness, moderation of status anxiety, establishment of distributive justice, provision of suspense or insulation, demarcation of group boundaries and atonement for unseen deviations.

Within this classic gift-giving literature, Veblen should hold a prominent position because he was the first who discussed the issue with reference to a status-driven behaviour, laying the foundations for subsequent scholars to follow[3]. To the lasting question of why people give gifts, Veblen offers the answer of "pecuniary emulation" and "conspicuous waste", describing the role of gift-giving as a means of conspicuous accumulation and display of wealth in the endless effort of the giver to establish and advance their prestige, recognition and power. Certainly, subsequent prominent scholars have pointed to the same direction. For example, Malinowski (1922/1985), in his study of the *Kula ring*, showed that objects of no-use were customarily exchanged by Trobriand Islanders, enabling participants to maintain social status and to establish social ties among them. Similarly, Mauss (1954, p. 39), in his discussion of the *potlatch* ritual, argued that competitive gift-giving among coastal indigenous American chiefs, along with the destruction of wealth, constituted a "fundamental act of public recognition in all spheres", bestowing prestige not simply to the individuals but essentially to the collectivities (families, clans, tribes, etc.) they represented.

However, whereas Malinowski and Mauss point out the reciprocal (due to custom or obligation) and collective nature of gift-giving, acknowledging it as a mechanism of social bonding, and, thus, of order and stability in a society, Veblen highlights its unilateral and "personal" dimension and the role gift-giving plays in corroborating (along with other acts of conspicuous waste) individuals' status and social position and, thus, in delineating social hierarchies and strata. Veblen, therefore, does not perceive gift-giving necessarily as a part of an obligatory mutual relationship defined by social contract[4] (as most subsequent theorists do), nor does he see gift-giving as a form of market exchange (a provocative issue for both anthropologists and sociologists). Instead, he apprehends gifts as a means of conveying information – they are signals, rather than loans or debt (Camerer, 1988) – and this perspective enables to embrace both reciprocal and non-reciprocal such behaviour. From this standpoint he advances understanding of not only the drivers of gift-giving behaviour but also its consequences on forming manners of life and social standards (in short, institutions) and by so prescribing the social structure of the time. Yet, Veblen's theory has not been put to test as far as ancient cultures are concerned, especially in order to understand how gift-giving was realised and practised and how it permeated the manners and the structure of the whole society.

The current chapter consolidates Veblen's theory seeking to understand gift-giving as an institution of status-driven conspicuous waste and to explore its role in shaping social values, customs and behaviour with specific reference to such an early stage of human development, which the Homeric epics describe. Homer's *Odyssey*, one of the oldest extant work of Western literature (dated around 700 BC), is used as a case study. This represents the socio-economic practices of *circa*, or right after, the Greek Dark Age[5] (1200 BC to 800 BC) (Finley, 1954; Morris and Powell, 1997) for which historical information is limited[6]. Interestingly, this is the epoch when the economic, social and political structures of the classic period have not been formed yet (Boutiras and Goulaki-Boutira, 2011; Donlan, 1997; Sakelariou et al., 1999), and which corresponds to an early phase of Veblen's institutional evolution, arguably the predatory and the quasi-peaceable stages (Arvanitidis and Papadopoulos, 2018). The poem delineates the characteristics and behaviour of the upper (leisure) class, reflecting the morals, social values, norms, customs and institutions of the time, and provides fertile ground for studying gift-giving behaviour at the dawn of Western civilisation. It is noteworthy to mention that although Veblen discusses extensively the early developmental stage that the Homeric era seems to refer to, he hardly mentions the Homeric epics (only in four places within the TLC), whereas there is no direct reference to the *Odyssey*.

This chapter is deployed in three sections. Following this introduction, the next section outlines the key notions of the TLC, whereas the third section moves to explore gift-giving in the *Odyssey* along the lines of Veblen's thought. Finally, the last section concludes.

The theory of the leisure class: a primer

Veblen's conception builds upon Morgan's (1877) scheme which identifies three successive societal stages of human progress: savagery, barbarism and civilisation. To these Veblen assigns four economic stages; the peaceable to the stage of savagery, the predatory and the quasi-peaceable to barbarism and the modern to civilisation. Obviously, the last Veblenian stage corresponds to the time in which Veblen lives and writes the TLC, which is the end of the nineteenth century. Within this frame, Veblen discusses the development and evolution of the behavioural propensities that drive humanity along its evolutionary path – called "instincts"[7] – the economic conditions of life in each stage, and the key institution of private ownership, which altogether mould the social structure and the economic behaviour of each class.

The key mechanism that, according to Veblen, determines the pace and direction of socio-economic evolution in each stage is a tension between basically two tendencies, or frames of mind, that are present to every human being and constitute the core makeup of all human societies. This notion is sometimes referred to as the Veblenian dichotomy and constitutes a central analytical tool of original institutionalism (Miller, 1978; Waller, 1982).

In particular, "industrial" or instrumental frames of mind (and habits of thought and action) are connected to the intrinsic human propensity for productive work and creativity, and refer to the ceaseless advance in scientific understanding involving development of "matter-of-fact" knowledge and reasoning from cause to effect. This is also associated with preference for efficiency or "serviceability" and an aversion to futility, waste or incapacity. Veblen calls this inclination and taste for accomplishment of some concrete, objective, effective and impersonal end, the "instinct of workmanship" and considers it to be the basis for technological development that leads to economic progress and advances human life as a whole.

In contrast, "pecuniary" or ceremonial frames of mind (and habits of thought and action) are regarded as related to the predatory aptitude of human nature, settled upon and habitually reproduced to serve "invidious" or "leisure" interests, legitimising abstention from productive work, rapacity, rivalry (called "emulation"), possessiveness and mastery as accepted schemes of life, and using the established status-quo and traditions for their warrant. Moreover, such behaviour is accompanied by a taste for wealth, esteem, reputability and power, and is more readily inclined to self-regarding, rent-seeking, guile, chicanery, fraud, pugnacity, coercion and aggression, inducing individuals to exploit and dominate other people. This tendency – called the "predatory instinct" – may stem from the conflict that humans are afflicted with on account of resource scarcity, or from the "invidious comparison" that inevitably is made between persons in terms of their capacities, creativity or efficiency (Arvanitidis, 2014), within the limits set by the "instinct of workmanship" (Waller, 2017). In any case, it is important to point out that the socio-economic process bears the character of a struggle between people for the possession of goods, giving rise to this propensity for "pecuniary emulation" (i.e. wealth acquisition and accumulation aiming to match or surpass others) and, in turn, to a number of social features (such as status and power structures), which sustain and support this tendency (Parker, 1918; Searle, 2005).

These qualities of the human essence, i.e. the instrumental vs. the ceremonial behavioural values, or the instinct of workmanship vs. the predatory instinct, constitute the core of the Veblenian ontology and the structural elements of his theory (Arvanitidis, 2014). These universal human dispositions and behavioural proclivities, and the institutions they give rise, set the parameters by which the socioeconomy operates and evolves. In particular, the instrumental aspects are progressive, serviceable and conducive to human development, whereas the ceremonial aspects are predatory, past-binding, resistant to change and thus impede or even undermine economic progress. The result is an evolving socio-economic system, where, in the context of technological progress, old institutions break down, fade away or, simply, change and new ones develop in the continuous process of selective adaptation to changing circumstances and exigencies of life.

The key feature of life in the first, peaceable, stage is the collaboration and solidarity of the community. The instinct of workmanship prevails and the emulation between the members of the community leads to cooperation and accomplishment of industrial serviceability for the benefit of the whole group. However, even in this stage, comparisons between persons in terms of efficiency set off invidious distinctions between individuals and the visible success becomes an end sought for its own value as a basis of esteem. In the next, predatory, stage, the material conditions of life improve substantially (in the sense that subsistence is obtainable on sufficiently easy terms and accumulation becomes possible) and the manifestation of emulation changes, giving space to the predatory instinct. Specialisation and differentiation of employments become more consistent and rigorous; industrial labour comes to be associated with submission, subservience and weakness, and as such it is seen as menial and unworthy, whereas predatory occupations that safeguard the property and life of the community become worthy, honourable and noble. Moreover, those engaged in the latter activities compete both with each other and with other warriors of other groups, in terms of prowess (e.g. killing formidable competitors) or "exploit". Thus, the exploit (rather than industry and creativity) becomes the sole criterion for social esteem and status in this stage. Tangible instances of prowess and exploit, such as trophies obtained by compulsion or the booty seized from the enemy (including food, tools, arms, livestock, even women) serve as a *prima facie* evidence of successful, predatory behaviour, and their possession and display attest the owner's eminence.

As such, property becomes the most easily recognised mark of a reputable degree of success as distinguished from signal or heroic achievement. This gives rise to the customs of individual ownership and property accumulation and eventually to the emergence of an early leisure class.

Over time, the direct manifestation of warlike prowess and exploit grow less available both in frequency and scope and the possession and ownership of goods and persons (primarily women) become an independent and dominant criterion of esteem. As we pass from the predatory to the quasi-peaceable manner of life (a time that, according to scholars, e.g. Arvanitidis and Papadopoulos, 2018, is reflected in the Homeric epics), the institution of private property establishes, pecuniary strength turns into a yardstick for reputability, and pecuniary emulation (i.e. the competitive struggle for wealth accumulation and display aiming to match or surpass others) materialises in full. By a further refinement, wealth acquired through inheritance from ancestors becomes even more honorific than wealth acquired by one's own labour. However, possession of wealth by itself is not enough to signal the owner's place in the social hierarchy. Status is conferred only when wealth is displayed and is made evident to others. This is accomplished in two ways. The first is called "conspicuous leisure" and concerns abstention from useful, productive, work. Leisure however, does not indicate indolence or idleness; it simply connotes non-productive consumption of time as an evidence of pecuniary strength and so, of high rank within society. Leisure class' time, therefore, is spent in quasi-scholarly or quasi-artistic activities or in the development of wasteful dexterities and skills, all of which do not conduce directly to the betterment of human life, such as learning of various forms of domestic music and other household arts, engagement in sports and games, taking care of pets and fancy-bred animals (usually dogs and race-horses), cultivating manners and the like. Overall, conspicuous abstention from labour and wasteful expenditure of time become the mark of pecuniary superiority, reputability and status within the social hierarchy.

It is important to note that, insofar as the pecuniary situation permits it, the conspicuous leisure extends beyond the person in concern, i.e. the head of the household. This is referred to as "vicarious leisure", where exemption from productive work is enjoyed progressively by the chief wife, the family and a portion of servants/slaves who are engaged in the personal service and attendance of the master and his household. Some of them are engaged in domestic duties of a ceremonial character and the maintenance of the household paraphernalia; so that it is leisure only in the sense that little or no profit-making work is performed by this group, and not in the sense that labour is totally avoided. Other servants, however, are employed mainly for show, rather than for services actually performed, which, in the end, become nominal only. Overall, vicarious leisure and conspicuous consumption engaged in by the wives, family and servants on behalf of the head of the household constitute a proof of the master's wealth, pecuniary reputability, power and social status.

The second trail of social display of wealth is called "conspicuous consumption" and concerns the wasteful expenditure of resources for the acquisition of (usually expensive) goods with low, if any, utility value to the owner beyond showing-off[8]. Typical examples of such goods today are luxury items and pricy fashion and branded products which consumers are willing to acquire at a much higher price in order to advertise their ability to do so and thus their social status (Amaldoss and Jain, 2005; Bagwell and Bernheim, 1996; Mazzocco et al., 2012). Similar to conspicuous leisure, Veblen acknowledges the case of "vicarious consumption", in which opulent clothing and other personal items are consumed by the wife, the family and the servants of the household as an evidence of pecuniary strength of the master. Interestingly, this extends even to friends, acquaintances and competitors. Thus, expensive presents, entertainments and feasts are given to known, whereas gifts, donations and alms are offered to other, even unknown, people, as a means of signalling wealth, rank and status, defining class boundaries, and cultivating peer bonding and loyalty relationships (especially in reciprocal giving) (Lampel and Bhalla, 2007; Mason, 1981). In that sense, the more wasteful and costlier is the gift or the good offered, the more efficient their function is performed. That is why practical and useful gifts are usually seen as crass or inappropriate, whereas lavish and impractical ones are desirable and pleasing (Camerer, 1988).

Conspicuous leisure and conspicuous consumption constitute the key methods of demonstrating the possession of wealth and together they compose the "canon of conspicuous waste" (i.e. conspicuously wasteful expenditure of time/effort and goods/substance), which imbues the leisure class scheme of life and drives the behaviour of the other classes. This is because the leisure class stands at the top of the social hierarchy and its manner of life and its standards of value provide the norm of reputability for the whole community. The result is that the members of each class accept as their ideal of decency the leisure class scheme of life and bend their energies to live up to that accepted code, not only in order to improve their social standing but also to retain their good name and their self-respect. As Veblen (1899/1912, p. 85) clearly argues "no class of society, not even the most abjectly poor", abstain from such a behaviour which acquires a customary status. In a sense, the leisure class scheme of life becomes incumbent upon all classes, defining in that way the behaviour, attitudes, tastes, habits, social values, norms and institutions of the society on the whole.

Passing to the last, modern, stage, further developments in technology, increase in productivity and industrial efficiency, and changes in the conditions of life in general, necessitate the adaptation of the foregoing behaviours and institutions. To start with, population increases in density, human relations grow more numerous, complex and impersonal, and economic and social mobility becomes easier, blurring the lines of demarcation among social classes. These circumstances reinforce the adoption and outspread of conspicuous waste behaviours, on the one hand (Bowles and Park, 2004, Charles et al., 2009), and facilitate the mitigation of extravagances and the permeation of lower-class values and manners into the leisure class scheme of life, on the other (Haight, 1997; Rojek, 1995). In addition, advances in the communication and the increased mobility of the population make clear to the individual that other persons have no other means of judging her reputability than the display of goods (and perhaps of breeding), which she is able to make while under direct observation. On these grounds, conspicuous consumption begins to hold over leisure as a customary measure of esteem, since the former provides more direct and recognisable indications of pecuniary strength and so, of social status, in comparison to the latter. As such, conspicuous leisure withers away and consumption gains in importance as an effective means of pecuniary ostentation in modern life (Arrow and Dasgupta, 2009; Bowles and Park, 2004; Haight, 1997). Such consumption is performed vicariously by the wife and children, especially in the case of typical businessman of today.

The relative decline in conspicuous leisure is due partly to an increasing relative effectiveness of consumption as a means of wealth display, but in part it is attributable to another force, the instinct of workmanship. Other circumstances permitting, that instinct inclines men to look with favour upon productive work and to deprecate waste of effort or substance. The instinct of workmanship, though present in all humans of all times, comes into effective play in modern societies, shaping the values and manners of the leisure class and asserting itself as an auxiliary, at least, mark of self-complacency. This is especially evident among with that part of the contemporary upper class whose low origin acts set them somewhat at odds with the dictates of the leisure-class principles.

Gift-giving as conspicuous consumption: the case of the *Odyssey*

Gift-giving in the Homeric epics, as Finley (1954, 1955) and Donlan (1982, 1997) have shown, represents a real historical phenomenon and it does not constitute a mere poetic invention (*pace* Snodgrass, 1974, who rejects the historicity of the Homeric world). This practice takes place primarily, but not exclusively, between members of the leisure class (aristocrats) and relates to certain aspects of the social life evident at *circa* or right after the Greek Dark Age (i.e. beginning of the Archaic Age)[9], such as the centred role of the *oikos* (household) and the importance of *xenia* (hospitality), a central feature of the *Odyssey*. While balanced exchange is the dominant practice between individual households and their heads (kings), examples of unilateral gift-giving, i.e. cases with no immediate reciprocation (even though this might be expected to take place at some point in the future), abound (Bertelli, 2014). These cases primarily reflect a social practice that gives honour, prestige and power to the donor, which, in the *Odyssey's* case, is usually the leisure class' king-chief. A *polis*/city in Homer is a collection of households (*oikoi*) each of which has a head, a king, who participates in the assembly (Peacock, 2013). The *polis* is ruled by the *primus inter pares*, who excels in wealth among the rest and demonstrates his pecuniary superiority also in the value of the gifts he offers. Of course, speaking of *oikos* in Homer, one refers to the *oikos* of the aristocrats or kings not of the lay people.

Gift-giving, as scholars have shown, is a mode to display status and power in Archaic Greek society and presumably in the Greek Dark Age as well (Domingo Gygax, 2013). The king, by showing generosity, holds prestige in his class, whereas the motivation of giving lies on the desire to augment fame and consequently honour and social status (Donlan, 1981, 1985, 1989). In addition to this, Finley (1954) sees in Homeric gift-giving a competitive ("emulative" or "invidious" in Veblenian terms) dimension. Gift-giving is a means of signalling wealth and status, as well as a way of defining classes boundaries and cultivating peer bonding and loyalty relationships (especially in the reciprocal giving). Veblen's theory of the leisure class and the canon of conspicuous waste can shed a new light on the institution of the Homeric gift-giving[10]. The wealthy aristocracy of the *Odyssey* develops such an elaborated institution along with other instances of conspicuous waste and vicarious consumption, such as feasts, entertainments, games and wedding ceremonies. Thus, the Homeric leisure class partakes in social events that require free time and great resources, and often engages in an antagonistic display of wealth, generosity and status.

Gifts are offered in the *Odyssey* most often in the contexts of *xenia* (hospitality and guest-friendship) and marriage, and less often as compensation/fine (e.g. 18.498, 23.312) or ransom, as the case is in the *Iliad*[11]. According to the ritual of *xenia*, gifts are offered by the host to the guest, usually a foreigner, who happens to visit the host during a journey. These gifts are provided before a feast in the guest's honour, or, most often, at his departure. When the stranger first arrives, he is welcome inside, is seated, is occasionally offered a bath and is invited to partake in a meal. Then, he is asked to reveal his identity and narrate the story of his travels. Finally, conveyance to homeland along with gifts is offered. These typical elements of the Homeric hospitality scene (Reece, 1993) reflect a social practice, which is ritualised. The way it is presented in the *Odyssey* includes a conspicuous waste of time and goods through gift-giving and the lavish hospitality-feast. The offer of a guest-gift marks a pact and a friendship, which has a lasting value and is even inherited to the descendants of guests-friends. In that way loyalty relationships within the leisure class are developed and inter-class ties are bolstered.

Although in the *Odyssey*, *xenia* is typically a leisure-class norm, performed by and for aristocrats, there are instances supporting the view that such practices permeate the whole social hierarchy. The case of the swineherd Eumaeus, a servant, who offers hospitality and provides his own cloak to Odysseus disguised as a beggar (14.513–514), is such an example. Eumaeus partakes in the aristocratic type of honour and prestige (Tracy, 2014). Even though in Greek society all persons despite their social status follow the rules of hospitality (since, due to religious conventions, Zeus protects guests), in the case of aristocrats, as we will show, such a behaviour is particularly ingrained and imbued with waste, prestige and authority. To this end, when Telemachus, in the absence of a king (his father Odysseus), offers Mentes (the disguised Athena), *xenia*, he reclaims his lost authority in his *oikos*. His offer of a gift, although denied by his guest, solidifies his capacity to employ his own property, which for ten years has been wasted by the suitors, as they wait idly for Penelope's choice of husband. In accordance with Veblen's theory, the suitors emerge as members of leisure class, who conspicuously abstain from labour, as they feast, play dice and ignore the guest (Mentes), being involved in their own festivities (1.105–108, 1.144–152). Even though they display the typical conspicuous leisure behaviour according to the norms of the leisure class scheme of life, they engage in an unauthorised vicarious consumption, since they do not own the property they ostensibly consume – a behaviour for which they are often condemned in the *Odyssey* (e.g. 1.260–262). The length of this consumption, ten years, is a marker of the owner's wealth, considering the consistent provision of supplies, and promulgates the status of Odysseus even in his absence.

In the *Odyssey*, narrative emphasis is given on three kings (Nestor, Menelaus and Alcinous along with his wife Arete), who play the role of the host to a guest and who conspicuously waste time and wealth as they exclaim on their generosity. All *oikoi* where *xenia* takes place are presented as rich. Menelaus' guests, Telemachus and Peisistratus, admire the palace of the king (4.43–44), which is compared to that of Zeus (4.71–75); this is a hyperbole that manifests, nevertheless, the ostensive display of riches. Menelaus does not accept the compliment that his palace rivals with Zeus' but acknowledges his great wealth, so laboriously collected and conspicuously displayed noticing that no one can rival him in his riches (4.78–81). The hospitality-feast, as well as other typical festivities of the household, such as wedding feasts or sacrifices performed often when the guest arrives, is marked by exuberance and abundance. Such practices are signs of pecuniary strength that presupposes conspicuous consumption. The display of wealth in the *xenia* feasts is marked by the abundance of resources (e.g. the roasted meat), various means of entertainment (dancing, lyre-playing) and even by gestures of conspicuous waste (e.g. the golden cup – in which they serve wine to their guests 3.40–41; a cup with which they also say prayers to Poseidon and pour libations). A full range of public festivities (dances, a bard's songs, games and feast) – an opportunity to consume and display wealth – are juxtaposed with gift-giving in the most elaborated hospitality scene, when Odysseys visits the island of Scheria/Phaiakia.

The value of the gifts and the manner in which they are handed mark the generosity of the host and attract attention to the act of giving. The superiority of the hospitality gifts is framed by their special place of storage, detailed description, significance of their previous owners and history. These elements that contribute to the high value of the gifts appear, for example, in the case of the departing gifts offered to Telemachus in Sparta. All members of the royal family (Menelaus, his son Megapenthes, and his wife Helen) provide gifts, which are retrieved from the special storeroom, where valuable items are kept – also a case of conspicuous waste, called "conspicuous hoarding" (Veblen, 1899/1912, p. 205) – some of which were acquired in the context of hospitality[12]. Objects of precious medals and high craftsmanship (a two-handled cup, a mixing-bowl of solid silver and fine handmade robes) are chosen (15.112–114). The host brings attention to his own generosity as he manifests his pecuniary strength (e.g. Menelaus announces to his host "Of all the treasures lying heaped in my palace/you shall have the finest, most esteemed" 15.124–125).

The body language, the way the gifts are provided as they are placed in the hands of the recipient, implies a highly ritualised practice that offers the opportunity to the host to exemplify his status. Menelaus' (15.120) and Helen's (15.130) gesture to place their gifts in Telemachus' hands gives a special value to the practice and contrasts with the gesture of the son of Menelaus, who places his offer in front of Telemachus (15.122). Conspicuous waste is demonstrated in the emphasis placed literally on the object. This is particularly achieved through the history of the gift that raises both the (symbolic and exchange) value of the offering (e.g. Menelaus' gift was forged to perfection by Hephaestus, the smith god, and it was a hospitality gift).

As a display of pecuniary strength, the value of the object is marked by its previous utilisation and history; the host, lists its previous owner, an aristocrat who also engaged in the practice of hospitality and provided it as a gift to the current owner. Gift-giving partakes in consecutive acts of conspicuous waste among members of the leisure class. In the case of Menelaus' gift, the two-handled cup which was forged by a god, Menelaus mentions that it belonged to an aristocrat, his royal friend, Phaedimus, king of Sidon, who gave it to him, when Menelaus was his guest. Circulation of gifts turns out to be circulation of wealth and prestige, since the gifts have both a material/use value and, perhaps more importantly, a symbolic value. The history of the object, which relates how the object came to the possession of the host, provides prestige to the host and donor, since he possesses such a valuable object, in the case of Menelaus a god's creation and a gift from another member of the leisure class. It is conspicuous and vicarious consumption to donate such a valuable object.

The enhancement of the value of a gift through its history is also evident in the case of Odysseus' bow, which was employed in a gift exchange. The history of the bow is pointedly mentioned when Penelope decides to use it for the contest of the suitors. The bow was a gift by Iphitus to Odysseus, in exchange of a spear and a sword (21.11–41). Both were guests at the house of Ortilochos and the gift exchange marks a guest-friendship. Odysseus refrained from using it at war and deprived it from a special value being used in an important action (Scodel, 2008). The bow lost its predatory (military) use and became a gift, a relatively useless ornament and eventually a stored keepsake, which functions as an indicator of the owner's honour and status. However, this gift attains a use value, even though in a unique, non-war context and receives a special honour as an instrument of revenge connecting even Odysseus, with Eurytus, the famous archer and father of Iphitus (Scodel, 2008).

To this end, the hosts' worth is manifested in the gifts they possess (not only in the ones they give), which are indicators of the pecuniary strength of their owner. The narrator mentions, for example, the gifts Menelaus and Helen received from the royal couple Alexandra and Polybius, who dwell in Thebes in Egypt, the locus of wealth *par excellence* (4.134–146). The reference to these gifts is prompted by an everyday scene, when the servant brings to Helen, a distaff and a silver basket, which were Alexandra's gifts. Through a short *analepsis*, a flashback, the narrator encapsulates the worth of these objects by presenting them as a part of a series of guest-gifts to Helen and Menelaus, which are enumerated. The status of the previous owners, members of aristocracy and leisure class, increase the value of the gift. Although usually gifts are stored and not used (a typical indication of conspicuous waste, and "conspicuous hoarding"), this is a rare example of an item of high material and symbolic value (since it is a guest-gift owned in the past by aristocrats), which is set in use[13].

The gifts convey the prestige of their current and previous owners but they are also commensurate to the honour of the guest. Gifts bring prestige to both, the giver and the recipient. This is evident in the case of the Phaiacians and Odysseus, whose identity is gradually revealed and accordingly the value of the gifts changes. The gifts are offered at different stages and in a climactic order as they ascend in value and importance. Bertilli (2014, p. 115) pointedly notices that "the obligation of gift-giving evolves together with progressive recognition of the *arete* of the guest" since, until *Od.* 8.386 a promise is given only for conveyance. However, when Odysseus shows his excellence in the games implying his aristocratic status, more gifts are promised. Later in the poem at a climactic moment, Arete impressed by her guest, who by then has revealed his identity and has narrated his encounters with queens in the underworld, encourages more offerings of gifts, since possessions abound by the will of the gods (11.336–341). Alcinous, equally amazed, asks Odysseus to stay longer so that he can accrue more gifts (11.388)[14]. Odysseus complies with this request on the account that his reputability and status are defined by his gifts: "the fuller my arms are the more respected and well received I will be" (11.408–409). Thus, the accumulation of gifts is translated into accumulation of honour. Even when specific gifts (which will be discussed next) are collected and stored in a chest for Odysseus at the end of Odysseus' narration, Alcinous (13.10–15), astonished by the turmoil of his guest, orders more gifts, a tripod and a cauldron. Alcinous tackles the issue of cost explaining that they (he and the other 12 kings) will be compensated later when they will collect the cost from the people, a kind of tax, since "it is hard to offer when there is no reciprocation" (13.14–15), which technically encompasses the practice of hospitality. The conspicuous waste appears to be out of proportion here, having exceeded the limits of the kings' resources. The lower classes have to contribute to their conspicuous waste.

This description of the sequence of gifts to Odysseus shows that honour and social position of the guest determine the value of the gifts. The relation between the prestige of the donor and the prestige of the recipient is worth exploring especially since conspicuous consumption is performed by Alcinous in collaboration and in competition with the other kings as *primus inter pares*. When first Alcinous promises his guest conveyance (8.363), this gift displays the superiority of the community of the Phaiacians, since this is a domain that they excel in (8.357). Similarly, when Odysseus exclaims after witnessing the Phaiacians' dance that they are the best dancers, Alcinous announces that the parting gifts a guest deserves should be offered (8.434). Gifts are provided in reciprocation for the good reputation that the Phaiacians will receive jointly. Collective conspicuous consumption is reciprocated with collective prestige. However, competitive gift-giving can be discerned as the value of gifts escalates. After Odysseus throws the disk during the games, Alcinous understands the special value of his guest and announces the gift-giving. Alcinous invites the 12 Kings, whose *oikoi* form the chiefdom of Phaiakia, to offer each of them a cloak, a tunic and a talent of gold (8.392–393). However, to these communal and identical gifts from the 12 kings, a personal one is added by Euryalus (8.403–405), who offers a highly valued gift to make amends with Odysseus, whom he challenged and insulted during the games, in Odysseus' honour. The gift is not a bar of precious medal like the other offerings, but his own precious sword, which as the detailed description emphasises, has silver studs and it was recently made. This personal gift is of less material value (not of gold but of bronze), but of excessive symbolic worth, since a warrior's offer of his armour metaphorically works as a sign of defeat. The gift, a type of compensation, is effective since Odysseus accepts it and reconciles with Euryalus (8.460). A second personal gift that contrasts (and competes) with the offerings of the rest comes from Alcinous. Alcinous (8.473) asks his wife Arete to bring a chest and put all gifts the other kings provided, including their own share, which comprises, however, only two of the three gifts that Alcinous had ordered, that is a cloak and a tunic (8.424–425). Instead of a talent of gold, Alcinous provides a goblet of gold (8.430–432), an item of high craftsmanship with ritual functions, demarcating his own personal worth and status but also his personal motive: Odysseus will remember Alcinous whenever he pours libations with this vessel.

In this scene therefore, it could be argued that there is competitive gift-giving, a practice that Scodel (2008, p. 42) rejects and recognises it only in the above scene but "on the margin". According to Scodel (2008) competition for prestige through gift-giving is not a Homeric practice, especially since reciprocation is not required, nor the recipient is deemed subordinate, if reciprocation is impossible. However, she acknowledges that such a strategy can be identified when more than necessary is wastefully offered for display and for gaining prestige[15]. However, Alcinous' offer of a valuable vessel, as a gesture of individualised (not communal) conspicuous consumption, contrasts ostensibly with the other offerings, not only the talent of gold but also Euryalus' gift, which was made of a lesser value medal. Alcinous' personal gift that alters the communal contribution solidifies his prominent ("first among equals") position. The competition of gifts, even on a small scale, echoes the pecuniary emulation among the members of the leisure class.

Judging from Alcinous' and Menelaus' similar gifts (a cup), we can identify a pattern in the offering of expensive ritual vessels, whose continuous use provides many opportunities for remembering the giver. In this respect, they are very effective gifts, since a primary reason for gift-giving is the commemoration of the host's generosity. Both hosts seek for eternal remembrance (e.g. 5.390), which equates with endless honour. The remembrance of gift-giving encapsulates the commemoration of the act of conspicuous waste and provides honour to the giver. The valuable gifts frame the good reputation of the host beyond the limits of the household, since the guest carries the gift to his own estate. For example, Telemachus notices (15.174–178) that if Odysseus were waiting in Ithaca he would tell him about the kindness with which he was treated by Menelaus "loaded down with all these priceless gifts". Odysseus promises that he will carry abroad ("he will sing") Alkinoous' praise presumably for his generosity (17.460–462). In all, both hosts and guests remember the gifts they offer and they receive (24.266–279). The prestige of the owner is transferred through the exceptional gift to the recipient, who in reciprocation preserves the memory of the donor (Crielaard, 2003).

Exceeding the capacities and expectations of the guest accentuates the effect of conspicuous waste / vicarious consumption. For example, the Phaeacians (5.38–40) offer more than what Odysseus had looted. And as we saw the promise for more gifts was enough for Odysseus to delay his return to Ithaca. In a similar example, Menelaus proposes a gift that Telemachus cannot accept. The initial offer of three horses, along with a chariot and a cup (4.589–592), marks the high status of the host and the guest, given that breeding race-horses is, for Veblen, a hallmark of the leisure class. In the case of Telemachus, however, the gift is an inappropriate offering, since, as he explains, the horses cannot be taken to rugged Ithaca that lacks meadows (4.600–608). Menelaus' gift is a display of wealth, a type of (attempted) vicarious consumption. Telemachus asks that the gift should be left as a keepsake and Menelaus agrees to change his offering (4.689), another sign of his chivalry and generosity. He expresses his intention to offer a solid silver cup (4.614–619), the most beautiful and honourable from the keepsakes he owns, made by Hephaestus (the smith god).

The storage of gifts (always great in number and value) is also an indication of the leisure-class practice of accumulation and presupposes conspicuous waste. Moreover, it manifests the wealth and the status of the giver. Gifts are usually kept in a store of treasures (e.g. Menelaus' and Odysseus'). In Ithaca, in view of the turmoil in Odysseus' palace, where neither hospitality is practised (see suitors ignoring a guest and maltreating a beggar, Athena or the disguised Odysseus) nor the host's property is respected (the suitors consume Odysseus' property in his absence while seducing his wife), the storage of gifts is peculiar. Piraeus transfers Telemachus' gifts to his house while Telemachus visits Eumaeus, and when they then meet at the palace Piraeus asks Telemachus to send some women to pick them up (17.78–80). Telemachus treats the gifts as his personal property that he can offer as heritance. To this end, in the case that the suitors kill him and confiscate his father's estate, he asks that Piraeus or another friend keep the gifts for their personal satisfaction. If, however, Telemachus kills the suitors then, they would bring the gifts to palace and share the joy (15.81–88). Telemachus violates the orders of Helen for storing and probably the customary practices of stowing gifts, but, as said, this is under extraordinary conditions.

The essence of the gift-giving as an institution, and the importance of its employment in forming and forging social relations, is revealed also in cases where gifts are not offered, violating in that way the customs, practices and norms of the leisure-class scheme of life of the time[16]. The example of the Cyclops' disinclination to offer a gift to Odysseus is particularly interesting. To most Homeric scholars (e.g. Brown, 1996; Newton, 2008) this is taken as a sign of barbarism, bestiality and defiance of gods. In our view, the Cyclopes' society employs practices that correspond to an early predatory stage, during which prowess and exploit, rather than conspicuous waste, constitute the primary mark of social esteem and status. In this society gift-giving is atypical; it has not established yet as a prevalent social institution, something that Odysseus terribly ignores. Loyal to the leisure-class norms of his society, he is willing to offer a hospitality gift with increased value due to its history: the wine that Maron gave to him as a present.

The defiance of the norms of the institution of gift-giving is also apparent in the scenes, where Odysseus arrives to Ithaca, disguises as a beggar by Athena and begs the suitors. In this case, another type of gift-giving takes place between members of different class: this is the case of gifts of food to beggars, a kind of alms. The scope of this type of offering is similar to that of hospitality in the context of the leisure-class ideals. Giving food to the beggars gathered at court is how the donors show that "they have superior status, decisive power, and surplus of means" (Cecchet, 2014, p. 160). Offering food to beggars is, therefore, a gesture of vicarious consumption. Telemachus abiding by the rules of the institution and knowing the real identity of his father receives Odysseus the beggar as a guest and treats him well, providing wine and food (20.257–298). He sets an example for the prototypical behaviour of the leisure class, which the suitors, nevertheless, ignore and therefore they maltreat Odysseus. The violation of the institution of gift-giving is encapsulated in the perverted use of the term guest-gift, which Ctesippus applies to a cow's hoof, which he hurls at Odysseus. Distorting the principles of Homeric gift-giving institution, Ctesippus asks Odysseus to share this prized gift with other servants (20.296–298) implying the circulation of gifts and a peculiar "conspicuous consumption"; in "an alternative gift economy" cow-hoofs are exchanged between low-class people, beggars and maids (Gottesman, 2010, p. 298).

Besides hospitality, in the context of another institution, that of marriage, wedding gifts are examples of vicarious consumption, although they perform additional functions. They are means to lure the bride's father or the bride herself (Bertelli, 2014). Penelope describes the practice of gift-giving in the case of a rivalry for a noble woman, when she tries to lure gifts from the suitors (18.275–279). Suitors, according to her, bring their own meat to feast the friends of the bride-to-be and shower her with gleaming gifts, and they do not devour the household's property (18.312–315). Penelope presents the behaviour of her suitors as unprecedented and contrary to what the norm, "the just" in her words, had prescribed by then. The suitors violate the institution of gift-giving in the context of marriage and transcend the prescriptions of the customary conspicuous waste.

As Penelope tricks the suitors by asking for gifts, presumably in order to choose a husband, a competition in gift-giving is implied (presupposing a kind of leisure-class pecuniary emulation). Antinous falls into the trap and encourages her to accept any offerings from the suitors, reminding her another facet of the institution of gift-giving often mentioned in the *Odyssey*, the fact that it is not proper to reject a gift. Moreover, he defends their conspicuous leisure, since they are stranded in the palace, until she picks a husband among them ("because we are not returning to our previous works/ estates or to any other location" 18.288). Four suitors are named (Antinous, Eurymachus, Eurydamas and Pisander), who offer splendid pieces of jewellery along with robes brought from their palaces by servants, pointing to the private ownership of these items (18.290–301). The gifts of the suitors are of dangerous type – gifts of metal and jewellery – that traditionally in myth make women betray men. As Lyons (2012, p. 74) notices "the good wife neither accepts gifts where she should not, nor gives away what must be kept". In this fake competition, there is no winner, since all gifts are described as "precious objects that bring pleasure and grace", with none of which emerging as exceptional in comparison with the rest. After the four suitors are named and their gifts are elaborately presented, a vague and generic description of the contributions of the rest of the suitors shows the equality of their gifts ("In the same way each of the Greeks brought one fair gift and one another" 18.295).

However, in other scenes the wedding gifts are presented as the criterion for Penelope's choice of husband, and thus gift-giving in the context of marriage is exceptionally competitive. When Athena urges Telemachus to return to Ithaca, she mentions that Penelope's father and brother press her to marry Eurymachus "who excels all other suitors at giving gifts and drives the bride-price higher" (15.17–18). Penelope as well, when she describes her situation to Odysseus, she mentions that the best suitor who will marry her will give her many/endless gifts (19.528–530). And Telemachus is invited by Agelaus to marry his mother to the best suitor who offers the most gifts (20.335–344). Moreover, after Leiodes fails to string the bow, he exclaims that a suitor who tries the bow should seek another woman to marry through gifts realising the difficulty of the competition. And Penelope should then (presumably after the failure of all) marry the one who offers more and who, therefore, will be her fated groom (21.157–162). Leiodes, therefore, proposes the conventional conspicuous antagonistic gift exchange instead of the antagonism of prowess in archery, which would be more appropriate in the predator stage.

Marriage gifts can go either direction and they are also provided to the groom. Telemachus, assuming the role of the household's head and showing his capacity to engage in conspicuous waste, he promises gifts to the groom his mother will choose (20.341–342). As in the case of his role as a host, Telemachus reclaims the authority of his household by participating in the rituals of gift-giving. In this context, it comes as no surprise that Penelope is called *polydoros* (many-gifted) (20.294), a term, which means the one who has gone to marriage with many gifts (no clarification if gifts are given or received), or "married with many gifts" (in this case with gifts received). The value of the bride is determined by the amount of gifts she can accrue and thus the more desirable she is, the more gifts her father will require, targeting at the higher social class who can afford such gifts (Leese, 2017). Penelope's characterisation as many-gifted implies her matching with an aristocratic groom.

While the scope of the chapter is not to record all instances of gift-giving, it is worth mentioning that outside the contexts of typical gift-giving institutions, i.e. hospitality and marriage, other instances of gift-giving are also attested. Gifts are promised to those who bring news for Odysseus' homecoming (e.g. 2.186, 15.537, 17.164, 19.310, 14.165), but most of the times they are denied, since the news for Odysseus' return are not trustworthy. In this case the value of the gift is questioned and thus it cannot be reciprocated. Moreover, it is not institutionalised to the same degree as other gifts. In contrast, another type of gift proves, according to Bertelli (2014), the institutional character of gift-giving, which transcends the limits of a simple custom. Bertelli (2014, p. 127) defines *geras* as "a special gift given by the community in recognition of kingly status"; it is, in a sense, a royal prerogative. Examples include a slave offered by the people to Alcinous (7.10) and higher portions of the booty offered to Odysseus (9.549–51). *Geras* demarcates social classes, since it is a gift received by a person of a higher rank than that of the giver. Moreover, the community as a whole emulates the conspicuous-consumption behaviour of the leisure class.

Conclusions

The question of why people give gifts and reciprocate has been the focus of considerable research in social sciences, traditionally in anthropology and sociology and more recently in economics and management. Yet, few scholars have acknowledged the pioneering work and influence of Veblen on the issue, let alone any attempt to explore his theory with reference to a specific spatiotemporal context. The current chapter has taken a small such step in outlining the Veblenian perspective on gift-giving as an institution, developed out of status-driven conspicuous-consumption behaviour of the upper-social ("leisure") class, and in exploring the emergence, development and practice of gift-giving in the earliest recorded period of European evolution.

Where most scholars (especially in economics) have stressed the reciprocal nature of gift-giving exploring its relation to market exchange, Veblen (long before) have perceived gift-giving as a means of conspicuous display of wealth in the endeavour of the giver to establish and advance their position within the social hierarchy, and so to achieve prestige, recognition and power. On this account, Veblen, pointing out the dual function of gift (as a means of signalling as well as maintaining social status and order), provided an explication of both the motives of gift-giving behaviour and its consequences on forming social standards and manners of life, and by so organising the social nexus of a time. Building upon this conception, the chapter has next attempted (for the first time, according to our knowledge) to shed light on the emergence and consolidation of gift-giving as an institution of the Homeric society. *Odyssey*, the second oldest (after Homer's *Iliad*) extant work of Western literature, was used as a case study. The poem, through the story of Odysseus' ten-year journey home after the Trojan War, reflects the socio-economic institutions and behaviour of the whole Homeric society, providing valuable information for analysing gift-giving behaviour in the early stages of human evolution and understanding the context and dynamics that gave rise to this institution. It should be noted that Veblen's theory, which (unlike other theories, e.g. Mauss's and Sahlins's) has never been applied on the field of Classics, provided valuable insights on the function and structure of ancient Greek society, and vice versa; its application on the Homeric society showed the latter's role in understanding the emergence and consolidation of the universal practice of gift-giving.

Delving into the Homeric society, as outlined by the class structure, scheme of life, institutional framework and socio-economic conditions and behaviour, it became evident that the *Odyssey* presents a social organisation that corresponds to the early quasi-peaceable stage of the Veblenian institutional evolution. Although behavioural traces of the previous developmental stage are still in force (as the scene of Cyclops exposes), it is clear that humanity has left behind its predatory, warlike past and it has entered a new period of socio-economic development with distinct peaceful characteristics and institutions. As Donlan (1981) aptly notices, plunder is replaced by circulation of gifts as a means of increasing wealth. Such institutions are those of private property, pecuniary emulation, and of course, the conspicuous leisure, conspicuous consumption and conspicuous gift-giving, which enable the Homeric leisure class to properly display their economic strength and, thereby, to achieve greater social status and power.

Focusing specifically on the Homeric gift-giving behaviour, it becomes clear that it has acquired the characteristics of an established institution that was, arguably, absent from the previous – predatory – developmental stage (again, as the Cyclops scene indicates). The Homeric leisure-class heroes not only turn to it in order to advertise their wealth (and as such to establish their social position), but also, they have attached to it a series of practices (e.g. circulation), religious morals (e.g. fear to god – 14.56–59) and rituals related also to other institutions (xenia, marriage), all of which facilitated its entrenchment in the scheme of life of the whole society. As such, gift-giving behaviour has become a customary norm of reputability and proper behaviour for all, even though it is primarily an aristocratic practice.

Certainly, gift-giving had a number of other functions (apart from status-motivated conspicuous consumption) and effects in the Homeric society. The circulation of objects as gifts is a circulation of prestige, but also a circulation and perpetuation of the owner's remembrance (*inter alia*: 15.591–592, 16.230, 19.281, 23.341). On these grounds, antagonism in gift-giving becomes an antagonism in generosity, fame and remembrance (e.g. 19.332–334). In addition, gift-giving plays another important role: it becomes the social mechanism to establish bonding relations between people (usually, of the same class), kings and chiefdoms. And since immediate or similar in value gift reciprocation is not always possible, the gift-giving creates commitment, indebtedness and loyalty between those engaged in the practice. All these concur in reducing transaction costs and increasing cooperation between people, both of the same class and in general. According to Tracy (2014, p. 6), such a gift-giving "cooperative generosity" is demanded by gods, practised by heroes and espoused by plain people, but it is principally motivated by a desire for *kudos*. In that sense, all these elements should not be seen as independent aspects of social organisation, but as facets of the wider institutional apparatus of the leisure-class scheme of life. On these grounds, Donlan (1980, p. 4) echoes Veblen when he writes:

> The possession of great wealth was a conspicuous sign of success – visible proof of prowess and leadership. It was also the means by which prestige and rank were enhanced, since it enabled the holder to give valuable gifts to guest-friends (*xeinoi*) and to reward followers, thereby insuring and increasing loyalty and dependency.

Notes

1 To use his own words "institutions are, in substance, prevalent habits of thought with respect to particular relations and particular functions of the individual and of the community" (Veblen, 1899/1912, p. 190), or "settled habits of thought common to the generality of men" (Veblen, 1909, p. 626).

2 According to Mauss (1954) there is no free or disinterested gift; giving, receiving and reciprocating are not only socially obligatory but the honour of the giver is also associated with the prestige of the receiver, since failure to receive and

reciprocate means "losing the competition for honour" (Douglas, 1990, p. xi). Malinowski (1922/1985, p. 175) as well points to the obligatory aspect of giving due to custom, arguing that it is motivated by the "fundamental human impulse, to display, to share, to bestow".

3 According to Diggins (1977, p. 360), Mauss was aware of Veblen's theory and admired him "as the only American sociologist of consequence", whereas Schwartz (1967) explicitly referred to Veblen's work.

4 According to Mauss (1954) collectivities rather than individuals inflict obligations for exchange, while for Malinowski (1922/1985) it is customary law that defines the system of gifts and counter-gifts.

5 Finley (1954) dates the Homeric society around the Greek Dark Age (tenth and ninth century BC), whereas others, e.g. Janko (1982) place it in the second half of the eighth century BC.

6 Note that the Linear B script, which was the written language of the time, disappeared with the fall of Mycenaean civilisation (in the thirteenth century BC), and writing, in the form of the Greek alphabet, appears much later in the eighth century BC.

7 It is important to distinguish between the Veblenian concept of "instinct" and what is usually understood as instinct in modern, scientific or common sense (Arvanitidis, 2014). For the latter, instinct is an innate biological impulse to behave or react in a particular way without involving rational conscious thought. For Veblen, instinct is a behavioural propensity, a salient quality of human essence, that has both biological and socio-cultural roots (Waller, 2007, 2017). "Instincts" emerged historically in a long process of socio-cultural evolution affected by our biological makeup, our contact with our environment and our relations with others. They are considered to be the restless propellants that drive human development by shaping cognition, beliefs and the criteria of knowledge and reality, and providing a basis to construct the canons of conduct which serve as guides and standards in socio-economic life. Yet, the form in which these forces come forth is also a function of culture and individual experience (Waller, 2017).

8 Although the institution of conspicuous consumption develops in full and consolidates in the quasi-peaceable stage (mainly due to the establishment of the private property), Veblen notes the emergence of conspicuous consumption even in the early phases of predatory life, when, for instance, top quality food and other goods are offered first to the warriors-hunters as a reward and a mark of their prowess and reputability.

9 According to Whitley (1991, pp. 36–37) the Homeric society can be dated either at the time of the composition of the Homeric epics (late eighth century) or even earlier (late ninth–early eighth century).

10 Interestingly, Hooker (1989) argues that Homeric gift-giving is a "a polite custom", rather than an institution, a view that Bertelli (2014), supporting Finley, has recently revaluated.

11 Other gifts include honour/*geras* to the king; see e.g. 7.10, 7.150, 11.176, 11.184, 15.522.

12 In the nexus of gift-giving, hosts pose as past guests, and guests are treated as future hosts. Menelaus recognises his duty to offer hospitality to Telemachus based on previous instances of hospitality shown to him (4.32–36).

13 Gifts, according to Finley (1954), are to be stored or to be given away, but as Peacock (2013) notices they can also be used. When they are not used they circulate in an elite class (Peacock, 2013).

14 When, however, Telemachus is encouraged by Mentes/Athena to leave Sparta right away to go to Ithaca, Pisitratus advises him to wait until next morning so that they will receive gifts. Pisistratus describes the proper type of *xenia*. The prospect of receiving gifts suffices to change Telemachus' opinion and a god's

order. Nevertheless, Telemachus on his return from Sparta asks Pisistratus not to stop to Pylos in order to receive more gifts, so that his journey would not be more delayed in danger that more of his property will be destroyed.

15 Scodel (2008) identifies competitive gift giving in the context of marriage.

16 For more examples of failures in hospitality see Tracy (2014).

References

Akerlof, G. 1982. Labor Contracts as Partial Gift Exchange. *Quarterly Journal of Economics*. **97**(4), pp. 543–569. DOI: 10.2307/1885099

Amaldoss, W. and Jain, S. 2005. Conspicuous Consumption and Sophisticated Thinking. *Management Science*. **51**(10), pp. 1449–1466. DOI: 10.1287/mnsc.1050.0399

Arrow, K. J. and Dasgupta, P. S. 2009. Conspicuous Consumption, Inconspicuous Leisure. *Economic Journal*. **119**(541), pp. F497–F516. DOI: 10.1111/j.1468-0297.2009.02318.x

Arvanitidis, P. 2014. *The Economics of Urban Property Markets: An Institutional Economics Analysis*. London: Routledge.

Arvanitidis, P. and Papadopoulos N. P. 2018. The "Theory of the Leisure Class" in Homeric Epoch. *Social Science Tribune*. **18**(69), pp. 121–144. [in Greek].

Bagwell, L. S. and Bernheim, B. D. 1996. Veblen Effects in a Theory of Conspicuous Consumption. *American Economic Review*. **86**(3), pp. 349–373.

Belshaw, C. S. 1965. *Traditional Exchange and Modern Markets*. Englewood Cliffs, NJ: Prentice Hall.

Bertelli, L. 2014. The Ratio of Gift-Giving in the Homeric Poems. In: Carla, F. and Gori, M. Eds. *Gift-Giving and the Embedded Economy in Ancient Greece and Rome*. Heidelberg: Winter, pp. 103–134.

Blau, P. 1964. *Exchange and Social Power*. New York: Wiley.

Boutiras, M. and Goulaki-Boutira, A. 2011. *The Ancient Greek Art and Its Radiance*. Thessaloniki: Institute of Modern Greek Studies. [in Greek].

Bowles, S. and Park, Y. 2005. Emulation, Inequality, and Work Hours: Was Thorsten Veblen Right? *Economic Journal*. **115**(507), pp. F397–F412. DOI: 10.1111/j.1468-0297.2005.01042.x

Brown, C. 1996. In the Cyclops' Cave: Revenge and Justice in "Odyssey." *Mnemosyne*. **49**(1), pp. 1–29.

Camerer, C. 1988. Gifts as Economic Signals and Social Symbols. *American Journal of Sociology*. **94**, pp. S180–S214. DOI: 10.1086/228946

Cecchet, L. 2014. Gift Giving to the Poor in the Greek World. In: Carla, F. and Gori, M. Eds. *Gift-Giving and the Embedded Economy in Ancient Greece and Rome*. Heidelberg: Winter, pp. 157–179.

Charles, K. K., Hurst, E. and Roussanov, N. 2009. Conspicuous Consumption and Race. *Quarterly Journal of Economics*. **124**(2), pp. 425–467. DOI: 10.1162/qjec.2009.124.2.425

Crielaard, J. P. 2003. Past or Present? Epic Poetry, Aristocratic Self-Representation and the Concept of Time in the Eighth and Seventh Centuries BC. In: Montanari, F. and Ascheri, P. Eds. *Omero tremila anni dopo*. Roma: Edizioni di storia e letteratura, pp. 239–295.

Diggins, J. 1977. Reification and the Cultural Hegemony of Capitalism: The Perspectives of Marx and Veblen. *Social Research*, **44**(2), pp. 354–383.

Domingo Gygax, M. 2013. Gift-Giving and Power Relationships in Greek Social Praxis and Public Discourse. In: Satlow, M. L. Ed. *The Gift in Antiquity. The Ancient World: Comparative Histories*. Oxford: Malden, pp. 45–60.

Donlan, W. 1982. Reciprocities in Homer. *Classical World.* **75**(3), pp. 137–175.

Donlan, W. 1985. The Social Groups of Dark Age Greece. *Classical Philology.* **80**(4), pp. 293–308. DOI: 10.1086/366938.

Donlan, W. 1989. The Pre-State Community in Greece. *Symbolae Osloenses.* **64**(1), pp. 2–29. DOI: 10.1080/00397678908590821.

Donlan, W. 1997. The Homeric Economy. In: Morris, I. and Powell, B. Eds. *A New Companion to Homer*, Leiden: Brill, pp. 649–667. DOI: 10.1163/9789004217607_029.

Douglas, M. 1990. Foreword, No free gifts. In: Mauss, M. Ed. *The Gift: Forms and Functions of Exchange in Archaic Societies.* London: Routledge, pp. ix–xxiii.

Finley, M. I. 1954. *The World of Odysseus.* New York: Harmondsworth.

Finley, M. I. 1955. Marriage, Sale and Gift in the Homeric World. *Revue International des Droits de l' Antiquité.* **s.3**(2), pp. 167–194.

Gerard-Varet, L. A., Kolm, S. C. and Ythier, J. M. Eds. 2000. *The Economics of Reciprocity, Giving and Altruism.* London: Palgrave Macmillan.

Gottesman, A. 2010. The Beggar and the Clod: The Mythic Notion of Property in Ancient Greece. *Transactions of the American Philological Association.* **140**(2), pp. 287–322.

Gouldner, A. W. 1960. The Norm of Reciprocity: A Preliminary Statement. *American Sociological Review.* **25**(2), pp. 161–78.

Haight, A. D. 1997. Padded Prowess: A Veblenian Interpretation of the Long Hours of Salaried Workers, *Journal of Economic Issues.* **31**(1), pp. 29–38. DOI: 10.1080/00213624.1997.11505889.

Hodgson, G. M. 1998. The Approach of Institutional Economics. *Journal of Economic Literature.* **36**(1), pp. 166–192.

Hodgson, G. M. 2014. Thorstein Veblen: The Father of Evolutionary and Institutional Economics. In: Reinert, E. S. and Viano, F. L. Eds. *Thorstein Veblen: Economics for an Age of Crises.* London: Anthem, pp. 283–295.

Homer. 1995. *The Odyssey.* [in English translated by Murray, A. T. and Dimock, G. E. 2 Vols. Cambridge, MA: Loeb Classical Library].

Hooker, J. T. 1989. Gifts in Homer. *Bulletin of the Institute of Classical Studies.* **36**, pp. 79–90.

Janko, R. 1982. *Homer, Hesiod and the Hymns.* Cambridge: Cambridge University Press.

Kolm, S. C. 2000. Introduction: The Economics of Reciprocity, Giving and Altruism. In: Gerard-Varet, L. A., Kolm, S. C. and Ythier, J. M. Eds. *The Economics of Reciprocity, Giving and Altruism.* London: Palgrave Macmillan, pp. 1–44. DOI: 10.1007/978-1-349–62745–5_1.

Kolm, S. C. and Ythier, J. M. Eds. 2006. *Handbook of the Economics of Giving, Altruism and Reciprocity, vol. 1: Foundations, vol. 2: Applications.* Amsterdam: Elsevier.

Lampel, J. and Bhalla, A. 2007. The Role of Status Seeking in Online Communities: Giving the Gift of Experience. *Journal of Computer-Mediated Communication.* **12**(2), pp. 434–455. DOI: 10.1111/j.1083–6101.2007.00332.x

Leese, M. 2017. An Economic Perspective on Marriage Alliances in Ancient Greece. In: Kehoe, D. P. and McGinn T. A. J. Eds. *Ancient Law, Ancient Society.* Ann Arbor: University of Michigan Press, pp. 32–45.

Lyons, D. 2012. *Dangerous Gifts. Gender and Exchange in Ancient Greece.* Austin: University of Texas Press.

Malinowski, B. 1922/1985. *Argonauts of the Western Pacific.* London: George Routledge & Sons.

Mason, R. S. 1981. *Conspicuous Consumption: A Study of Exceptional Consumer Behavior.* New York: St. Martin's Press.

Mauss, M. 1954. *The Gift: Forms and Functions of Exchange in Archaic Societies.* London: Cohen and West.

Mazzocco, P. J., Rucker, D. D., Galinsky, A. D. and Anderson, E. T. 2012. Direct and Vicarious Conspicuous Consumption: Identification with Low-status Groups Increases the Desire for High-Status Goods. *Journal of Consumer Psychology.* **22**(4), pp. 520–528. DOI: 10.1016/j.jcps.2012.07.002

Miller, E. S. 1978. Institutional Economics: Philosophy, Methodology and Theory. *The Social Science Journal.* **15**(1), pp. 13–25.

Morgan, L. H. 1877. *Ancient Society; or, Researches in the Lines of Human Progress from Savagery, through Barbarism to Civilization.* London: Macmillan.

Morris, I. and Powell, B. Eds. 1997. *A New Companion to Homer.* Leiden: Brill.

Newton, R. 2008. Assembly and Hospitality in the "Cyclôpeia." *College Literature.* **35**(4), pp. 1–44.

Parker, C. H. 1918. Motives in Economic Life. *American Economic Review.* **8**(1), pp. 212–231.

Peacock, M. 2013. *Introducing Money.* London: Routledge.

Reece, S. 1993. *The Stranger's Welcome: Oral Theory and the Aesthetics of the Homeric Hospitality Scene.* Ann Arbor: University of Michigan Press.

Rojek, C. 1995. Veblen, Leisure and Human Need. *Leisure Studies.* **14**(2), pp. 73–86. DOI: 10.1080/02614369500390071

Sahlins, M. 1972. *Stone Age Economics.* Chicago, IL: Aldine-Atherton.

Sakelariou, M. B., Maltezou, X. A. and Despotopoulos, A. I. Eds. 1999. *Greek History, Book 1: Prehistoric and Archaic Times.* Athens: Ekdotike Athenon. [in Greek].

Schwartz, B. 1967. The Social Psychology of the Gift. *American Journal of Sociology.* **73**(1), pp. 1–11. DOI: 10.1086/224432.

Scodel, R. 2008. *Epic Facework: Self-Presentation and Social Interaction in Homer.* Swansea: Classical Press of Wales.

Searle, J. R. 2005. What is an Institution? *Journal of Institutional Economics.* **1**(1), pp. 1–22. DOI: 10.1017/S1744137405000020

Snodgrass, A. M. 1974. An Historical Homeric Society? *Journal of Hellenic Studies.* **94**, pp. 114–125. DOI: 10.2307/630424

Tracy, C. 2014. The Host's Dilemma: Game Theory and Homeric Hospitality. *Illinois Classical Studies.* **39**, pp. 1–16. DOI: DOI: 10.5406/illiclasstud.39.0001

Veblen, T. 1909. The Limitations of Marginal Utility. *Journal of Political Economy.* **17**(9), pp. 620–636.

Veblen, T. 1912[1899]. *The Theory of the Leisure Class: An Economic Study of Institutions.* New York: Huebsch.

Waller, W. T. 2017. Reconsidering Thorstein Veblen's Use of Instincts. In: Plotkin, S. Ed. *The Anthem Companion to Thorstein Veblen.* London: Anthem Press, pp. 39–67.

Waller, W. T. 1982. The Evolution of Veblenian Dichotomy: Veblen, Hamilton, Ayres, and Foster. *Journal of Economic Issues.* **16**(3), pp. 757–771. DOI: 10.1080/00213624.1982.11504031

Waller, W. T. 2007. Veblen's Missing Theory of Markets and Exchange, or Can You have an Economic Theory Without a Theory of Market Exchange. In: Knoedler, J. T., Prasch, R. E. and Champlin, D. P. Eds. *Thorstein Veblen and the Revival of Free Market Capitalism.* Cheltenham: Edward Elgar, pp. 87–126.

Weiner, A. B. 1992. *Inalienable Possessions: The Paradox of Keeping-While-Giving.* Berkeley: University of California Press.

Whitley, B. C. J. 1991. *Style and Society in Dark Age Greece: The Changing Face of a Pre-literate Society 1100–700 BC.* Cambridge: Cambridge University Press.

7 The fluid nature of gifts and grants

An institutional application to the Marshall Plan

Stefan Kesting

Introduction

In his "Grant's Economics", Boulding proposes a particular communication-based way of dealing with reciprocity in gift relationships. My chapter will explore how his approach differs in terms of its institutional foundation from the standard approach to reciprocity suggested for gift relationships in economic anthropology (e.g. Mauss, 1990; Polanyi, 1957 and Sahlins, 2004[1972]). The particular strength of Boulding Grant's Economics of love and fear as an analytical framework is that, it allows for the non-reciprocal nature of the gift (a sacrifice) deemed as important by Elder-Vass (2016 and 2019). This is more inclusive than the standard Maussian notion of the gift as solely enticing an obligation to reciprocate. Moreover, Boulding's theory of grants also allows for some utilitarian calculation applied to gift-giving which would be shunned by most economic anthropologists. Thus, Boulding's approach includes and distinguishes three distinct norms or values for gift or grant giving, which makes it a much richer instrument of analysis. I will show the usefulness of this analytical tool by applying it to the Marshall Plan as a historical example of a grant.

Boulding's grant economics of love and fear (1981) takes Gouldner's (1973) emphasis on the gift relationship of "receiving something for nothing" seriously. In other words, he takes a clear ontological stance in favour of a potential for non-self-interested behaviour and follows an alternative notion of rationality than the one typically employed in mainstream economics. A gift as sacrifice (Eagleton, 2018) can potentially break the spell of the Nash Equilibrium in the Prisoners' Dilemma and lead a society from a war of all against all to a peacefully cooperating society (Marchionatti and Cedrini, 2017; Sahlins, 2004[1972]). In Gouldner's (1973) words: "In exploring the system-maintaining function of the norms of beneficence, one other function of this norm deserves special mention; it serves as a mechanism for *stopping vicious cycles* of social interaction" (p. 274). Boulding (1981) writes:

> One of the most important aspects of the grants economy is the role it plays in the building up of integrative structures and communities – that

> is, groups of people who have some feelings of identification and benevolence toward each other.
>
> (p. 27)

In arguing on the basis of benevolence (love) vs. malevolence (fear) and combining these concepts with utilitarian calculus and the opportunity cost principle, in his Grants Economics, Boulding goes beyond the conventional wisdom about the potential for social cohesion and peace initiated by the gift in the literature on economic anthropology. He tries to integrate debates about norms of reciprocity vs. norms of altruism or sacrifice. Though distinguishing the gift clearly from exchange of equivalents ("the market"), Boulding manages to apply a couple of standard mainstream instruments of economic analysis to the gift relationship or what he calls grants. A rational criterion for an effective grant is in Boulding's words:

> … if the utility derived from the activity itself, plus the contemplation of increased benefits to others with whom the actor identifies and is benevolent toward, exceeds the utility cost involved in the sacrifice of alternative uses of time and their product.
>
> (p. 31)

This chapter aims at discussing the fluid transition and potential fruitful combination of the three conceptually distinct institutions (habits of thought in Veblen's sense)[1] inherent in gifts and grants: (a) utilitarian calculus, (b) altruism, sacrifice or giving something for nothing, and (c) reciprocity when applied and implemented in real-world political economic settings. Though the basic motivation may often be benevolence in a gift or a grant and I see utilitarian calculation with Boulding in this instance, as an additional institution to protect the grantor from being overly generous or silly, I chose the institutions in this order because this will be the logic (from a) to b) to c)) I will use in my interpretation of the Marshall Plan. This notion of institutions follows Geoff Hodgson's definition of them as rules, conventions, norms, values and customs that have been established formally or informally (Hodgson, 2006, p. 18). To support this threefold interwoven institutional framework with empirical evidence and demonstrate its analytical fruitfulness, it will be applied to the historical case study of the Marshall Plan implemented after the Second World War.

The institutional transition of the gift from sacrifice to reciprocity

What I will try to show in this section is the significant function of the gift to overcome a social stalemate exemplified by the Prisoners' Dilemma – the power of "giving something for nothing", which can break the spell of self-interested strategic behaviour and even take the risk of an unfulfilled expectation of reciprocity. The social and economic importance and crucial distinction of a gift from trade, i.e. exchange of equivalents is its inherent acceptance of taking this risk, relying on beneficence (Gouldner, 1973).

Creating social bonds, obligations, trust and peace: the potential to overcome the Prisoners' Dilemma

The neoclassical microeconomist Robert H. Frank (2003) wrestles with the question of why people give gifts like leaving a tip at a motorway restaurant where they in all likelihood will never be customers ever again. It is hard to see gains that may incentivise such behaviour for rational self-interested utility maximising individuals. For a neoclassical economist this creates a conundrum: these people give something for nothing. Why do they do this?

Frank's answer is that such gifts involving short-term losses are motivated by an interest in entering long-term profitable contracts *in general* in all kinds of aspects of economic life (for instance: business, employment, marriage and renting accommodation opportunities). According to him, for people operating under neoclassical assumptions, there are two mechanisms that drive them to forgo short-term gains or to take risks of short-term losses. These mechanisms are concerns of reputation and a life-long overall psychological make-up which will suffer if people always take advantage of others in dealings that involve typical prisoners' dilemma situations. The main argument is that potential fruitful long-term relations will be foregone if contractual partners will either know from our reputation or detect from our habitus and aura that we are crooks and not trustworthy.[2] His microeconomic approach bears strong resemblance with Camerer's mainstream view of the gift as a signalling device for further relationship-specific intentions of investment (1988) and Kaplan and Ruffle's argument about gifts as welfare enhancing (2009). He stresses that the main objective of gift-giving in communicating with others and behaving cooperatively is fostered by emotional bonds and sympathy. This behavioural pattern is conceptually at odds with rational choice theory and Frank implicitly admits that his attempt to integrate gift-like and especially sacrificing behaviour as rational in a self-interested maximising framework of analysis is problematic. This is because rational choice models do not usually integrate moral emotions. Moreover, he admits that according to rational choice logic, self-interest would tend to crowd out other-regarding behaviour in an individualistic Darwinian framework of competition (Frank, 2003, p. 27). However, Frank's urge to cling to the unitary neoclassical theory is stronger than to be logically consistent or to propose a less conventional and more realistic theoretical framework. Frank claims to propose a broader theory, but his approach leads to contradictions if other-regarding and self-interested motivations are intertwined with and subsumed under a rational choice framework. In my view, a clear conceptual distinction of these motivations allowing for inner conflict will be more fruitful to disentangle how they work together and overlap empirically in real social interactions. Such alternative theories of inner self-conflict are presented for instance by Lutz and Lux (1988) as a dual self where individuals can either follow Kantian norms of a higher self or self-interested hedonistic urges of a lower self. Another alternative theory is Etzioni's communitarian notion of "the I needs a We to be" (1990, p. 9), that is, a dual self where individuals based on emotional bonds forged by their community follow either social rules and norms or a more individualistic utilitarian calculated self-interest.

Frank's theoretical starting point is the prisoners' dilemma (PD). The only way to break out of this self-interested logic of the PD is to have a meta-strategy, which will overrule the dominant strategy. To come up with a meta-strategy entails leaving the strict behavioural rational choice assumptions that underpin game theory and replace them by some notion of a self with potentially conflicting motivations. Work by economic anthropologists suggests the gift by applying the institutions of sacrifice and reciprocity can potentially break the spell of the Nash Equilibrium and lead a society from a war of all against all to a peacefully cooperating society.

So, in this way the reciprocity inspired by a gift may transpire through society anonymously and the initiated reciprocity is not necessarily targeted at the giving person by the receiving person in a particular situation. The gift fosters social bonding and trust in a general way. That such a process of spreading gratitude and goodwill can happen on a large scale will be shown in the interpretation of the Marshall Plan. This is a slightly different interpretation from the symbolical gift exchanges described by Mauss (1990) who stresses the ritualised rivalry in the Potlatch for instance or the interpretation by Sahlins who emphasises the diplomatic peacekeeping nature of gift exchange:

> Intergroup exchange does not simply answer to the "moral purpose" of making friends. But whatever the intent and however utilitarian, it will not do to make enemies. Every transaction, as we already know, is necessarily a social strategy: it has a coefficient of sociability demonstrated in its manner, and in its rates by the implied willingness to live and let live, the disposition to give full measure in return. As it happens, the safe and sane procedure is not just measure-for-measure, a reciprocity precisely balanced. The most tactful strategy is economic good measure, a generous return relative to what has been received, of which there can be no complaints.
>
> (2004[1972], p. 303)

Note that both Mauss and Sahlins see the institution of reciprocity at the centre of the gift relationship.

Ethnographic studies show the "... deep tendency to create social ties through exchange of gifts" (Marchionatti and Cedrini, 2017, p. 174). However, Gouldner's (1973) emphasis on giving something for nothing is of particular importance for this potential of breaking social stalemates, confrontation and solving conflicts:

> Norms of beneficence also serve as a "starting mechanism" helping to initiate social interaction. … To use a crude analogy: the norm of beneficence is an ignition key that activates the starting engine (the norm of reciprocity) which, in turn gets the motor – the ongoing cycle of mutual exchanges – to turn over.
>
> (p. 275)

This argument can be seen as an alternative yet supportive one for *doux commerce* (Hirschman, 1977 and 1982).[3] Gouldner criticises Malinowski for giving in to Mauss' argument that all gifts are motivated by reciprocity. The distinctive power of the gift is in danger of being lost when the norm of beneficence is overlooked:

> Gouldner's analysis has the merit of making the tension between reciprocity and gift-giving explicit, recognizing it as something that cannot be eliminated – unless one decides to concentrate on gift exchange as exchange of equivalents, on the symmetry of the exchange itself, thus running the risk of coming close to the reciprocity inherent in market exchange.
>
> (Marchionatti and Cedrini, 2017, p. 176)

Note that reciprocity is treated here as a motivation or expectation. However, this informal institution can be formalised in a more structured relation between parties (i.e. a contractual relation).

While acknowledging the tension inherent in the gift between the two institutions (behavioural and motivational patterns) of giving something for nothing and reciprocity, Gouldner stresses the fluidity in the transition between the two institutions. Though the initial motivation for the gift may be beneficence, the possible, potential and most probable consequence may be a cycle of reciprocity. The probable, but not guaranteed reciprocal effect of the gift exerts an underlying principle of hope (Bloch, 1959). In his three-volume magnum opus *The Principle of Hope*, the German philosopher Ernst Bloch describes the progressive power of optimistic utopia, which has its origin in day dreams of a better life and finds its expression in theatre, art, cinema, opera, technology, literature, religion, etc. and sees the concrete world as a laboratory for a potential better world. It is the notion of the sacrifice (Eagleton, 2018) that lends the potential power of social integration to the gift:

> The paradox is this, there is no gift that brings a higher return than the free gift, the gift given with no strings attached. For that which is truly given freely moves men deeply and makes them most indebted to their benefactors. In the end, it is beneficence that transcends this world and can make men weep the tears of reconciliation. If such prodigies of social interaction are rare, it is not for want of knowing how to produce them.
>
> (Gouldner, 1973, p. 277)

Boulding's grant (the economics of love and fear)

Boulding is definitely one of the few economists who take the tension of the gift and its distinction from exchange seriously (Marchionatti and Cedrini, 2017, pp. 136, 146). He insists that reciprocity is formally unconditional while exchange is not. He refers to Malinowski, Gouldner, Titmuss and Mauss when introducing his own take on the gift which he relabels as grant. Boulding's idea of the grant is a transfer without the expectation of return, the intentions of the donor of a grant matter because they distinguish it clearly from exchange. His microeconomic approach departs methodologically radically from typical neoclassical assumptions which underlie mainstream approaches to the gift-like: Camerer's mainstream view of the gift as a signalling device for further relationship-specific intentions of investment (1988), Kaplan and Ruffle's argument about gifts as welfare enhancing (2009) or Andreoni et al.'s work on private donations and crowding out and crowding in effects (2011 and 2014) or their ethical and religious specificity (2016).

In Boulding's framework, a grant is either motivated by benevolence or malevolence, which is clearly perceived as such by the recipient and may be accompanied by utilitarian considerations on the side of the donor. The grant (especially the benevolent one) will most likely lead to reciprocal behaviour by the recipient in the future. His research question is: "… what elements of the social system make some conflicts creative and fruitful and some conflicts destructive and damaging to all parties?" (Boulding, 1973, p. 1). The grant provides the potential for unlocking the Prisoners' Dilemma and is instrumental for the transition from destructive to creative conflict resolution.[4] For Boulding the grant encompasses the gift – i.e. a grant given out of love. However, he distinguishes a second kind of grant given out of fear which he calls a tribute. Apart from adding a second motive for grant or gift-giving: malevolence motivated by a threat, to benevolence (beneficence in Gouldner's terminology) motivated by love, Boulding's arguments are quite similar to Gouldner's.[5] He also insists on the crucial institutional distinction of reciprocity from exchange: "Reciprocity, even though it looks superficially like exchange, has integrative aspects that exchange does not" (Boulding, 1981, p. 25). Moreover, he stresses the importance of serial reciprocity for modern societies (ibid., p. 26). Boulding also repeats Gouldner's argument about the igniting character of the gift and in true Keynesian fashion calls this phenomenon a "reciprocity multiplier … the original gift giver becomes a source of infection of benevolence" (ibid., p. 27).

According to Boulding, grants are necessary to provide public goods (ibid., p. 6) and states: "… a grants system which is neutral in terms of the distribution of resources is extremely unlikely" (p. 7). Moreover, Boulding writes these distributional effects of grants should be used to foster equality (p. 8). So, in contrast to Sahlins's (2004[1972]) description of affluence or absence of scarcity found among hunter and gatherer peoples in ethnographic field work, Boulding's concept of the grant is based upon the economic standard assumption of relative scarcity and applies a utilitarian calculus and the opportunity cost principle to grant giving. To illustrate the utilitarian calculation of the donor, he writes for instance: "Thus, if by sacrificing a dollar I perceive that somebody else is four dollars better off, my perception of the efficiency of the grant is 4" (p. 11). Moreover, he advises the provider of a grant to apply the opportunity cost principle: a grant is worthwhile

> … if the utility derived from the activity itself, plus the contemplation of increased benefits to others with whom the actor identifies and is benevolent toward, exceeds the utility cost involved in the sacrifice of *alternative uses* of time and their product.
>
> (p. 31)

So, while economic anthropologists working in the tradition of Marcel Mauss are generally suspicious of utilitarianism[6] and see the reciprocity of the gift as culturally embedded and in opposition to a utilitarian calculus – for instance, the chief giving away everything[7] in a Potlatch – in Boulding's mind a grant, though sincerely benevolent and not self-interested, can be in part motivated by utilitarian considerations. The result is a possible fluid transition in gift and grant giving from the rational choice institution of utilitarian calculus to the empathy-based institution of sacrifice and further to the fairness norm of reciprocity. This kind of fluid transition from one institution to the next can be shown at the example of the Marshall Plan.

The Marshall Plan

Note, that the Marshall Plan, formally known as the European Recovery Programme, was probably the first historical example of foreign aid in the form of an enormous grant. A large literature (e.g. Bermeo, 2018; Veen, 2011 and Holden, 2009) questioning the efficiency of foreign aid and its motivations does exist (Harrison, 2018); however, this contemporary debate focuses on more or less conditional financial assistance provide by developed countries for developing countries, whereas the Marshall Plan was a grant from one industrial nation (the United States) to 16 European industrial nations. Moreover, the Marshall plan proved to be normatively and economically successful while more recent examples of foreign aid tend to be condemned as inefficient and morally questionable. So, this literature seems not particularly relevant for the specific historical case under investigation, which predates the more modern cases of foreign aid.

In this section, I will discuss in which way the Marshall Plan can be interpreted as a gift or grant and I aim to show how particularly the igniting function of the gift as beneficence, followed by a cycle of reciprocity, can be demonstrated as the example of this historical case. Moreover, I will demonstrate that though the Americans had certainly utilitarian motives while initiating the Marshall Plan, they were also following norms of benevolence and this institution was perceived by the recipients, which led, in turn, to them applying norms of reciprocity. In other words, the Marshall followed Boulding's institutional logic of a grant. Heins, Unrau and Avram (2018) have also interpreted "the Marshall plan as iconic and controversial example" (p. 126) to support their application of Mauss' concept of gift-giving at the international level. However, they limit their analysis to the institution of reciprocity and do not discuss utilitarian elements or beneficence. Moreover, Heins et al. (2018) do not consult the work of economic historians, but base their interpretation of the Marshall Plan merely on the memoires of Jean Monnet and on sociological and philosophical literature (Bataille, 1949; Chomsky, 2004; Dillon, 1968).

My main source is Benn Steil's magnum opus *The Marshall Plan* (2018), which presents a fresh account based on very thorough historical research and a vivid and encompassing, up to date engagement with the relevant literature. Steil's book is particularly appropriate for my purpose, because contrary to my conceptual foundation he builds his historical case focusing on just the instrumental utilitarian institution:

> The book situates the Marshall Plan more directly at the center of the emerging Cold War than earlier accounts, highlighting the seriousness with which Stalin treated the threat it presented to his new, hard-won buffer zone in central and eastern Europe.
>
> (2018, p. xii)

and: "Containment successfully navigated between appeasement and war for four decades, and the Marshall Plan played a principle role in bonding the West together for the struggle" (ibid., 2018, p. 373).

Despite Steil's mono-motivational utilitarian self-interested Cold War explanation of the Marshall Plan, I can use his rich historical description to answer my question: how did the fluid combination of the three characteristic institutions of the gift work to make the Marshall Plan a success in overcoming a geostrategic Prisoners' Dilemma? That even his book provides me with enough material to show that the Marshall Plan was indeed a gift which contained and was motivated by its three characteristic institutions: utility, sacrifice and reciprocity, underpins the analytical fruitfulness of this framework.

This threefold institutional interpretation will be further supported by three other older sociological and economic accounts expressing a similar theoretical view as mine (Bataille, 1988[1967]; Galbraith, 1994; Perroux, 1948, 1961) and some other historical literature.

Georges Bataille not only discusses the mixed motivations of the American donors but also emphasises particularly the element of giving something for nothing:

> The Marshall Plan is an isolated reaction, to be sure; it is the only undertaking that results from a systematic view opposing the Kremlin's will

> to world domination. … It is not essentially the struggle of two military powers for hegemony; it is the struggle of two economic methods. The Marshall Plan offers an organisation of surplus against the accumulation of the Stalin plans.
>
> (1988[1967], p. 173)

Moreover, he adds: "It was necessary to deliver goods without payment: It was necessary to give away the product of labor" (ibid., p. 175). And referring to a book on the Marshall Plan written by Francois Perroux (1948), Bataille writes: "The operation was prepared, decided, and will be conducted on the basis of political options and macroscopic calculations which classical analysis does not really help to understand (pp. 172–173)" (ibid., p. 177). In Bataille's interpretation: "The Marshall Plan is the consequence of a working-class agitation that it tries to remedy with a rise in the Western standard of living" (p. 184). "The Marshall Plan is also, from the start, a means external to capitalism of raising the standard of living" (ibid., p. 185).

What was the Marshall Plan? – A short description

Benn Steil describes the deal of the European Recovery Program (ERP)[8] in a nutshell:

> … the United States would underwrite a basic standard of living in the participating countries to afford them the space to liberalize and integrate their economies. In essence, the State Department was tendering the largest foreign aid program in history as a social shock absorber for the largest structural adjustment program in history.
>
> (2018, p. 166)

Was the MP a gift?

The short answer to the question is definitely: yes. Steil points to the unusual economic mechanism chosen by the American government: "The financial assistance aspect of the Marshall plan also departed from earlier American efforts by abjuring the creation of unbroken circles of loans to pay back loans, relying instead on grants-in-aid" (ibid., p. 370). This motivation finds support in John Kenneth Galbraith book *The World Economy since the Wars,* 1994, p. 157: "… the earlier experience warned and intervened [the Treaty of Versailles] i.e. creating an international debt had to be avoided! There was only one solution; that was to give the money" (ibid., p. 157). Galbraith points here to the utilitarian notion of the grant donor wanting to maximise its effect. Moreover, the European imports from America resulted in a balance of payments deficit. "The latter deficit would then be covered by the Marshall Plan aid" (ibid., p. 158).

> When the Marshall Plan came into being, therefore, its creators were motivated both by an unselfish compassion for economically afflicted people and by a deep and insistent concern that the Soviet Union might otherwise occupy a depressed and vulnerable Western Europe.
>
> (Ibid., p. 161)

As the German economic historian Werner Abelshauser (2004, pp. 130, 151) argues, contrary to popular beliefs in Germany, the Marshall Plan did not significantly contribute to the German economic miracle during the years of reconstruction following immediately after the Second World War. Expectations of receiving much needed resources and capital goods by German politicians and industrialists were thwarted because the Americans did not oblige to German wish lists, but focused on their own domestic interests in terms of the kind of raw materials they delivered and the provision of machinery and vehicles was comparatively small (Abelshauser, 2004, pp. 136–138). Nonetheless, apart from facilitating the politico-psychological integration of the wider West German public into the Western capitalist world, Abelshauser concludes that the Marshall Plan provided help for the Germans to help themselves (2004, p. 151) and to return to foreign trade as Kramer adds (1991, p. 156).

The opportunity for self-help provided by the ERP is also apparent in the British experience: From England, *Time* offered the stirring story of a Birmingham car plant that had been on the verge of shutting down, with a loss of 10,000 jobs, before Marshall aid began flowing. The firm had been unable to buy carbon black, an essential element for a third of each tire's carcass and tread, owing to the country's paltry dollar reserves, until counterpart funds began financing the imports. "We've never had to worry since", said one of the workers. "Marshall aid saved us from catastrophe" (Steil, 2018, p. 314).

Who received what?

Looking at the enormous dimension of the American transfer and how it was distributed among the Europeans underpins the perception of the Marshall Plan as a gift by the recipients. According to Steil:

> Between 1948 and 1952 (four and a quarter years), the United States transferred $13.2 billion to the sixteen Marshall Plan countries. Accounting for inflation over those years, the total was $14.3 billion (that is, in 1952 dollars). … The largest recipients were the U.K. ($3.2 billion, or $32 billion today), France ($2.7 billion, or $27 billion today), Italy ($1.5 billion, or $15 today), and West Germany ($1.4 billion, or $14 billion today). Austria and Norway were the biggest beneficiaries per capita. … In today's dollars, total Marshall aid was worth $130 billion. But if the United States had run a Marshall Plan of equivalent size as a proportion of GDP (1.1 percent) from 2012 to 2016, this would have amounted to a

> vastly higher *$800 billion*. The total aid figure is higher still if we account for non-Marshall military and other assistance.
>
> (2018, p. 342)

> Although in retrospect it may seem otherwise, the Marshall Plan was of greater material significance to France and other recipient nations than to West Germany. … On a *per capita* basis it is even more apparent why Abelshauser calls West Germany the "stepchild" of the Marshall Plan: in the second year of the plan, while France received total aid of $21.7 per head of population, Austria $36.2 and The Netherlands as much as $45, West Germany received – including the GARIOA aid – only $12 dollars *per capita*.
>
> (Kramer, 1991, p. 154)

According to Abelshauser (2004, p. 144), the United States defined the Marshall Plan aid purposefully as a grant and not a loan in the contracts with participant countries to secure their influence in Europe, but Germany was an exception. Contractually, the "claim against Germany" had to be paid back in dollars, but this was not expected at the time by the US administration and this special arrangement fulfilled the purpose of averting any future demands for reparations by other countries (ibid., p. 145). However, no matter whether the ERP grant for Germany was a loan in disguise or not, Steil emphasises:

> Aid figures ignore the vast and consequential write-off of the country's debt. Germany's total official public debt after the war, 86 percent of which was domestic, amounted to nearly four times the country's 1938 GDP. The United States abolished it through the 1948 currency reform that introduced the deutschmark. Banks holding the debt received compensating assets to prevent their collapse. As regards external debt, the 1953 London Agreement reduced the principal and interest on obligations incurred through 1933 (when the country defaulted) and postponed settlement of obligations subsequently created until sometime after a future German unification, when a reparations conference could be held.
>
> (2018, p. 358)

The interpretation as the ERP as a "pure gift" in Gouldner's sense (1973) is further supported by the relative freedom to use the financial funds as they saw fit. Germany was an exception to this (Steil, 2018, pp. 356–361). However, Britain used the money to pay back their government debt with the United States (ibid., p. 348), while the French financed a planned programme of investment into public infrastructure (ibid., p. 350) and Italy focused on stabilising the economy by reducing inflation and poverty (ibid., p. 354).

Utilitarian motives

The Americans had at least three utilitarian motivations for providing their generous gift: (1) to stabilise the continent politically, (2) to favour their own domestic economy and (3) to improve their position in the Cold War with the Soviet Union.

First, as already alluded to in the quote from Galbraith (1994, p. 157) above, the Truman administration in a series of international conferences in the late 1940s pushed for and assured European integration and cooperation to prevent yet another war in Europe. While doing so, the Americans had to face constant unwillingness and opposition exemplified in this British comment:

> We are being asked … to join the Germans, who started two world wars; the French, who had in 1940 collapsed in the face of German aggression; the Italians, who changed sides; and the Low Countries, of whom not much was known but who seemed to have put up little resistance to Germany.
>
> (Steil, 2018, p. 305)

The second utilitarian argument is that the United States wanted to prevent a recession at home by creating demand for American products in Europe and to recycle their output surplus after the war. This thesis is put forward by Varoufakis (2011) and Bataille (1988[1967]). Moreover, it is presented by Steil quoting Stalin's economic advisor for the Soviet view: "… Washington must, in its own interest … grant much greater credits than it has done heretofore – just to rid itself of surplus goods at home" (2018, p. 121) as well as wishful thinking by certain American industries: "Industry groups representing specific sectors, such as tobacco growers and flour dealers, were naturally enthusiastic at the prospect of having their commodities distributed abroad with government dollars" (ibid., p. 200). However, the leading manager of the ERP Paul Hoffman had to curb such enthusiasm:

> Some American companies, he would tell his new staff, had "come to consider [the ERP] a bonanza in which everyone can share as an exporter who has anything to sell." But it needed to be "understood that the full recovery program [actually] contemplates a lower rate of exports from this country." This aim contrasted with Soviet caricatures of the program's purpose.
>
> (Ibid., p. 263)

Third, as Steil writes citing president Truman's advisor George F. Kennan, the Marshall plan was a primary instrument of the American containment strategy:

> Since the Russian threat "is more than a military threat", Kennan said at a War College lecture in October 1947, it could not "be effectively met entirely by military means". It meant "marshal[ling] all the forces at your disposal on the world chessboard … in such a way that the Russian sees it is … in his interests to do what you want him to do". The Marshall Plan

> was the centrepiece of Kennan's thinking. Victory would be defined as the revival of a democratic, capitalist western Europe without military confrontation.
>
> (Ibid., p. 340)

That the Americans saw the ERP as taking "a calculated risk" (ibid., p. 92) especially when not knowing whether Stalin would allow Eastern Europe and even the Soviet Union to be part of it (ibid., p. 133) means, they were aware of making a sacrifice that may not pay off (ibid., p. 197). Steil writes: "In chess, such a move is known as "a sham sacrifice": appearing to blunder into loss of a piece to gain tactical advantage" (ibid., p. 340).

So, it seems pretty clear that the USA had at least geostrategic utilitarian motives for the ERP, but was the Marshall Plan also a sacrifice i.e. giving something for nothing?

Europe after the war could be certainly seen as a Prisoners' Dilemma situation in need for a meta-strategy to prevent famine and chaos. In Steil's description:

> Local economies of sorts continued to function, but often only in their most Hobbesian form. During the war, the right to property had dissolved, with occupiers and resisters taking and distributing, retaking and redistributing, in the cause of war, justice, or opportunity. In the process, trust in authority and one's fellow had been shattered.
>
> (Ibid., p. 17)

Americans travelling through Europe in 1946 like Will Clayton were "… genuinely alarmed that Europe was on the brink of disaster … His stories of fearful peasants, workers, and merchants hoarding to avoid hunger were vivid and compelling …" (ibid., p. 99). So the humanitarian motive was surely part of the American relieve effort: "Spontaneous public initiatives sprang up to supplement the Marshall Plan" (ibid., p. 201).

However, not all recipients across the Atlantic saw the Marshall Plan as a sacrifice:

> …public opinion was split as to the main American objective …. In both France and Britain, one in four thought it was humanitarian; the same proportion thought it was economic self-interest. One in seven believed it was to stop Communism. Italians were more generous: one in three thought the main motive was humanitarianism. The Dutch were sceptical: only one in ten believed this. Four times as many believed it was economic self-interest.
>
> (Ibid., p. 227)

"Leading European politicians and the press supported the motive of generosity" (ibid., p. 261). Moreover, there was: "a massive, carefully orchestrated public relations campaign – a Marshall Plan to sell the Marshall Plan" (ibid., p. 199).

"Spending on media publicity would grow from $500,000 in 1948 to about $20 million annually by 1952 ($182 million in today's money)" (ibid., p. 315).

Historian Alan Kramer (1991) manages to pin down the widespread popular myth in the German public about the Marshall Plan in one sentence plugged from a report produced by the Advisory Council of Economists to the German Federal Economics Ministry in 1950: "The generous assistance of the Marshall Plan made it possible to restart the economic process in Germany" (p. 148). Moreover, during the late 1940s West German politicians fostered the message of the generous gift by the Americans in what Kramer calls "a massive public relations campaign" (1991, p. 151). And there was some truth in this message. Due to Marshall Plan aid and its predecessor the GARIOA (Government and Relief in Occupied Areas) programme food imports from 1947 onwards raised the nutritional level of the German population above the critical level. Since foodstuffs provided by the Marshall Plan were of higher quality than the preceding GARIOA ones, the Anglo-American aid had a profound politico-psychological effect on the German population (Kramer, 1991, p. 150).

The ERP was certainly seen by parts of the American public as "giving something for nothing" and it faced substantial political opposition: "But Truman's challenge was to convince many more Republicans that the Marshall Plan was the answer to communism, rather than being communism itself" (ibid., p. 193). And:

> At home in the United States, the Marshall Plan became legislation against all odds. By contemporary standards of cross-party cooperation and public support, it was a remarkable triumph. The Republican 80th Congress had been in no mood to devote vast new funds to foreign aid.
> (Ibid., p. 371)

To conclude, at least in large parts of the population on both sides of the Atlantic the Marshall Plan was definitely perceived as a sacrifice – a pure gift.

Did the ERP lead to reciprocity?

A main American strategic objective catered to by the Marshall Plan was to keep France off Germany's back. In the spirit of the Versailles treaty, at the end of the war the French wanted the Saar, some control over the Ruhr and reparations from Germany (ibid., p. 66). The ERP instilled a sense of reciprocity into France and compensated it for refraining from demanding reparations and halting the removal of industrial equipment from their occupied part of Germany (ibid., pp. 108 and 249):

> After the launch of the Marshall Plan, France found it increasingly difficult to use its occupation zone as a bargaining chip for economic and

> security concessions. France not only wanted Marshall aid, but needed it once the United States began shutting off its avenues to extracting reparations, territory, and underpriced commodities from Germany. American power in Germany ultimately obliged Paris to accommodate itself to Washington's western integration agenda.
>
> (Ibid., p. 356)

As a consequence, France and Germany stopped seeing each other as arch enemies and began friendly cooperative relations which led to forming the predecessors of the EU.

> The first important offshoot would be the Schuman Plan of 1950: the French foreign minister's scheme, devised by Monet, for French and West German steel and coal production to be placed under a single authority. This would form the basis of a wider European effort in 1952, with the addition of Italy and Benelux, in the form of the European Coal and Steel Community, and the European Economic Community (the "Common Market") in 1958.
>
> (Ibid., p. 153)

The spirit of European integration based on relations characterised by reciprocity was kick started by the Marshall Plan (ibid., pp. 101, 305). Underwritten by it, the Americans insisted on the European countries to cut quantitative import restrictions massively and to collaborate on the creation of a payments union to eliminate currency barriers to trade. "... it was again the American and not European initiative which pushed Western Europe further on the road to greater cooperation and integration" (ibid., p. 306). Varoufakis (2011) does also stress the leading role of the Americans in not only encouraging but ensuring European integration after the end of the Second World War.

It can be concluded that since the Marshall Plan led to reciprocity, it was a positive, successful grant in Boulding's sense of creating a community and keeping peace. If it would have failed to generate reciprocity, then it would have still been a grant based on benevolent intentions, but it would not have succeeded in some of its utilitarian motives and as a meta-strategy in a PD to foster cooperation and reciprocity.

That the grantor in the case of the Marshall Plan is a government representing the American population and not an individual person as certainly envisioned in Boulding's theory does not devalue the argument put forward here. To the contrary, if Boulding's grants economics is viewed from and supported by Etzioni's I & WE paradigm this makes perfect sense, since Etzioni (1990) argues that collective bodies are better equipped to deal with complex decisions based on multifaceted motivations and potentially conflicting decision rules (Table 7.1).

Table 7.1 Evidence for and Against an Interpretation of the Marshall Plan as a Gift

<table>
<tr><th>Gift Characteristics</th><th>Other Characteristics</th></tr>
<tr><td>All European countries except Germany received the ERP as a grant. However, a large chunk of Germany's post-war debt was written off.</td><td>The American containment strategy – a utilitarian political instrument during the Cold War to prevent communism from spreading to Western Europe.</td></tr>
<tr><td>Bataille's (1988[1967]) interpretation of it as redistributing surplus without payment.</td><td>The Americans used it to favour their own domestic economy by boosting aggregate demand for their exports.</td></tr>
<tr><td colspan="2">Galbraith: "When the Marshall Plan came into being, therefore, its creators were motivated both by an unselfish compassion for economically afflicted people and by a deep and insistent concern that the Soviet Union might otherwise occupy a depressed and vulnerable Western Europe" (1994, p. 161).</td></tr>
<tr><td>Marshall Plan aid rescued industrial production in England by filling crucial resource gaps that would otherwise not have been available.</td><td>At least in the case of Germany, it was not delivered what was needed, but what the Americans wanted to get rid of (Abelshauser, 2004).</td></tr>
<tr><td>Large parts of the population in the 16 receiving European countries perceived the American transfers as a gift.</td><td>Equally, large parts of the population in the 16 receiving European countries perceived the American transfers as motivated by self-interest and utilitarian motives.</td></tr>
<tr><td>The European countries were free to use the grant freely as they saw fit.</td><td></td></tr>
<tr><td colspan="2">One motive of the Americans was to stabilise the European continent and prevent yet another war in the near future. Though this motive is utilitarian it nonetheless fits Sahlins's (2004[1972]) main conceptual peace ensuring motive of the gift.</td></tr>
<tr><td>In the United States, "Spontaneous public initiatives sprang up to supplement the Marshall Plan" (Steil, 2018, p. 2010)</td><td></td></tr>
<tr><td>Food imports from America from1947 onwards raised the nutritional level of the German population above the critical level.</td><td></td></tr>
<tr><td>Its critics in the United States saw the Marshall Plan as a gift.</td><td></td></tr>
<tr><td>The ERP instilled a sense of reciprocity into France and compensated it for refraining from demanding reparations from Germany. As a consequence, France and Germany stopped seeing each other as arch enemies and began friendly cooperative relations, which led to forming the predecessors of the EU. The spirit of European integration based on relations characterised by reciprocity was kick started by the Marshall Plan.</td><td></td></tr>
</table>

Conclusion

Boulding's Grants Economics takes the institutional tension of the gift seriously and presents its potential to overcome social and economic conundrums that cannot be solved by market exchange. He clearly states the motivational foundation: benevolence (malevolence) and ensuing expected reciprocity. Assuming conditions of scarcity, he adds a utilitarian and an opportunity cost argument.

A grant in Boulding's perspective is a transfer motivated by love or fear, without an expectation of reciprocity arising for certain, but with the hope and potential of reciprocity in the future. The fluid mix and progression from a variety of institutions signifying particular intentions and norms are key to his theory. This distinguishes his approach from the mono-institutional views put forward by most economists stressing self-interested utilitarian motives and social anthropologists emphasising reciprocity. Moreover, following Boulding, it matters very much how a transfer is perceived by the recipient.

This interpretation showed that the Marshall plan had characteristics of:

a altruism, sacrifice or giving something for nothing,
b utilitarian calculus and
c creating reciprocity.

The significance of all three institutions: sacrifice based on beneficence, reciprocity and utilitarian calculation can be seen in the working of the Marshall plan as a case study of a grant. As I have shown, this theoretical differentiation and paying attention to how these institutions work fluidly and in conjunction helps to understand the motivations of the Truman administration for initiating and implementing the Marshall Plan against considerable odds and opposition and how it was perceived by Americans as well as Europeans and therefore, worked as a mechanism to achieve peace and cooperation. That each European country experienced it differently as well as the flexibility and moderate control imposed by the Americans is itself a defining aspect of the Marshall Plan and makes it a true gift characterised by an element of generosity and contingency in achieving its intended outcomes.

Notes

1 For Veblen institutions are a mix of motivations (instincts), behavioural patterns and ways of thinking or norms. This comes through in the following two quotes by authors publishing in the leading Veblenian academic journal:

> According to Veblen, "[instincts] are the prime movers in human behaviour" (1914, p. 1) and the starting point of his theory of institutional change. Veblen ascribed the origins of institutions to learned habits and ultimately to innate instincts, which provide a set of basic drives of human action, in the context of particular material conditions (Edgell, 1975).
>
> (Cordes, 2005, p. 1)

Moreover:

> Veblen produced a complex and hierarchical theory of human mind and human nature in which instincts, habits, volitions, and actions all played important roles in how we think and feel and believe. While he relied upon instincts in his hoisting of essentialists, he used the full range of instincts, habits of thought, and other elements of a very complex theory of human mind and human nature to criticize the hedonism and utilitarianism of neoclassical economists.
>
> (Dugger, 2006, p. 658)

2 Unlike Dorian Gray in Oscar Wilde's novel, we do not have a surrogate picture stashed away in the attic which will miraculously take all the wrinkles and scars that would show our past bad behaviour to the world and can thus, camouflage this malicious psychological make-up from potential business partners.

3 In his investigations into the history of thought, Hirschman uncovered that one way to legitimise capitalism and prepare societies to accept it was to argue that trade between countries is good for preventing them to go to war with each other – the doux commerce thesis. The argument about the gift as beneficence initiating a cycle of reciprocity, which may lead to trade relationships and foster social interaction as well as peaceful relations has some parallels with the doux commerce thesis, while the difference is that a gift is not similar to and precedes exchange.

4 "One of the most important aspects of the grants economy is the role it plays in the building up of integrative structures and communities – that is, groups of people who have some feelings of identification and benevolence toward each other" (Boulding, 1973, p. 27).

5 While Boulding makes the malevolent element in the grant explicit, it is also implicitly discussed by Gouldner when he links beneficence to the hegemony of the upper class who show their dominance by exploiting the lower classes, but establish their hegemony even further when they give some of this bounty back to the lower classes as charity (1973, p. 272). In the gift relationship the power is with the donor: "In its institutionalized forms, the wish for something for nothing is acknowledged only as an obligation to give, never as a right to receive" (ibid., p. 268).

6 Mauss himself makes his anti-utilitarian stance very clear in the second part of his conclusion (social and economic) at the end of *The Gift* (1990[1925]).

7 Note that this is not some carefully calculated social optimum.

8 This is the official name of the Marshall Plan.

References

Abelshauser, W. 2004. *Deutsche Wirtschaftsgeschichte seit 1945*. Munich: Verlag C. H. Beck.

Andreoni, J. and Payne, A. 2011. Is Crowding Out Entirely Due to Fundraising? Evidence from a Panel of Charities. *Journal of Public Economics*. **95**, pp. 334–343. DOI: 10.1016/j.jpubeco.2010.11.011

Andreoni, J., Payne, A. and Smith, S. 2014. Do Grants to Charities Crowd Out Other Income? Evidence from the UK. *Journal of Public Economics*. **114**, pp. 75–86. DOI: 10.1016/j.jpubeco.2013.10.005

Andreoni, J., Payne, A., Smith, J. and Karp, D. 2016. Diversity and Donations: The Effect of Ethic and Religious Diversity on Charitable Giving. *Journal of Economic Behavior and Organization*. **128**, pp. 47–58. DOI: 10.1016/j.jebo.2016.05.010

Bataille, G. 1988[1967]. *The Accursed Share: An Essay on General Economy, Vol. I: Consumption* (translated by Robert Hurley). Cambridge, MA: The MIT Press.

Bauman, Z. 2000. *Liquid Modernity.* Cambridge and Malden, MA: Polity Press.

Bermeo, S. B. 2018. *Targeted Development: Industrialized Country Strategy in a Globalizing World.* Oxford: Oxford University Press. DOI: 10.1093/oso/9780190851828.001.0001

Bloch, E. 1959. *Das Prinzip Hoffnung.* Frankfurt am Main: Suhrkamp. [in English translated by Neville Plaice, Stephen Plaice and Paul Knight as: *The Principle of Hope.* Cambridge, MA: The MIT Press, 1995].

Boulding, K. E. 1981. *A Preface to Grants Economics: The Economy of Love and Fear.* New York: Praeger.

Camerer, C. 1988. Gifts as Economic Signals and Social Symbols. *American Journal of Sociology.* Supplement: Organizations and Institutions: Sociological and Economic Approaches to the Analysis of Social Structure. **94**, pp. S180–S214.

Chomsky, N. 2004. *Language and Politics.* Oakland: AK Press.

Cordes, C. 2005. Veblen's Instinct of Workmanship, Its Cognitive Foundations, and Some Implications for Economic Theory. *Journal of Economic Issues.* **39**(1), pp. 1–20. DOI: 10.1080/00213624.2005.11506778

Dillon, W. S. 1968. *Gifts and Nations: The Obligation to Give, Receive and Repay.* The Hague: Mouton de Gruyter. DOI: 10.4324/9780203790755

Dugger, W. M. 2006. Veblen's Radical Theory of Social Evolution. *Journal of Economic Issues.* **40**(3), pp. 651–672. DOI: 10.1080/00213624.2006.11506939.

Eagleton, T. 2018. *Radical Sacrifice.* New Haven, CT and London: Yale University Books.

Edgell, S. 1975. Thorstein Veblen's Theory of Evolutionary Change. *American Journal of Economics and Sociology.* **34**(3), pp. 267–280. DOI: 10.1111/j.1536–7150.1975.tb01185.x

Elder-Vass, D. 2016. *Profit and Gift in the Digital Economy.* Cambridge: Cambridge University Press. DOI: 10.1017/CBO9781316536421

Elder-Vass, D. 2019. Defining the Gift. *Journal of Institutional Economics.* **16**(5), pp. 1–11. DOI: 10.1017/s174413741900033x

Etzioni, A. 1990. *The Moral Dimension – Toward a New Economics.* New York: The Free Press.

Frank, R. H. 2003. *What Price the Moral High Ground?* Princeton, NJ: Princeton University Press.

Galbraith, J. K.1994. *The World Economy since the Wars.* London: Mandarin.

Gouldner, A. W. 1973. The Importance of Something for Nothing, Chapter 9. In: Gouldner, A. W. Ed. *For Sociology – Renewal and Critique in Sociology Today.* Harmondsworth: Pelican Books, pp. 260–299.

Harrison, G. 2018. Aid. In: Brown, G. W., McLean, I. and McMillan, A. Eds. *A Concise Oxford Dictionary of Politics and International Relations.* [Online]. 4th ed. Oxford: Oxford University Press. [Accessed 29 April 2020]. Available from: https://www.oxfordreference.com/view/10.1093/acref/9780199670840.001.0001/acref-9780199670840, DOI: 10.1093/acref/9780199670840.001.0001

Heins, V. M., Unrau, C. and Avram, K. 2018. Gift-giving and Reciprocity in Global Society: Introducing Marcel Mauss in International Studies. *Journal of International Political Theory.* **14**(2), pp. 126–144. DOI: 10.1177/1755088218757807

Hirschman, A. O. 1977. *The Passions and the Interests: Political Arguments for Capitalism before Its Triumph.* Princeton, NJ: Princeton University Press.

Hirschman, A. O. 1982. Rival Views of Market Society. *Journal of Economic Literature*. **20**(3), pp. 1463–1484.

Hodgson, G. 2006. What Are Institutions? *Journal of Economic Issues*. **40**(1), pp. 1–25. DOI: 10.1080/00213624.2006.11506879

Holden, P. 2009. *In Search of Structural Power: EU Aid Policy as a Global Political Instrument*. London and New York: Routledge. DOI: 10.4324/9781315588148

Kaplan, T. and Ruffle, B. 2009. In Search of Welfare Improving Gifts. *European Economic Review*. **53**, pp. 445–460. DOI: 10.1016/j.euroecorev.2008.09.002

Kramer, A. 1991. *The West German Economy 1945–1955*. New York and Oxford: Berg and St Martin's Press. DOI: 10.1080/03612759.1992.9950714

Lutz, M. A. and Lux, K. 1988. *Humanistic Economics – The New Challenge*. New York: The Bootstrap Press.

Marchionatti, R. and Cedrini, M. 2017. *Economics as Social Science – Economics Imperialism and the Challenge of Interdisciplinarity*. London and New York: Routledge. DOI: 10.4324/9781315694047

Mauss, M. 1990[1925]. *The Gift: The Form and Reason for Exchange in Archaic Societies*. London and New York: Routledge.

Perroux, F. 1948. *Le Plan Marshall ou l'Europe nécessaire au monde*. Paris: Librairie de Medicis.

Perroux, F. 1961. *Zwang, Tausch, Geschenk – Zur Kritik der Händlergesellschaft*, Stuttgart: Curt E. Schwab (French original: *Économie et Société – Contrainte, Échange, Don*. Paris: Presses Universitaires de France, 1960).

Polanyi, K. 1957[1944]. *The Great Transformation – The Political and Economic Origins of Our Time*. Boston, MA: Beacon Press.

Polanyi, K. 1968[1947]. Our Obsolete Market Mentality. In: Dalton, G. Ed. *Primitive, Archaic, and Modern Economies – Essays of Karl Polanyi*. New York: Anchor Books, pp. 59–77.

Sahlins, M. 2004[1972]. *Stone Age Economics*. London and New York: Routledge.

Steil, B. 2018. *The Marshall Plan: Dawn of the Cold War*. London: Simon and Schuster.

Varoufakis, Y. 2011. *The Global Minotaur: America, the True Origins of the Financial Crisis and the Future of the World Economy*. London: Zed Books.

Veblen, T. 1914. *The Instinct of Workmanship, and the State of the Industrial Arts*. Reprint in: New York: Cosimo Classics (2006). DOI: 10.4324/9781315132686

Veen, van der, M. 2011. *Ideas, Interests and Foreign Aid*. New York and Cambridge: Cambridge University Press. DOI: 10.1017/CBO9780511842177

8 An institutional analysis of the dowry system in South Asia

Kalpana Khanal and Ruchira Sen

Introduction

Dowry is a marriage gift, the giving and receipt of which creates the conditions for a marriage contract. Marriage comprises a set of formal and informal norms, rules and behaviours regarding the exclusivity of the contract, economic solidarity and long-term sexual intimacy (Boyer and Peterson, 2012). Negotiating marriage contracts involves a complex interplay of strategies between contracting parties, and among such strategies is the system of gift-giving or dowry. Specifically, South Asian dowry systems present certain peculiarities with respect to the theory of the gift. As in the work of Marcel Mauss (1990), South Asian dowry systems involve little separation between gifts and persons (Graeber, 2000). The bride, herself, is a dowry "gift". The groom, however, is not expected to present himself as a "gift" in return. In fact, both convention and religious scripture expressly forbid the return of any kind of dowry gift – including separation or divorce where the bride returns to her natal home. Meanwhile, though dowry gifts around the world have become economically irrelevant, prospective South Asian grooms have continued to demand increasingly large dowries, with larger proportions of market goods, to settle marriage contracts (Rao, 1993).

The question of the continued prevalence of dowry as an institution in South Asia has been taken up in several studies relying on mainstream economics and formalist anthropology.[1] Such studies have missed the question of interactions between dowry and the evolution of the market system, which is essential to explain the role of dowry in the contemporary market economy. In this chapter, we will apply the substantivist methodology to conceptualise the motives of gift-giving within dowry systems and the interactions between dowry and markets.

The substantivist tradition epitomised by the work of Karl Polanyi (1944) illustrated the need for a method that combined economic history and comparative anthropology for economy-society configurations in which economic activity exercised a social function. It also installed the imperative in a generation of anthropologists to describe the differences between traditional economies and market economies. Much of Polanyi's *opus* is devoted to documenting alternative economic arrangements in non-capitalist contexts, and specifically in pointing out myriad ways in which the economy has been embedded in social institutions (Arensberg et al., 1957; Polanyi, 1966).[2]

Substantivist economics analyses "the economy as an instituted process of interaction serving the satisfaction of material wants" (Polanyi, 1977, p. 31; Stanfield, 1986, p. 36). In non-capitalist systems, economies exist within a cultural context. That is, economy is "embedded" in society. The individual pursuit of material self-gain is generally discounted and collective goals are established that link economic and other types of social processes (Parry and Bloch, 1989, p. 25; Waller and Jennings, 1991, p. 488). In these non-market contexts, an entirely different set of analytical concepts is required to explain the material process of making a living. Polanyi referred to such social livelihood processes as the "substantive" dimensions of the economy (Rankins, 2004, p. 27). The substantivist school constructed its mission to document livelihood processes and understand their underlying principles. The resulting research produced taxonomy of forms of exchange and distribution not conforming to neoclassical principles of economic rationality (ibid., p. 28).[3]

A long-standing fascination with gift-giving – the phenomenon of giving wealth away rather than accumulating it, exists within the substantivist school. Most economic anthropologists in the pre-1970s era were concerned with non-commercial exchange using the language of gifts. They were trying to understand the moral obligation to give, receive and repay gifts based on a radically new theory of value that had the notion of reciprocity at its core (Gregory, 2015). The idea of reciprocity in the substantivist school challenged the Smithian assumption of a "propensity to truck, barter and exchange" within human nature. The substantivists did not see gifts as part of individual "transaction" or "exchange" but as an enduring social contract. Unlike in Smithian political economy, contracting parties were not individuals but whole communities. Contracts were not enforced through natural propensity but through considerations of shame, power and prestige. In fact, gifts were thought to include acts of politeness, ritual, military services and festivals more often than market goods. The seminal work in the tradition of gifts as social contract was Mauss's, *Essai sur le don*, published in 1925 (and translated into English in 1954) well before the substantivist-formalist debate even got under way. Mauss sought to investigate the "spirit of the gift" or the legal and spiritual obligations underlying gifts as a form of social contract. Herein, gift exchanges exist within a legal, social and cultural framework of obligation rather than in isolation. Similar to Polanyi, Mauss also took on a field-based method where he examined gift systems in various institutional contexts from Polynesian reciprocal exchanges to gift systems in ancient Rome and India.

In applying a substantivist lens to the problem of motives of dowry giving and the interactions between dowry and market systems in South Asia, we will focus on extending the arguments of Mauss and Polanyi. In section "The prevalence of non-reciprocal dowry systems" of this chapter, we will use a

Maussian lens to enquire into why dowry gifts are given when scriptural authorities forbid the return of dowry gifts. In section "The institution of dowry through colonial processes", we will use a Polanyian double movement framework to examine the modernisation of dowry practices along with the emergence of property rights in the colonial era. The last section will conclude the chapter.

The prevalence of non-reciprocal dowry systems

A Maussian analysis of dowry in South Asia

The institution of dowry is in no way unique to South Asia. In fact, contrary to the British colonists' disgust with dowry in India, dowry systems were prevalent across Europe – lasting well into the 1970s. In his 1972 case study on family marriage strategies in the French Pyrenees, for instance, Pierre Bourdieu (2002) found that dowries were as essential to negotiating desirable marriage contracts as birth order and education. Goals of dowry negotiation varied from acquiring property, to bringing in more labour to reproduce the household to negotiating a family member's position in the household s/he married into. For example, parents of younger daughters tried to ensure their daughters would marry older sons who would inherit property and enjoy a higher status in terms of birth order. Therefore, they were obliged to make larger dowry gifts. Both brides and grooms required dowries for the marriage contract, though dowries for women tended to be larger than those for men. In societies outside the Indo-European regions, dowry could also involve systems of gift exchange. For example, the gifts of emblazoned matting in Samoa were given by the bride's family to the groom's family as "tonga", which obliged the groom's family to make a reciprocal gift of "oloa" (Mauss, 1990).

The case of dowry in the Brahmanical, Hindu societies of South Asia, however, is peculiar.[4] Unlike in the case of the French Pyrenees only brides bring in dowry. According to the Codes of Manu, a scriptural authority on laws and norms in Hindu society, dowry gifts must be made with no expectation of return. Accepting any form of gift in return for the daughter of a house is considered unlawful (Buhler, 1886).[5] Dowry gifts can therefore, guarantee nothing – neither the brides' status nor position nor social protection as the bride's parents are legally obliged to accept nothing in return for the gift of their daughter. Thereby, unlike in the case of Polynesia, there is no reciprocity norm in the case of dowry gifts in South Asia. Dowry in South Asia remains prevalent not only into the 1960s, as in the French Pyrenees, but till today. Dowry gifts in modern Hindu society are no longer always voluntary. Instead, brides' families are subjected to demands for large dowries increasingly comprising of market goods. Often, brides are subjected to harassment and death-threats in the in-law's residence as a pressure tactic to extract larger dowries from their families. Dowry-related harassment remains one of the primary forms of violence against women in South Asia.[6]

Consequently, an analysis of dowry in Sanskritic societies in South Asia yields important insights into a theory of the gift. What does gift-giving mean in the absence of the moral, cultural or legal obligation to reciprocate? Studying the ancient Hindu texts, Mauss found several references supporting an obligation to give gifts without return – even when such gifts would ruin the donor. In the Mahabharata, for instance, Prince Yudhishthira found himself compelled to stake his kingdom, his brothers and wife in a dice game.

While Mauss's analysis of the role of the reciprocity norm in gift-giving received most of the attention from his followers, primarily Sahlins (2012) and Levi-Strauss (1987), his discussion of non-reciprocal gift-giving in ancient India was largely ignored (Parry, 1986). However, ancient India was important to Mauss who considered it a "fossil record" for Europe (Parry, 1986).[7] Bringing his "theory of the gift" closer to home for his European readership, Mauss sought to show that only in particular historical conditions, and only in the context of particular religious doctrines, do we find the emergence of "disinterested giving". Mauss's insights into the peculiar case of India enable South Asian scholars to understand the continued prevalence of dowry gifts even in modern times.

Mauss understood non-reciprocal gift-giving from the concept of danadharma. Danadharma is the religious obligation to give gifts. Mauss drew his analysis of danadharma from the Anushasanaparvan (Book VIII of the Mahabharata, which has both smriti (tradition), and shastra (living law) value).[8] The Anushasanaparvan tells of the tendency for all gifts (or *dana*) to return to the donor in the next life – in this regard, while there may be no reciprocity norm in this life, there is certainly the expectation that returns would be made in the next one. Gifts are personified as living creatures who share in the contract. Gifts of land and food ask to be given away. It is understood that the very nature of food and wealth is to be shared and distributed to those worthy of it (usually the Brahmins), else there is little pleasure in partaking of it. There is no obligation for the Brahmins to reciprocate – at any rate, in this life.

The Anushasanaparvan maintains strict rules about which gifts may be accepted and from whom.[9] Gifts are at the same time, the livelihood of the Brahmins but they are also an object of fear. Gifts bear the spirit of the donor – the sum of the donor's experiences or the burden of the donor's sin; Parry (1980) refers to the Benares Brahmins who see themselves as absorbing the burden of sin in the form of gifts from donors. They believe they are a moral sewer to absorb the impurities of their donors and if they are not worthy to absorb these sins, they would become a cesspit and rot. In accepting a gift, some ceremony may be performed to separate the gift from the donor – to unburden the donor of the gift. In case of dowry gifts, a separation of this sort is especially significant.

Danadharma includes *kanyadan* or "the gift of a virgin daughter", which is considered one of the highest gifts a man can give. Since in a patriarchal system, a woman's body and labour are controlled by the men of the household, "wife giving" is an important aspect of *dana* – a spiritual gift that the household is obligated to give. The bride herself is part of her dowry. Since she is a gift from her community, or more specifically, her father or closest male relative, she embodies the spirit of her donor. Female characters in both Mahabharata and Ramayana tend to be associated with their fathers. Draupadi in the Mahabharata, for example, draws her name from her father, Drupada. Sita in the Ramayana is also known as Janaki, which is drawn from her father's name, Janaka. Marriage in patriarchal and patrilineal households involves a transfer of the bride and her dowry from her natal household to her marital household. To ensure that she does not return to her natal home and thereby break the system that preserves patriarchal marriage, a special ceremony must be performed to sever the bride's connection with her natal household. This is called the *kanyadan* and accompanies most Hindu wedding rituals. Following the *kanyadan*, it becomes understood that both the dowry and the marriage are irreversible.

According to the Codes of Manu, it is considered "reprehensible" if a father does not give up his daughter in marriage (Buhler, 1886). The virgin daughter intimates the burden of sin, impurity and inauspiciousness. Every time an unmarried daughter menstruates, the father bears the sin of the loss of prospective human lives that could have been borne (Tambiah, 1989). In this case, taking on the burden of a father's sin elevates the son-in-law who is considered to be performing an act of benevolence much like the Benares Brahmins in the work of Parry (1980). Moreover, since burdens can only be transferred to someone worthy of bearing them, "gifts" of virgin daughters must be made to sons-in-law who are from higher castes or income groups, i.e. there is a tendency to hypergamy.[10] Consequently, the marriage must be performed with ostentatious condescension on the part of the bridegroom while the father is obliged to meet the expenses of an elaborate ceremony and make a sizeable gift of money, market and non-market goods to accompany the daughter to her marital home.

While in modern times, girl children are considered a burden because dowries must be found for them, it appears that dowry itself is contingent on the idea of girl children as a burden of sin as in the Codes of Manu (Parry, 1980). The Codes of Manu decree that it is a spiritual obligation for fathers to "gift" their reproductively capable virgin daughters and be relieved of them. The consequent relief is not a matter of neoclassical market exchange. It is the fulfilment of a scriptural norm which must be performed with ceremony and ostentation through the ritual of the *kanyadan*. Unlike a market transaction between anonymous individuals, as in the work of Gary Becker, the act of dowry and bride-giving is a legal, ceremonial and social obligation between contracting communities.

What happens when market forces interact with a patriarchal system imbued with notions of sin and purity, burden and alleviation? Sheel (1997), Tenhunen (2008) and Oldenburg (2003) note the increasing proportion of money gifts and gifts of marketable goods within dowries. As market processes impose private property rights drawn up in the name of the family patriarch, they "masculinize" the economy. With the advent of market processes, the proportion of market goods in dowry gifts starts to rise. Grooms who have become more powerful and more visible as owners of property and labour are now in a position to bring market processes into the marriage relation. Their families can now make dowry demands and hold brides hostage until demands are met. Sheel (1997) and Oldenburg (2003) try to identify how various policies legitimised during British colonial period affected the law of marriage and hence dowry. The next section of this chapter will analyse the evolving pattern of institution of dowry in India using a Polanyian framework.

Dowry in South Asia: a Polanyian analysis

The modern dowry system in the Indian subcontinent is rooted in the practices of *kanyadan* (gift of the virgin bride), *varadakshina* (voluntary gifts given by the bride's father to the groom), and *stridhan* (voluntary gifts given by relatives and friends to the bride) (Diwan, 1987; Srinivasan and Lee, 2004; Van der Veen, 1972).[11] Traditionally these gifts would be in the form of small tokens from well-wishers. More recently dowry involves a substantial transfer of wealth from the bride's family to the groom's and has become a major factor in marriage negotiations (Nadagouda et al., 1992; Teja, 1991). Traditionally in a virilocal society like Hindu India where institutional or legal barriers to women's right to inherit property existed, dowry could serve as a culturally established method of bequest (Zhang and Chan, 1999). In such societies marked by poor protection of women in their in-laws' households, dowry was seen as a way to improve brides' position, thereby improving women's welfare (Brown, 2009). All of these explanations view dowry as a transfer specifically to the daughter who could access it freely. In cases where dowry wealth was controlled by in-laws and not by the bride, dowry systems were possibly, less benign.

Nonetheless, even to the extent that dowry systems could be seen as traditional systems of inheritance and bequest, today, several scholars follow the Beckerian neoclassical model and address dowry as a price (Banerjee, 1999; Oldenburg, 2003; Srinivas, 1984; Tambiah, 1973).[12] We argue that the neoclassical reading of dowry as price is problematic. Instead, the evolution of dowry must be understood in terms of not only cultural symbols and social practices of marriage as an institution, but also through structural dimensions of property and gender hierarchies inherent in it (Sheel, 1997, 1999).

Mainstream literature on dowry relies on the price model first formalised by Becker (1981) and sees dowries as transfers between families, in which brides do not directly benefit. Most of these explanations are grounded in a model of dowry as a price that clears the marriage market (Arunachalam and Trevon, 2008). Three dominant reasons are discussed in mainstream literature regarding the dowry practice. First, dowry is seen to serve as a form of inheritance for women because by ancient Hindu tradition, only men are entitled to inherit family property (Sharma, 1980). Second, dowry is seen as a way of compensating the groom and his family for the economic support they would provide to the new wife, because women had little or no role in the market economy and would be dependent upon their husband and in-laws (Boserup, 1970). Third, dowry is seen as a gift that lends itself to hypergamy (Tambiah, 1989, 1973).

Sharma's inheritance argument may be critiqued in that women often have limited access to their dowries as seen in the field reports of Vatuk (1975) and Tenhunen (2008). Dowry gifts may be re-gifted as dowries for the groom's sister's in-laws. Thereby, dowries cannot always be thought of as a reliable inheritance for daughters. Boserup's compensation argument has been critiqued because if the economic dependence of women were causally linked to the institution of the dowry, women's increasing role in the market economy should bring about a decline in dowries. However, despite an increasing participation of women in the labour force over the twentieth and twenty-first centuries, dowries are becoming more common. Dowry magnitudes have been inflating rapidly, such that the expenses of daughters' weddings have become financially burdensome for their parents (Srinivasan and Lee, 2004, p. 1109).[13] Some other scholars situate inflation in dowry price within the context of growing consumerism in Indian culture (Krishnaawamy, 1995; Nadagouda et al., 1992) and argue that some young men and their families have come to see dowry as a route to sudden affluence and rapid upward mobility (McCoid, 1989). Tambiah's notion of dowry as compensation for hypergamy confuses cause and effect. Hypergamy is not why dowry gifts are made. Instead, because dowry gifts must be made as a religious obligation (as in the Codes of Manu), a worthy recipient must be found for them, which, in turn, results in hypergamy.

The institution of dowry through colonial processes

To explain the changing practices of dowry, we revisit Polanyi's notion of "double movement". That is, emergence of capitalism involves two phases, "marketization" followed by "protection" via regulation. Polanyi (1944, p. 71) saw marketisation as causing disruption of social bonds and argued that market forces tend to takeover non-market forces with profound social consequences, implying a reorganisation of the entire social fabric. Therefore, according to Polanyi, societies tend to design constraints on markets. Such constraints are not inherently beneficial to everybody, and may be oppressive, but they keep the system functioning (Khanal and Todorova, 2019).

All dowry does not lead to abuse and violence and even though dowry is a cultural practice, violence associated with dowry is not (Rastogi and Therly, 2006). Scholars such as Srinivas (1984) call the evolution or more appropriately the degradation of dowry system, the "new dowry". He also sees this phenomenon as entirely "the product of the forces let loose by

British rule such as monetization, education and the introduction of the organized sector".

> The attempt to equate the huge sums of cash, jewellery, clothing, furniture, and gadgetry demanded of the bride's kin by the groom's, to "dakshina", is only an attempt to legitimize a modern monstrosity by linking it up with an ancient and respected custom, a common enough and hoary Indian device.
>
> (Srinivas, 1984, p. 13)

Sheel (1997, p. 1709) reinterprets and rearticulates the caste system as arising out of the colonial State's codification of the social order. The establishment of the British rule in India led to a new interpretation of Indian, especially Hindu traditions, rituals and customs to facilitate the colonial State's subjugation of the native population.[14] The most significant impact of the British occupation had to do with the caste system. British ideals of societal hierarchy transformed previously fluid Indian institutions into the more rigid terms of class, caste and gender (Shrivastava, 2019). British occupation also accelerated the process of the institutionalisation of a single form of marriage. The newly "invented tradition" suppressed the diversity and complexity of all forms of marriages in India. First, it institutionalised the form of marriage, which was most intrinsically linked with dowry. Second, it universalised that form of marriage by encouraging all social groups to emulate Brahmanical marriage practices (Sheel, 1997). Carroll (1989, p. 2) notes the process of propagating values of orthodox Hinduism and "Hinduising" the castes and tribes on the fringes of Hinduism, during the colonial period. This process accorded State legitimacy to the Brahmanical rules and laws of social order over customary local practices of various rural groups. This provided legal sanction to certain patriarchal practices to the disadvantage of a majority of Hindu women. This also impacted the marriage customs and inheritance norms followed by a majority of population. One of the important aspects of the trend towards the brahminisation was the establishment of the legality of the Brahma form of marriage (or the practice of *kanyadan*) as recognised by judicial bodies.[15]

The reinforcement and expansion of the Brahma form of marriage, with dowry as an important component, took place in a situation where the local socio-economic conditions were getting restructured (Sheel, 1997, p. 1712). The colonial State used its own brand of market capitalism to reshape social mobility. Land settlement was one of the tools used to reallocate ownership on the basis of contracts rather than status. Within the context of private property and free market, the rajas, zamindars, tax collectors, etc. were displaced in some places and re-empowered in other places. The restructuring of economic order also included the commercialisation of agriculture, the emergence of new market centres along the newly introduced railway routes and the creation of the service sector for colonial administration. This led to speeding of the restructuring process, which caused the decline of indigenous industry and the development of urban industries, as well as the incorporation of regional economies into a single unified economy linked with the world capitalist economy (ibid., p. 1713).

The nineteenth-century Indian social and economic order was substantially different from that of a century back. As Bayly (1988, p. 144) states "the more homogenous society of peasants and petty moneylenders which emerged in the nineteenth century was a more appropriate basis for a semi-European colonial State". Sheel (1997) further argues the colonial State's compulsion to extract surplus, expand revenue collections and control a wider area of society effectively led to the creation of settled agriculture and peasant petty-commodity production. The pluralist and mobile cultural traditions of nomadic tribes were restricted by the introduction of revenue assessment (private property rights).

The colonial period witnessed increasing social mobility with the expansion of the State and the monetisation of the economy. The process of social mobility caused by the colonial structure was male oriented (Sheel, 1997). During the colonial period the role of women diminished in the production activities. Turner (1933, p. 53) noted that female workers and working dependents were proportionally lower in the post-1931 census period than they had been at the two censuses before that. Some scholars have argued that the growing economic dependency into which women were forced strengthens the idea that men must be compensated for taking on the burden of providing for women, i.e. the dowry system. The link between the decline of women's contribution in productive economic sphere and the rise of the dowry system has been noted in *Stree Darpan* 1915 (VI), December, pp. 418–424.

In brief, the Brahma form of marriage along with the practice of dowry was institutionalised and universalised by its legal recognition as the most approved form of marriage. The relationship between women's property rights and the Brahma form of marriage is closely associated with the shift from tribal agricultural society and the emergence of patriarchy (Srivastava, 2019). The sexual subordination of women was affected by an enforced economic dependence on the male head of the household. Property came to be regarded as a crucial indicator of the balance of power between women and men (Lerner, 1986; Hirschon, 1984, p. 1).[16]

Setting out to trace the roots of the "dowry problem", Oldenburg (2003) digs deep into the colonial past. Her study on Punjab tracks the course of the dowry system's changing perceptions and functions over time and observes how cash and property began to increasingly form dowry composition when land became a marketable commodity during the colonial period.

> As large chunks of the subcontinent fell under the domination of the colonial government, a revolution in property rights transformed the social and economic world of the peasant. The introduction of the idea of land as a commodity and therefore entirely alienable, by sale or foreclosure, also gave men precise, titular ownership, at the cost of all subsidiary

> claims or entitlements that were traditionally ordained. The customary rights of women were the heaviest casualties of this transformation of a peasant economy into an unevenly modern and capitalistic one.
>
> (Oldenburg, 2003, pp. 20–21)

The outstanding discovery of recent historical and anthropological research is that the economy, as a rule, is submerged in social relationships. People do not act to safeguard individual interest in the possession of material goods; they act to safeguard social standing, social claims and social assets. People value material goods only in so far as they serve this end (Polanyi, 1944, p. 46).[17] Polanyi showed that even though the institution of market precedes the nineteenth century, its role in non-capitalist systems was limited and secondary: "markets were merely an accessory feature of an institutional setting controlled and regulated more than ever by social authority" (ibid., p. 67). Most of these were societies where reciprocity and redistribution were the dominant forms of integration, which assured order in production and redistribution (Joao, 2004). Because of that, human motivations in those societies are considered to be highly varied when it came to gift-giving. As discussed in section "The prevalence of non-reciprocal dowry systems" one of the unique features of the Indian institution of gift-giving was that it was not based on reciprocity. Nevertheless, Indian gift-giving, specifically the tradition of dowry is embedded in the general fabric of social, political, religious and moral life. In pre-colonial India, dowry was not necessarily a "problem" but could provide support for married women, also serving as a mark of their social status and providing a safety net (Oldenburg, 2003, p. 4).

> Dowry, as a subset of *stridhan* became vulnerable to the new market economy that abruptly replaced the old order of obligations and reciprocities among those who had shared the produce of the commonly controlled land. Indeed, the concept of a woman's right to property, even in its unequal and usufructuary way, seemed to have been entirely forfeited (and had to be fought for anew in the twentieth century), and dowry seemed to have become a matter for aggressive negotiation by the groom's family.
>
> (Oldenburg, 2003, p. 21)

Oldenburg looks at the influence of the colonial enterprise of codifying custom into textual law and its implementation in the legal systems in Punjab, on various existing practices, particularly on the rights of women and the notions of dowry.[18] The transformation of the basic relationship between peasants and their land and the simultaneous codification of customary law caused much of the infamous indebtedness of the Punjab peasant. These two intertwined events became central in altering the texture of women's lives, their implicit rights and entitlements in their families as daughters, wives, and widows, by making men the sole proprietors. This, in turn, transformed the notions of women's wealth, property rights, and dowry (ibid., p. 12).

To understand the changing meanings of dowry and the processes that underwrote the change, it is imperative to understand how the notion of property and land rights were differently constituted in pre-colonial and colonial times (ibid., p. 14).

With the creation of male individual property rights in land, the British decided to create the individual peasant owner as the centrepiece of their modern revenue policy. These new circumstances altered the generally symbiotic relationship between borrower and lender. In pre-colonial times moneylenders had advanced small loans; the object was never to let a debt be paid off entirely, in order to keep the debtor as a permanent client. The new breed of moneylenders, with an appetite for appropriating their debtors' land emerged as a cause of suffering in the countryside during these changed circumstances. The critical difference was that land was now a commodity that could be alienated from the original proprietor and auctioned (ibid., p. 14). Chronic indebtedness became the other side of the coin of marketisation for the vast majority of small peasant proprietors. As the colonial State sought to collect land revenue, leading to chronic indebtedness across the countryside, land prices and rents began to rise.

Putting landed property in exclusively male hands and holding males solely responsible for the payment of revenue had the effect of creating the Indian male as the dominant legal subject; this happened throughout British India and even in the Princely States. The effects were disastrous to the lives of women (p. 15). The establishment of property rights for peasants, inflexible tax demands and collection regimens, and a host of other imperial measures prepared the ground for worsening gender inequality which, in turn, increased the vulnerability of women to violence in both their natal and marital homes (ibid., p. 5).

By the turn of the century, making dowry demands for market goods and money became pervasive across most parts of colonial North India. The dowry brought in by a bride, was no longer preserved as a woman's exclusive wealth but was now used to pay off debts or to marry off daughters in the husband's family, and "if the sum is considerable it is used to cover the expenses of the education of the son in England or to add to family property holdings, and to buy Government promissory notes" (Bose, 1914, p. 27). These were radically new uses for a woman's *stridhan*, and certainly could be marked as the beginning of a trend where dowry became as an evil and problematic social practice.

Since India achieved Independence, the State has continued to play the role of social reformer. The emergence of the notion of dowry as something evil continued to haunt the deliberations of the Hindu Code Bill in the early 1950. And eventually these debates led to the Dowry Prohibition Act of 1961. The Act made any dowry negotiation illegal and punishable by imprisonment and fines. A loophole remained; families could still provide "gifts" to the bride at the time of marriage, that was not "excessive" (loosely defined) in financial value. A record of the gifts had to be maintained and the gifts were to be held in trust for the bride (Banerjee, 2014; Basu, 2001). Later in August 1983, the Law Commission of India published the 91st Report on Dowry Deaths and Law Reform. Its publication led to the amendment of the Hindu Marriage Act, 1955, the Indian Penal Code, 1860, and the Indian Evidence Act, 1872 (Sarkar, 1983). The Criminal Law Act of 1983 defined "cruelty" as an offense under the Indian Penal Code Section 498-A. Based on this law cruel acts related to demands of property by husband or relatives of a woman are considered a punishable offence (Newman, 1992). The Dowry Prohibition Amendment Act of 1984 helped narrow the loopholes in the Dowry Prohibition Act and increased the punishment associated with dowry negotiations. The concept of "dowry death" was added as an amendment to this act making it an offense (Shenk, 2007). In addition, a woman's death occurring within the first seven years of marriage requires investigation (Newman, 1992). The Protection of Women from Domestic Violence Act was passed in 2005. The law is comprehensive, including all forms of violence against women, including those related to dowry. In July 2009, the Bombay High Court determined that the provisions of the new law would apply retroactively (Ghosh and Choudhuri, 2011).

These laws and regulations can be seen as State protection mechanisms or the countermovement *à la* Polanyi, in the evolution of the "new dowry" process. These laws have presented alternatives to many urban victims. However, there is still some serious limitation in legal measures to curb domestic violence and much remains to be done to ensure gender justice in a patriarchal society (ibid., p. 2). Others argue bans of dowry have taken the form of largely ineffectual "paper laws", and momentum needs to be gained among activists and policymakers to make the prohibition of dowries actually work in reality. Publicising regulations in urban and rural areas equally, increasing the penalties for violations, making reporting to authorities safer and more attractive are some of the steps that need to be taken to make these laws more effective (Basu, 2005; Menski, 1998).

Conclusion

While mainstream literature, based on neoclassical economics and formalist anthropology, discusses dowry as groom-price, its ahistorical approach fails to account for the evolution of otherwise pre-capitalist dowry systems in modern capitalism. This chapter uses a substantivist method that combines economic history, culture and anthropology to explain the problem of motives of dowry giving and the interactions between dowry and market systems in South Asia. First by using the Maussian lens, it enquires into the "spirit of the gift" despite the peculiar lack of reciprocity in the South Asian dowry system. The Hindu notions of *Danadharma*, which includes *Kanyadan* and *Stridhan*, are analysed by bringing in relevant artefacts from cultural, anthropological studies and religious scripts. Second, the Polanyian framework is used to examine the modernisation of dowry practices along with the emergence of property rights in the colonial era. Moreover, the paper goes beyond Polanyi's exclusive focus on the corrosive effects of commodification of land upon the institution of dowry. It also delves into some injustices within Indian society, including injustices, such as patriarchy, caste and class systems "that depend on social constructions of labour, land and money, precisely as non-commodities" (Fraser, 2014, p. 544).

British occupation in India had a significant impact on the caste system. British ideals of societal hierarchy transformed the fluid Indian institutions of societal hierarchy as more visible and rigid in terms of class, caste and gender (Shrivastava, 2019). This process also accelerated the process of the institutionalisation of a single form of marriage system, that is the *Brahma* form, which required dowry. Additionally, the introduction of the idea of land as a commodity and therefore entirely alienable, by sale or foreclosure, shifted the ownership of land entirely to men. This led to the masculinisation of the economy and the customary rights of women, including rights over their own dowry, were heavily impinged upon. This led to the gradual shift of dowry as bequest to dowry as price, "new dowry".

Even though several laws were enacted, and regulations have been passed in order to protect women from the outcomes of the new notion of dowry, much needs to be done in terms of implementing those laws. A twenty-first-century mechanism for protecting women from dowry violence should go beyond Polanyi's idea of double movement. More work needs to be done in terms of factoring in struggles of women for emancipation, alongside those for marketisation and social protection. As Fraser (2014, p. 555) emphasises the new mechanism must analyse the struggles of modern women in terms of triple movement, in which marketisation, protection and emancipation combine and collide.

Notes

1 See Sen (1998), Caplan (1984), and Rao (1993).

2 It is important to note here that, several critiques including Hodgson (2016, pp. 4–5) note that Polanyi uses the term "economic" in two peculiar ways. One meaning of "economic" in several passages of The Great Transformation points towards the behaviour motivated by gain (Polanyi, 1944: pp. 30, 41, 46, 49, 53, 268, 269). By gain Polanyi seemed to focus on "material goods" and their use as ends rather than means. Another meaning of "economic" is when conjoined with words such as "system", which implies production and distribution of economic goods. In his 1957 essay Polanyi also notes two meanings of the word "economic", namely, substantive and the formal meaning. The substantive meaning derives from man's dependence for his living upon nature and his fellows … [hence] supplying him with the means of material want satisfaction. The formal meaning of economic derives from the logical character of the means-ends relationship, as apparent in such words as "economical" or "economizing" (Polanyi et al., 1957, p. 243).

3 We consider the substantivist approach for the purpose of this chapter as opposed to the neoclassical model, or "formal" economic model because the latter is a model of choice under scarcity. The latter approach is problematic because all

economic choices are not necessarily made under conditions of scarcity. The non-scarcity determinants can be very complex and shaped by numerous institutions outside the realm of markets and the substantivist approach tends to embrace these determinants (see Dalton, 1990, 1969; Elardo and Campbell, 2015 for details).

4 Brahmanical societies in ancient India refer to strictly hierarchical social systems where Brahmins hold all socio-religious political power arising from the sole right to interpret the Hindu scriptures. Brahmanical society is characterised by a preoccupation with ritual purity to preserve caste privilege among the Brahmins and the perpetuation of atrocities such as untouchability and violence against the lower "castes". In ancient Brahmanical societies, certain types of work were to be undertaken by certain castes only. For example, Brahmins were to perform religious ceremonies and impart education, the warrior castes were to govern and wage wars, the trading castes were intermediaries in an economic system of producers and consumers and the "Dalits" or lower castes were to undertake most tasks of production – especially those considered "unclean" such as cremating the dead, working with leather and undertaking tasks of sanitation. Today, mainstream Hindu societies across South Asia are still Brahmanical in that Brahmins are overly represented in academia and government services. Caste-based violence against Dalits is common. "Dalits" are still overly represented in tasks of sanitation and manual cleaning of sewers in still prevalent.

5 Vatuk (1975) describes a situation where one of the Gaur Brahmin women she interviewed in western UP reported that she had to hide while journeying through the affinal village of one of the daughters from her household. Being seen accepting the hospitality of a son-in-law's kin group was considered a sin.

6 In India, for example, 32.56% of crimes against women in 2016 were crimes of "cruelty by husband or his relations" – typically in the form of dowry demands (Authors' calculations from National Crime Records Bureau Report 2016, p. xix).

7 Mauss referred to "Aryan colonization" where Eurasian tribes migrated into the Indian subcontinent and subdued the earlier migrants or the Dravidians (Mauss, p. 70). In this regard, ancient India was intimately bound with European tradition and revelations about the gift from ancient India would bring the theory of the gift closer to home for Mauss's European readership. Mauss is careful to note that his understanding of ancient Indian society comes from texts written by Brahmins who laid out tradition and law to serve their own interests (Mauss, p. 70).

8 Mauss is careful to note that his understanding of ancient Indian society comes from texts written by Brahmins who laid out tradition and law to serve their own interests (Mauss, p. 70).

9 Mauss notes that it is almost comical that a caste which lives almost exclusively on gifts (the Brahmins) sanctions against gifts received from kings. Brahmins are considered superior to kings and may not accept gifts that would make them dependent on kings.

10 Pocock (1972, p. 64) explains hypergamy as

> a practice in which a family of lower status but not necessarily of inferior wealth attempts to raise its position and its prestige by contracting a superior marriage for its daughters and sisters. Here there is an exchange of status for wealth, and no doubt the dowry-givers can themselves get their return by demanding higher dowries from their own wife-givers.

11 Oldenburg (2003, p. 19) argues that it is difficult to define contemporary dowry with the simplicity and clarity that Manu gave to the term *stridhan*, or the "six fold property of a woman", almost two millennia ago. However, what he decreed has lingering echoes in the legal and moral worlds of colonial and contemporary

India. *Stridhan* subsumed a woman's dowry – which he did not designate separately or name – and this aggregate term has been revived in legal discourse since the passage of the Hindu Code Bill in 1956.

12 By 1938 Altekar suggested that dowry, which had been "a voluntary gift of pure affection and presented no impediment in the settlement of a daughter's marriage" until the middle of the previous century, had for the past 50 years "begun to assume scandalous proportions", and it was now "high time to put an end to this evil custom" that had driven "many an innocent maiden to commit suicide". He feared that the custom "was becoming unpopular and odious", and exhorted youths to rise in rebellion against it (Altekar, 1938, cited in Oldenburg, 2003).

13 Anderson (2003, pp. 269–270) reviews various evidence-based studies to show that real dowry payments, the transfer of wealth from bridal families to grooms, and their families at the time of marriage, have risen over the last five decades. Rao (1993a, b) and Deolalikar and Rao (1998) show that, from 1921 to 1981, when grooms' characteristics are held constant, the wealth of both families is controlled for, and a real price index is imposed, the price of husbands went up significantly. A case study in Delhi by Paul (1985) did not estimate dowries, but in his raw sample, average real dowry payments increased from 3,998 rupees in 1920–1929 to 71,173 rupees in 1980–1984. Interviews from a study in Goa by Ifeka (1989) showed that highest-quality grooms who received a dowry of 2,000 rupees in 1920 could demand between 500,000 and one million rupees in 1980 (there was a 14-fold increase in prices over this time period). In the sample used by Deolalikar and Rao, average dowries are equal to 68% of total assets before marriage and can amount to six times the annual wealth of the bridal family. Case studies document payments between as much as US$60,000 and $130,000 (see, e.g. Billig, 1992 and Joshi, 1992, as cited in Anderson, 2003).

14 During the colonial period the British officials observed the predominantly Hindu culture through a European lens and incorporate facets of this culture into their reasoning for why this progress was necessary. The notion of introducing this progress became known as the "civilizing mission" one that Britain could characterise as a duty of discipline and education and not simply an economic exploit (Mann, 2004, p. 6).

15 The transformation of complex customs and practices into a unified Hindu Family Law entailed comprehending ancient religious literature and applying it to the modern legal framework. For this purpose Sanskrit Pundits, who were Brahmins (highest caste) by caste, were attached to the courts (Sheel, 1999, p. 67). This led to the transformation of Brahmanical or high-class Hindu family norms into universal statutory Hindu Law. Customs and norms approved by the Brahmanical code of conduct became the yardstick to validate or invalidate socio-cultural practices prevalent among other sections of the differentiated Hindu society.

16 The Western notion of class was crucial to the overall evolution of marriage ideologies and accompanying status of women because class stresses the individual and family unit, whereas caste stresses an entire group. While individuals could change class status through acquisition of property, the status mobility of a caste occurred only slowly over time (Liddle and Joshi, 1985, p. 79).

17 Social scientists concerned with economic behaviour such as gift-giving often invoke a dichotomy between market societies and non-market societies. Non-market societies are thought to be moral economies in which economic behaviour is embedded within noneconomic social relationships and socially prevalent ideas of morality. In the "moral economy" social justice comes first before the logic of the market. That is in non-market economies economic action was embedded in broader social norms (Prasad, 1999, pp. 182–183).

18 Oldenburg acknowledges the fact that the changes in the practice of dowry are uneven and ongoing and coexist in time and space and can be best seen on a continuum rather than sharply drawn opposites of "traditional" and "modern" dowry. Her careful reading of historical sources related to interviews conducted in a village in Punjab in the 1870s does not describe dowry as gifts demanded by the groom's family. In 49 separate volumes of customary law in an equal number of districts in the vast territory that constituted colonial Punjab – present-day Pakistan and Indian Punjab, Haryana, Jammu, Delhi and Himachal Pradesh – this definition of dowry was reiterated (Oldenburg, 2003, p. 10).

References

Altekar, A. S. 1938[1956]. *The Position of Women in Hindu Civilization*. Delhi: Motilal Banarsidass.

Anderson, S. 2003. Why Dowry Payments Declined with Modernization in Europe but Are Rising in India. *Journal of Political Economy*. **111**(1), pp. 269–310. DOI: 10.1086/367679

Arensberg, C. M., Pearson, H. W. and Polanyi, K. 1957. *Trade and Market in Early Empires*. New York: Free Press.

Arunachalam, R. and Trevon D. L. 2016. On the Heterogeneity of Dowry Motives. *Journal of Population Economics*. **29**(1), pp. 135–166. DOI: 10.1007/s00148-015-0544-1

Banerjee, K. 1999. Gender Stratification and the Contemporary Marriage Market in India. *Journal of Family Issues*. **20**(5), pp. 648–676. DOI: 10.1177/019251399020005005

Banerjee, P. R. 2014. Dowry in 21st –Century India: The Sociocultural Face of Exploitation. *Trauma, Violence and Abuse*. **15**(1), pp. 34–50. DOI: 10.1177/1524838013496334

Basu, M. 2001. *Hindu Women and Marriage Law: From Sacrament to Contract*. New Delhi: Oxford University Press.

Basu, S. 2005. *Dowry and Inheritance*. London: Zed Books.

Bayly, C. A. 1988. *The New Cambridge History of India: Indian Society of the Making of the British Empire*. New Delhi: Orient Longman.

Becker, G. S. 1981. *A Treatise on the Family*. Cambridge, MA and London: Harvard University Press.

Billig, M. S. 1992. The Marriage Squeeze and the Rise of Groom Price in India's Kerala State. *Journal of Comparative Family Studies*. **23**(2), pp. 197–216.

Bose, R. B. C. 1914. *Marriage-Dowry*. Calcutta: Hindu Marriage Reform League.

Boserup, E. 1970. *Women's Role in Economic Development*. London: Allen and Unwin.

Bourdieu, P. 2002. On Marriage Strategies. *Population and Development Review*. **28**(3), pp. 549–558. DOI: 10.1111/j.1728–4457.2002.00549.x

Boyer, P. and Petersen, M. 2012. The Naturalness of (Many) Social Institutions: Evolved Cognition as their Foundation. *Journal of Institutional Economics*. **8**(1), pp. 1–25. DOI: 10.1017/S1744137411000300

Brown, P. H. 2009. Dowry and Intrahousehold Bargaining: Evidence from China. *The Journal of Human Resources*. **44**(1), pp. 25–46.

Caplan, L.1984. Bridegroom Price in Urban India: Class, Caste and "Dowry Evil" Among Christians in Madras. *Man*. **19**(2), pp. 216–233. DOI: 10.2307/2802278

Carroll, L. 1983. Law, Custom and Statutory Social Reform: The Hindu Widow's Remarriage Act of 1856. *The Indian Economic and Social History Review*. **20**(4), pp. 363–388.

Dalton, G. 1968. Economic Theory and Primitive Society. In: LeClair, Jr., E. E. and Schneider, H. K. Eds. *Economic Anthropology: Readings in Theory and Analysis*. New York: Holt, Rinehart and Winston, Inc., pp. 143–167. (Reprinted from: Dalton, G. 1961. Economic Theory and Primitive Society. *American Anthropologist*. **63**, pp. 1–25). DOI: 10.1525/aa.1961.63.1.02a00010

Dalton, G. 1990. Writings that Clarify Theoretical Disputes Over Karl Polanyi's Work. In: Polanyi-Levitt, K. Ed. *The Life and Work of Karl Polanyi*. Montreal: Black Rose Books, pp. 161–170.

Deolalikar, A. B. and Rao, V. 1998. The Demand for Dowries and Bride Characteristics in Marriage: Empirical Estimates for Rural South Central India. In: Maithreyi, K. R., Sudershan, R. M. and Shariff, A. Eds. *Gender, Population and Development*. Oxford: Oxford University Press, pp. 122–140.

Diwan, P. 1987. *Dowry and Protection to Married Women*. New Delhi: Deep and Deep. DOI: 10.1177/1524838005283927

Elardo, J. A. and Campbell, A. 2015. Choice and the Substantivist/Formalist Debate: A Formal Presentation of Three Substantivist Criticisms. In: Wood, D. C. Ed. *Choice in Economic Contexts*. Published online: 10 March, pp. 267–284. [Accessed 29 April 2020]. Available from: http://dx.doi.org/10.1016/S0190-1281(06)25012-1

Engels, F. 2000. Origin of the Family, Private Property and the State, Marx/Engels Internet Archive. [Accessed 29 April 2020]. Available from: https://www.marxists.org/archive/marx/works/download/pdf/origin_family.pdf

Fraser, N. 2014. Can Society Be Commodities All the Way Down? Post-Polanyian Reflections on Capitalist Crisis. *Economy and Society*. **43**(4), pp. 541–558. DOI: 10.1080/03085147.2014.898822

Ghosh, B. and Choudhuri, T. 2011. Legal Protection Against Domestic Violence in India: Scope and Limitations. *Journal of Family Violence*. **26**(4), pp. 319–330. DOI: 10.1007/s10896-011-9369-1

Graeber, D. 2000. *Give It Away, In These Times*. [Accessed 29 April 2020]. Available from: https://inthesetimes.com/issue/24/19/graeber2419.html

Gregory, C. A. 2015. Preface to the Second Edition. In: Gregory, C. A. Ed. *Gifts and Commodities*, 2nd ed. Chicago, IL: Hau Books, pp. xix–li.

Hann, C. 2006, The Gift and Reciprocity: Perspectives from Economic Anthropology. In: Kolm, S. and Mercier Ythier, J. Eds. *Handbook on the Economics of Giving, Reciprocity and Altruism*. Amsterdam: Elsevier, pp. 207–223.

Hirschon, R. 1984. *Women and Property: Women as Property*. London: Croom Helm.

Hodgson, G. M. 2017. Karl Polanyi on Economy and Society: A Critical Analysis of Core Concepts. *Review of Social Economy*. **75**(1), pp. 1–25. DOI: 10.1080/00346764.2016.1171385

Ifeka, C. 1989. Hierarchical Woman: The 'Dowry' System and Its Implications Among Christians in Goa, India. *Contributions Indian Sociology*. **23**, pp. 261–284. DOI: 10.1177/006996689023002003

Khanal, K. and Todorova, Z. 2019. Remittances and Households in the Age of Neoliberal Uncertainty. *Journal of Economic Issues*. **53**(2), pp. 515–522. DOI: 10.1080/00213624.2019.1603763

Knight, F. H. 1941. Anthropology and Economics. *Journal of Political Economy*, **49**(2), pp. 247–268.

Krishnaswamy, S. 1995. Dynamics of Personal and Social Factors Influencing the Attitude of Married and Unmarried Working Women toward Dowry. *International Journal of Sociology of the Family*. **25**, pp. 31–42.

Levi-Strauss, C. 1987. *Introduction to the Work of Marcel Mauss*. London: Routledge and Kegan Paul.

Liddle, J. and Rama, J. 1985. Gender and Imperialism in British India. *Economic and Political Weekly*. **20**(43), pp. 72–78. DOI: 10.1177/026272808500500206

Mann, M. 2004. Torchbearers Upon the Path of Progress. In: Fischer-Tine, H. and Mann, M. Eds. *Colonialism as Civilizing Mission*. London: Anthem Press, pp. 1–28.

Mauss, M. 1990. *Essai sur le don* (The Gift). London and New York: Routledge.

McCoid, C. H.1989. *Dowry Deaths in India: A Materialist Analysis*, Working Paper No. 188. Michigan State University, East Lansing.

Menski, W. 1998. *South Asians and the Dowry Problem*. London: Trentham.

Nadagouda, S. G., Krishnaswamy, S. and Aruna, R. 1992. Influence of Socioeconomic Factors on the Employed Hindu Woman's Attitude toward Dowry. *Indian Journal of Social Work*. **53**, pp. 679–688.

National Crime Records Bureau. 2017. *Crime in India 2016*. New Delhi: NCRB.

Newman, A. 1992. For Richer, for Poorer, 'til Death Do Us Part: India's Response to Dowry Deaths. *Journal of International Law*. **27**, 109–141.

Oldenburg, V. T. 2003. *Dowry Murder: The Imperial Origins of a Cultural Crime*. New Delhi: Oxford University Press.

Parry, J. 1980. Ghosts, Greed and Sin: The Occupational Identity of the Benares Funeral Priests. *Man*. **15**(1), new series, pp. 88–111. DOI: 10.2307/2802004

Parry, J. 1986. The Gift, the Indian Gift and the "Indian Gift." *Man*. **21**(3), new series, pp. 453–473. DOI:10.2307/2803096

Parry, J. P. and Bloch, M. 1989. Introduction: Money and the Morality of Exchange. In: Parry, J. P. and Bloch, M. Eds. *Money and the Morality of Exchange*. Cambridge: Cambridge University Press, pp. 1–32.

Paul, M. C. 1985. *Dowry and Position of Women in India: A Study of Delhi Metropolis*. New Delhi: Inter-India Pubs.

Piot, C. 1999. *Remotely Global: Village Modernity in West Africa*. Chicago, IL: The University of Chicago Press.

Pocock, D. F. 1972. *Kanbi and Patidar: A Study of the Patidar Community of Gujarat*. Oxford: Clarendon Press.

Polanyi, K. 1944. *The Great Transformation*. Boston, MA: Beacon Press.

Polanyi. K. 1966. *Dahomey and the Slave Trade: An Analysis of an Archaic Economy*. Seattle: University of Washington Press.

Polanyi, K. 1977. *The Livelihood of Man*. New York: Academic Press.

Polanyi, K., Arensberg, C. M. and Pearson, H. W. 1957. *Trade and Market in the Early Empires*. Chicago, IL: Henry Regnery.

Prasad, M. 1999. The Morality of Market Exchange: Love, Money, and Contractual Justice. *Sociological Perspectives*. **42**(2), pp. 181–214. DOI: 10.2307/1389627

Rankin, K. N. 2004. *The Cultural Politics of Markets: Economic Liberalization and Social Change in Nepal*. Toronto and Buffalo: University of Toronto Press.

Rao, V. 1993. The Rising Price of Husbands: A Hedonic Analysis of Dowry Increases in Rural India. *Journal of Political Economy*. **101**(4), pp. 666–677.

Rastogi, M. and Therly, P. 2006. Dowry and Its Link to Violence against Women in India: Feminist Psychological Perspectives (Commentary). *Trauma, Violence, & Abuse*. **7**, pp. 66–77. DOI: 10.1177/1524838005283927

Rodrigues, J. 2004. Endogenous Preferences and Embeddedness: A Reappraisal of Karl Polanyi. *Journal of Economic Issue*. **38**(1), pp. 189–200. DOI: 10.1080/00213624.2004.11506671

Sahlins, M.1993. Goodbye to Tristes Tropes: Ethnography in the Context of Modern World History. *The Journal of Modern History*. **65**(1), pp. 1–25.

Sahlins, M. 2012. *Stone Age Economics*. Abingdon, Oxon: Routledge.

Sarkar, L. 1983. *91st Report on Dowry Deaths and Law Reform: Amending the Hindu Marriage Act of 1955, the Indian Penal Code, 1860, and the Indian Evidence Act, 1872*. New Delhi: Law Commission of India.

Sen, B. 1998.Why Does Dowry Still Persist in India? An Economic Analysis Using Human Capital. In: Menski, W. Ed. *South Asians and the Dowry Problem*. London: Trentham Books Limited.

Sharma, U. 1980. *Women, Work, and Property in North-West India*. London: Tavistock.

Sheel, R. 1997. Institutionalisation and Expansion of Dowry System in Colonial North India. *Economic and Political Weekly*. **32**(28), pp. 1709–1718.

Sheel, R. 1999. *The Political Economy of Dowry*. New Delhi: Manohar Publishers.

Shenk, M. K. 2007. Dowry and Public Policy in Contemporary India: The Behavioural Ecology of a Social Evil. *Human Nature*. **18**, pp. 242–263. DOI: 10.1007/s12110-007-9006-0

Shrivastava, A. 2019. Born to Marry: The Political Economy of Dowry in India. [Accessed 5 September 2019]. Available from: https://editorialexpress.com/cgi-bin/conference/download.cgi?db_name=IAFFE2011&paper_id=230

Srinivas, M. N. 1984. *Some Reflections on Dowry*. Centre for Women's Development Studies. New Delhi: Oxford University Press.

Srinivasan, P. and Lee, G. R. 2004. The Dowry System in Northern India: Women's Attitudes and Social Change. *Journal of Marriage and Family*. **66**(5), pp. 108–1117. DOI: 10.1111/j.0022–2445.2004.00081.x

Stanfield, J. R. 1986. *The Economic Thought of Karl Polanyi*. Houndmills, Basingstoke and New York: Palgrave Macmillan.

Tambiah, S. J. 1973. Dowry and Bride Wealth and the Property Rights of Women in South Asia. In: Goody, J. and Tambiah. S. J. Eds. *Bride Wealth and Dowry*. Cambridge: Cambridge University Press, pp. 59–169.

Tambiah, S. J. 1989. Bride Wealth and Dowry Revisited: The Position of Women in Sub-Saharan Africa and North India. *Current Anthropology*. **30**(4), pp. 413–435.

Teja, M. K. 1991. *Dowry: A Study of Attitudes and Practices*. New Delhi: Inter-India.

Tenhunen, S. 2008. The Gift of Money: Rearticulating Tradition and Market Economy in Rural West Bengal. *Modern Asian Studies*. **42**(5), pp. 1035–1055. DOI: 10.1017/S0026749X06002629

Turner, A. C. 1933. Census of India-1931 (United Provinces of Agra And Oudh) Part II and I. The Superintendent, Printing and Stationery, United Provinces: Allahabad.

Van der Veen, K. W. 1972. *I Give Thee My Daughter: A Study of Marriage and Hierarchy Among the Anavil Brahmans of South Gujarat*. Assen, Netherlands: Koninklijke Van Gorcum.

Vatuk, S. 1975. Gifts and Affines in North India. *Contributions to Indian Sociology*. **9**(2), pp. 155–196. DOI: 10.1177/006996677500900202

Waller, W. and Jennings, A.1991. A Feminist Institutionalist Reconsideration of Karl Polanyi. *Journal of Economic Issues*. **25**(2), pp. 485–497. DOI: 10.1080/00213624.1991.11505182

Zhang, J. and Chan, W.1999. Dowry and Wife's Welfare: A Theoretical and Empirical Analysis. *Journal of Political Economy*. **107**(4), pp. 786–808.

9 In search of relevant financial regulation

Some lessons from the gift-economics

Faruk Ülgen and Marina Sakovich

Introduction

The purpose of this essay is to determine whether gift-economics can provide a relevant analytic direction for an institutional framework in order to design an alternative financial regulation that could strengthen systemic stability in market-based capitalist economies. We regard "gift-economics" as a proxy for different terms such as gift-economy, gift-exchange, gift-transactions, gift-giving, etc. However, there could be crucial differences among them; some concepts relying on neoclassical transactional approaches while some others might mean alternative non-utilitarian perspectives. For instance, Akerlof (1982) argues, from a neoclassical perspective of efficiency-seeking incentive mechanisms, that gift-rules might affect employer-employee relations, and assumes that when they are better (more poorly) paid, workers would feel an obligation (an incentive) to produce a higher (lower) value of output per unit of time even if this "implicit cost equivalence" criterion is not an element of the work contract. In a similar vein, Mercier Ythier (2006) gives a comprehensive analysis of gift-giving as an element of equilibrium redistribution of wealth. With regard to the transaction cost issue but developing on the informational and cultural characteristics of gift relations, Dolfsma et al. (2009, p. 325) consider gift-exchange as a complement to legal contractual arrangements and argue that "Gift exchange can lead to lower transaction costs since it allows individuals to trade with one another without relying solely on formal mechanisms such as legal contracts and litigation". From a more holistic perspective, Sahlins (1972) regards the economy as a category of culture and politics related to the material life process of society and focuses on reciprocity as a social common denominator that could enable society to stabilise inter-individual relations. This way of embedding economic relations within a more general societal framework that would be resting on reciprocity as a social cement/social glue is very close to the Polanyi's approach to the capitalist economy (Polanyi et al., 1957).

This chapter seeks to assess the relevance of the gift-rules, to name (mainly), *reciprocity and mutual engagement*, as possible references that could contribute to frame stabilisation rules in the working of financial markets whether these rules could be interpreted in an individualistic way or in a holistic way. Using a well-known Maori proverb, *Ko Maru kai atu Ko Maru kai mai Ka ngohe ka ngohe*[1], one can regard the rule of reciprocity in the organisation of society as a central element of "time-consistency", i.e. capacity to allow social relations to develop in a sustainable way and then stabilise the functioning of society. This reciprocity can be considered as the immediate expression of a gift-economy.

However, this chapter argues that in a capitalist society, reciprocity cannot be organised *spontaneously* through decentralised market relations between individuals since the latter is mainly resting on selfish private individual decisions that seek private performance (capital accumulation). In a non-cooperative environment, market incentives rely on opportunistic possibilities that might impede collective stability. In the absence of some cooperation mechanisms able to direct players to trust one another, the economic relation (the transaction, the game) would result in defection and suboptimal outcomes as players might implement strategies that would potentially give them the best payoff without regard for what would be the optimum for the overall system (Harsanyi, 1976, p. 158). This could mean that as a relevant "alternative" solution to suboptimal non-cooperative frameworks, reciprocity can be considered as a rule of institutionalised coordination provided that it is framed and managed by the institutions of collective action in order to become effective. In this case, reciprocity-including regulation can be regarded as a holistic mechanism enlarging the scope of collective action in markets, going beyond the usual opposition between constraint-imposing public regulator and social-restriction-avoiding opportunistic private interests. This assertion will be studied in this essay with regard to financial market regulation.

Many institutionalist economists focus on the crucial role of institutions to design financial structures that are consistent with regard to the characteristics of a capitalist economy. Hyman Minsky (1986a) is one of them and points to the endogenous instability of a monetary/finance-based capitalist economy. In this tradition, socio-cultural norms, habits, group-membership, societal rules, etc., may all influence individuals' strategies. These elements also contribute to the complexity of the individual decision-making process, while individuals are assumed to be rational profit-maximisers or not. Parallel to this, works on economic psychology, in relation with cognitive psychology, also develop on some similar assumptions and place the emphasis on group-centred rules, goals and behaviour in society (Baddeley, 2019; Katona, 1975).

In this line, reciprocity might be a relevant angle of reflection when it comes to the design of an institutional regulatory framework consistent with the characteristics of monetary capitalist economies. However, a specific study of a possible contribution of gift-economy dynamics to an institutional reflection on an alternative financial regulation aiming at dealing with recurrent financial instabilities of capitalism has not yet been done.[2] This essay aims at exploring the possibility to fill this gap between a rich analytical tradition on the gift-economics and the research done on financial instability and regulation. We suggest an institutional analysis of the possible corrective effects of gift-rules as determining social and cognitive factors, on the recurrent financial instabilities in capitalist economies. The departure hypothesis is that a gift-economics approach may provide a social rules-related guide to shape individuals' behaviour within society. The core purpose is then to investigate how to match reciprocity and the macro-prudential approach, both resting on the idea that the organisation of society should rely on some social/ collective constraints in order to lead to social stability and coherence. In the gift-based environment, those constraints are usually implicit and conventional while in a market-based capitalist society, written rules are needed and a constraint-related macro-regulatory framework is required.

For this aim, the second section presents the major features of a monetary capitalist economy and the concerns that arise from its financialisation in a loosely regulated institutional environment since the late 1970s. The third section presents some of the characteristics of gift-economics and questions the possibility of considering alternatives to liberal and micro-prudential financial regulation that could be based on the reciprocity rule of gift-economics and then lead to a consistent institutional environment able to provide a sustainable financial regulation. Although some directions are suggested in terms of relevant alternative financial regulation, we do not give a list of collective actions that should be implemented to reframe financial markets, but rather indicate the necessary institutional analysis of financial regulation. The last section concludes.

An institutionalist analysis of financialisation and liberal financial regulation

Capitalism as a monetary economy

Capitalism is a historically identifiable social structure where economic relations are resting on some specific features. One of these features that determine the reproduction possibilities of the economy is the monetary and financial system and the underlying institutional structure. The institutionalist approach (Dillard, 1987; Mitchell, 1916; Veblen, 1904; among others) develops a relevant analysis of capitalism as a "money economy" where money plays a central role in economic evolution. Minsky (1982, p. 92) states that the mode that actually rules at any time depends upon institutions, the structure of financial linkages, usages and policies. In a capitalist economy, the monetary and financial structure is at the heart of the economy since all economic relations require the use of money and generate financial operations (Ülgen, 2018). This framework displays some features resting on a specific schema called a payments system that allows private individuals to set up multiple relations in society and develop their plans in a decentralised way. Money is the name of the payments system, a set of rules that permits the creation-circulation-repayment process of debts within the economy. These debts flow through the entire economy as money.

Consequently, a core feature of such an economy lies in the financing process of decentralised private plans without any central (external) decision control mechanism. In this "endogenous money" environment, all economic activities need to be financed to become effective. This usually results in private debt contracts between the spending units (mainly the enterprises) and the banking system. Debts generated through these operations must be repaid according to their maturity. The debt-financing process and resulting financial operations enable private economic units to undertake their own plans according to their expectations (the Keynesian animal spirits of entrepreneurs) once they are financed by the banking and/or financial system (Ülgen, 2019).

In such a social institutional framework, money has two core characteristics: ambivalence and transversality.

First, money is ambivalent, private and public. On the one hand, it is generated through decentralised private decisions and actions as a means of financing profit-seeking activities. On the other hand, it is public since its threefold use – as a general unit of account, a means of payment, and the only society-wide means of settlement of debts – rests on its publicness that gives it its supra-individual power[3]. Although created in a private (endogenous) way, money stands as a public system of accounts through payment-repayment relations and draws its objective validity from public (non-market) power (such as an extra-market central bank, public rules and constraints imposed on private debt operations, obligation to repay debts, limited access to money and credit, etc.).

Second, money is transversal to all economic relations whether they directly or indirectly involve individuals in these operations. Everyone uses money, contributes to financial operations, and is affected by the systemic consequences of these operations (and related policies) without being necessarily directly engaged in monetary and financial transactions in markets.

The efficiency of the working of a capitalist economy is then related to the relevance of its monetary and financial institutional framework in force. Given this crucial role of the payments system,

> … money and finance can be seen as capitalism-specific public utilities. Without their regular provision, a capitalist society cannot develop. At the same time, their sustainable provision cannot rest on decentralized market mechanisms that evolve through uncertainty in a non-ergodic world. The provision of money and finance often requires policies and intervention by a public power.
>
> (Ülgen, 2018, pp. 543–544)

However, two major concerns arise in the "normal" working of a capitalist economy and depend on the aforementioned specific characteristics of money: the tendency to financial instability and the tendency too loose regulation. These two concerns recurrently provoke systemic instabilities and crises and call for corrective measures to calm down market's ardour and potential to generate imbalances.

Financial instability and financialisation

Minsky (1982, p. 66) states that in a private debt-financing economy instability is an endogenous feature since serious business cycles are due to the financial attributes that are essential to capitalism: "the fundamental instability of a capitalist economy is upward. The tendency to transform doing well into a speculative investment boom is the basic instability in a capitalist economy".

This idea follows Keynes' Chapter 12 of *The General Theory* where the development of the exchange market is assumed to be mainly relying on speculation that often results in instability: "When the capital development of a country becomes a by-product of the activities of a casino, the job is likely to be ill-done" (Keynes, 1936, p. 159).

This "Financial Instability Hypothesis" (FIH), developed by Minsky, is very close to Polanyi's disembedded economy analysis where capitalist evolution may destroy the sustainability of the social environment through its incentive-mechanism, the accumulation process (Polanyi, 1944). Therefore, the principle of entropy may enter into the picture as "Economic activity cannot create energy and thus produces negentropy. In essence, it destroys environmental resources and biodiversity" (O'Hara, 2007, p. 31). Here are some of the consequences of the inability of market mechanisms to operate in a stable path of evolution. This would require public interventions to counterbalance the tendency of individual behaviours to generate systemic crises. This propensity to generate endogenously instability is exacerbated through the financialisation process that major market economies experienced during the last four decades, displaying some features of Minsky's FIH. Indeed, the financialisation of capitalist economies from the 1980s onwards rested on the transformation of the capital development into a by-product of casino-like activities that developed on financial efficiency criteria seeking rapid speculative rents.

Financialisation can be identified as the evolution of economies when financial relations and aims become increasingly important and dictate how decisions should be assessed as efficient choices over the whole economy. This results in the implementation of short-sighted financial efficiency criteria[4] as the best way of improving the economy's performances. Then the money manager capitalism of Minsky (Minsky, 1991; Wray, 2009) can emerge through complex new financial vehicles. Epstein (2005, p. 5) argues that some of the effects of financialisation "in concert with neo-liberalism and globalization – have been highly detrimental to significant numbers of people around the globe". Such a process resulted in a worldwide catastrophe in 2007–2008 (henceforth "the crisis"), "the worst in modern history" (Bernanke, 2010), that began in the United States and then spread to the entire planet. This turmoil continues to threaten, 12 years later in 2020, the viability of globalised and interdependent economies.

This crisis obviously challenges the efficient financial market ideology (Lepper, 2011) and liberal financial regulation, still in force in major advanced and emerging market economies. Financialisation is a systemic result of the implementation of market individualist ideology that resulted in the worldwide catastrophe (Hodgson, 2009). At the roots was the belief that liberalised market mechanisms could not only allocate resources efficiently, but also redistribute risks among those better prepared to bear them. Not only the international organisations but also scholars and policy-makers did share the same belief: the "good" institutions should be market-friendly, and private-interests-incentive mechanisms could contain self-adjusting dynamics. Numerous works draw attention to the possible consequences of such an evolution over the real economy and point to various analytical weaknesses that played a role in the failure to identify risks and give clear warnings. To point to the weaknesses of this approach, Galbraith (2008, p. 5) maintains that nothing in this consensus could lead to a correct and relevant anticipation of the ongoing financial crisis since what one could find in this approach is: "a resolute, dogmatic, absolutist belief that monetary policy should not – should never – concern itself with such problems". Indeed, the irrelevance of such a synthesis stems from the fact that it cannot allow questions about financial instability since it does not allow questions about booms and busts, about insolvency and illiquidity to be asked (Buiter, 2009).

The Independent Evaluation Office of the International Monetary Fund (2011, p. 17) states that:

> The prevailing view among IMF staff – a cohesive group of macroeconomists – was that market discipline and self-regulation would be sufficient to stave off serious problems in financial institutions. They also believed that crises were unlikely to happen in advanced economies, where "sophisticated" financial markets could thrive safely with minimal regulation of a large and growing portion of the financial system.

Minsky (1991, p. 17) underlines the fragile working of liberalised markets that evolve through subjective transformation of uncertainty into mere risk calculations:

> The way markets price capital and financial assets often reflects an heroic assumption that the unknowable can be known: that propositions about fundamentally uncertain situations can be derived by assuming that what happens can be viewed as if it is a sample from a well-defined probability distribution.

As Keynes (1936) remarks, that it is mass psychology which allows individuals to take heroic decisions and then enter into fragile financial positions. But this heroism develops on financial markets in an uncertain world which are fundamentally precarious: "Day-to-day fluctuations in the profits of existing investments, which are obviously of an ephemeral and non-significant character, tend to have an altogether excessive, and even an absurd, on the market" (ibid., pp. 153–154). Harvey (2010, p. 4) states then that such behaviour "while this enables economic activity to take place despite uncertainty, it also inspires agents to anticipate increasingly favourable economic outcomes in times of plenty", contributing to increase fragilities and preparing the roots of the future instability.

The environment in which the current crisis occurred is partly the outcome of some regulatory changes supported by the New Classical/New Keynesian synthesis (Arestis, 2009; Buiter, 2009). This synthesis theoretically relies on the assumption that free markets are globally self-stabilising without restrictive exogenous public intervention and active monetary and financial policies (Ülgen, 2017). Greenspan (1997) assumes, for instance, that detailed rules and standards have become both burdensome and ineffective, if not counterproductive. He then asserts that a consistent regulatory rule must be to make that effective risk management systems are in place in the private sector (accountability, compliance and disclosure of information) in order to foster financial innovation without imposing rules that inhibit it. Such a perspective gained strength and became a common ground of agreement among policy-makers in major capitalist economies.

Liberal regulation as a crisis generator

The regulatory structure that frames the behaviour of economic units plays a crucial role in economic evolution. The way of functioning of markets is determined by the way financial systems are organised by the authorities of regulation. The regulatory framework provides markets and agents with collective rules and means of acceptable actions in order to maintain separate individual strategies within a viability zone. The very issue is to find the right way (e.g. a relevant way with regard to the objectives and consistent with regard to the constraints and capabilities) to make decentralised private actors' plans compatible with systemic stability of society within which these plans could be built up and implemented.

In major market economies, regulatory reforms were designed and implemented in favour of a loose regulation of financial markets from the 1980s with a large retreat of public supervisors from macro-prudential mechanisms for the benefit of the models of self-regulation of markets[5]. This resulted in a sharp reduction of the public regulatory power over the financial markets (Hake, 2005; Wray, 2011). Such an evolution of financial systems during the last decades was a conscious and voluntary institutional orientation resting on the hypothesis of financial market efficiency. The dominant approach of regulation assumes that self-control mechanisms can globally ensure the stability of financial systems and maintains that the individual safety of banks and financial institutions at the micro level is the major concern with regard to systemic stability. Therefore, it is argued that if relevant micro-prudential measures can be framed, markets would not require restrictive public supervision. This (dominant) liberal regulatory approach builds systemic stability on individual risk instruments through the mechanisms of self-control. This phenomenon, also called the deregulation process, is actually a specific liberal financial regulation that reframed the working conditions and incentive-mechanisms of markets.[6]

Such a process failed to result in a more stable and time-consistent financial system able to answer to the needs of the real economy. The crisis pointed to the weaknesses of micro-prudential and market mechanisms-related regulatory framework. Several concerns can be pointed out in such an approach. We will only develop a few of them specifically related to the limits of micro-rationality with regard to systemic stability.

One of the analytic explanations of the malfunctioning of the market-based regulation models is that these models rely on the assumptions that the decisions and actions of decentralised units (e.g. micro-rational strategies) would result in social harmony (the so-called Pareto-optimum), thanks to the self-adjustment capacity of market mechanisms (usually summarised by the encounters between private individuals' supply and demand through market prices)[7]. However, there is a crucial difference between micro-rationality and macro-stability. The former is limited as it is based on private information about the microeconomic environment while macroeconomic stability seeks at assessing the situation of the whole system and then to evaluate its possible deviation from the sustainability/viability range through time. In this sense, microeconomic rationality-based behaviour transforms, in the private decision process, the Knightian authentic uncertainty into risk though this does not reduce the potential systemic instability at a macroeconomic level. In the absence of macro regulation there is no other mechanism that could prevent decentralised private decisions from resulting in a general crisis. The macro-regulatory structure lies in a specific institutional structure built on some collective principles aimed at the sustainable reproduction of the economic system. Liberal regulation ignores, by its own logic, the missing bridge between micro-coverage of risks and systemic stability concerns, skipping parts of necessary prevention-based prudential policies.

Another point of interest is the cognitive bias (Janis, 1982) which is the tendency among homogeneous, cohesive groups to consider issues only within a certain paradigm and not challenge its basic premises. This can be related to what Akerlof and Dickens (1982) call the *cognitive dissonance* such that people who are able to exercise some choice about belief given available information can also manipulate their own beliefs by selecting sources of information likely to confirm "desired" beliefs. Economic actors usually believe that their speculative strategies are safe, but in this line, they do not experience the unpleasant feelings of constant fear or unsettling doubts about how wise it was to take such dangerous direction. When they convince themselves their decisions are safe, they potentially make judgement errors due to the discrepancy between their beliefs and the true state of the world. But at the individual (microeconomic) level the true state of the world (e.g. the systemic macro situation) cannot be observed but *a posteriori*. One may also add to this picture of human decision complexity the *planning fallacy* such that the market players (the insiders) are inclined to assume that they are always right and overestimate their ability to overcome obstacles and neglect to look at contingencies that are opposite or contrary to their beliefs (Kahneman, 2011).

Such a complex decision process may obviously generate macular degeneration that is permitted by the absence of collective constraints and lack of social reference. The result is a new regime of (financial) accumulation that generates speculation-oriented financial products and processes and transforms financing relations into Ponzi schemes (Minsky, 1982, 1986b, 1992). In the period before the crisis, the economy turned out to a bubble environment based on real-estate-related debt leveraging in search of capital gains: "The annual rise in land prices has far outstripped growth in national income since the late 1960s, becoming the driving force in today's financialised mode of 'wealth creation'" (Hudson, 2010, p. 4). The regime of accumulation therefore moved towards more short-term criteria. Financial operations, and new products and processes were directed towards speculative opportunities that became the main helm of not only the private decisions but also public policies. This evolution was obviously related to a specific institutional environment that allowed actors and markets, and especially banks, to adopt fragile strategies. With the financial liberalisation-liberal regulation in financial markets, banks were more incited to enter into competition for the collection of deposits by offering higher interest rates to the expenses, often, of their balance-sheet stability and thus entered into excessively optimistic and short-sighted positions by financing holding companies' LBO operations without questioning their financial and economic soundness at the long-run. Obviously, accompanied by the limited liability of banks in the (de)regulatory system, such a situation creates an environment dominated by the moral hazard; the highly risky investments – the cost of bankruptcy of which is partially transferable on public funds – becoming more attractive.

Ahearne et al. (2005) then remark that:

> Financial deregulation has often been pointed to as a possible culprit for the large run-up in house prices experienced by many countries in the late 1980s. Indeed, (...) in the 1980s a large portion of the countries in our sample experienced some sort of mortgage market deregulation. By the end of the 1980s, most constraints in most industrial countries had been lifted. Much of the deregulation eased constraints on household

> borrowing. In the United Kingdom, the United States, France, Canada, and Denmark, the deregulation increased the pool of potential lenders by lifting constraints on eligible lenders. In Australia, Denmark, Finland, Japan, Sweden, and the United States, removing the regulations pertaining to the interest rates paid by borrowers and the interest rates paid to lenders increased the willingness and ability of borrowers and lenders to arrange mortgages. These changes may also have boosted competition in the lending market as financial institutions sought to establish or protect market share.

In a similar way, the *Special Report on Regulatory Reform* of the US Congress (2009, p. 10) documents that unregulated and weakly regulated financial markets have historically shown a tendency towards excessive risk taking and instability. The reasons for this are many:

> To begin with, financial actors do not always bear the full consequences of their decisions and therefore are liable to take (or impose) more risk than would otherwise seem reasonable. For example, financial institutions generally invest other people's money and often enjoy asymmetric compensation incentives, which reward them for gains without penalizing them for losses. Even more troubling, the failure of a large financial firm can have systemic consequences, potentially triggering a cascade of losses, which means that risk taking by the firm can impose costs far beyond its own shareholders, creditors, and counterparties. The freezing up of the credit markets in 2008–09, because even healthy banks are afraid to lend, is an especially serious example of this phenomenon.

Therefore, in the aftermath of the crisis, Bernanke (2010) asks what policy implications should we draw. Bernanke argues:

> … the best response to the housing bubble would have been regulatory, not monetary. Stronger regulation and supervision aimed at problems with underwriting practices and lenders' risk management would have been a more effective and surgical approach to constraining the housing bubble than a general increase in interest rates.

In this vein, it is maintained that the roots of the crisis mainly rest on the institutional regulatory structure of financialised capitalism. Economic instability is a result of cumulative euphoric expectations in the absence of consistent institutional-policy framework. Dugger (2005) states that a market is the result of collective action backed by the state. The role that policy-makers play in market economies should be reconsidered with the aim of strengthening the resilience of macroeconomic structures to possible negative consequences of private micro decisions.

Gift-economics: elements for an alternative regulatory framework?

Financial regulation after the crisis: some directions

In the aftermath of the crisis, scholars as well as central bankers called for a necessary "revision" of financial regulation and maintained that a more macro-prudential approach would be suitable to strengthen financial stability. However, after more than one decade of reforms, relevant regulatory structures are not in place to ensure the systemic resilience of banks and financial markets:

> eight years after the passage of Dodd–Frank, and nearly a decade after the banking agencies began to work on stronger capital and liquidity regulation, the new regulatory framework in place is still not completed, with numerous proposed regulations not having been finalized.
>
> (Tarullo, 2019, p. 70)

Major remarks that are brought forth are mainly related to increasing debt positions and the persistency of risky practices that feed vulnerabilities while an appropriate regulation of liquidity and short-term finance is still not in place (Tarullo, ibid., p. 62). Tarullo (ibid., pp. 70–71) also argues that the relative resilience that large banks recovered during the last years thanks to new regulatory measures does not rest on long-term sustainable change and may become degraded over time. It is worth noting that while US Congress legislated some changes to the Dodd–Frank Act in early 2018 that eliminated regulatory requirements for small- and mid-sized banks, the banking agencies have moved towards relaxing regulation for the largest banks as well. Tarullo (ibid., p. 71) reports that these agencies have proposed reductions in the leverage ratio surcharge for the eight banks designated as being of global systemic importance and effective reduction in capital requirements for the three "super-regional" banks. Tarullo (ibid., p. 70) then maintains that: "The future degradation of the resiliency of large banking organizations is by no means foreordained...".

Moreover, Clark and Large (2011, p. 25) insist that sources of systemic financial vulnerability that stem from unsustainable evolution in financial aggregates over time still reinforce an unstable pattern of financial exposures, and structural weaknesses. Even though some significant progress has been made in the field of bank capital and liquidity regulation during the last decades, new sources of risk are emerging. Financial innovations keep on developing also outside the perimeter of regulated banking organisations; notably from forms of shadow banking, and new financial instruments, practices and forms of business activity may become the impetus for another crisis (Tarullo, ibid., p. 63).

It is worth noting that technologies and financial market participants are transforming, and this can lead to new risks: "Technology is transforming the payments and banking industry and, together with opportunities, it brings with it new risks" (Saporta, 2018, p. 8). In addition, market participants trying to reduce the cost of regulation change their behaviour and adapt to regulation. Therefore, "core capital and liquidity regulations need continual refinement, both to combat arbitrage efforts by the banks and to adapt to new financial products and conditions" (Tarullo, ibid., p. 70). Monitoring the creation and development of new instruments and the emergence of new forms of business activity can give important clues to potential sources of risk. From this perspective, the macro-prudential approach should seek to identify systemic vulnerabilities and sources of risk. It is important to maintain the results achieved in reducing the risks of the banking sector while it is clear that the regulation approach should be system-wide. An important feature of macro-prudential regulation is to fix the rules in normative legal acts in order to make their implementation mandatory for financial system participants.

Various tools are currently being used to prevent future financial crisis, smooth the financial cycle and mitigate the effects of the financial crisis. Risk-weighted requirements, minimum capital ratios, stress tests, tail risks, etc., can lead to identify globally and systemically important banks: "Three significant accomplishments seem reasonably apparent: tiering of bank regulations by size of institution, greater financial resiliency for bank-related financial institutions, and movement toward an orderly resolution mechanism for failing banks" (Tarullo, ibid., p. 64). From this perspective, Saporta (ibid., p. 12) notes that "horizon scanning draws on supervisory and market intelligence, macroeconomic analysis, and thematic analysis of trends in key financial markets".

The use of such tools has contributed to the increase in financial system's stability. Saporta (2018, p. 4) reports, for instance, that: "UK banks' buffers of liquid assets have increased by over 40 percent since 2010". Tarullo (ibid., p. 64) argues that

> the post-crisis regulatory regime has led to a dramatic increase in the resiliency of the prudentially regulated part of the financial system, as measured by (1) the quality and quantity of capital both required and actually maintained by banks; (2) the greater stability of funding sources for banks; and (3) the risk management capacities and practices of banks.

When making adjustments of regulation in response to emerging risks, it is important to remember the main goal of the reforms and verify compliance with this goal: "It is important to remember the aim of these reforms. Their aim was to reduce excessive variability of banks' risk-weighted assets, and in doing so making banks' risk-based capital ratios more transparent and comparable" (Saporta, ibid., p. 4). The selection and implementation of an appropriate tool is an important foundation for successful macro-prudential policies. However, it is important to understand that the financial environment is actively changing and new sources of risks arise. Therefore, it is important to adapt the tools to current conditions: "It is by making dynamic adjustments that we can ensure the regulatory framework continues to deliver on the reforms' objectives and ensures that the resilience that policy makers injected into the system post-crisis endures" (Saporta, ibid., p. 9). [8]

To implement successful macro-prudential policy, institutions are needed:

> Macroprudential regulation advocates were able to present practical policy proposals that promised to limit future potential market losses, to reduce future calls on public finances and to minimise the loss to macroeconomic output that came with episodes of financial distress. This increased the appeal of these ideas to both public and private sector representatives.
>
> (Baker, 2013, p. 18)

It is clear that a successful framework requires the input and engagement of a number of institutions, with a shared objective of delivering financial stability.[9]

An interesting question is to consider the possibility of imagining an institutional regulatory framework based on the rules of gift-economics in that the latter is based on social constraints that would act as social institutions and link individual choices to societal constraints and choices required for the social recognition of each community member.

Institutions and gift-economics

The research on financial regulation points to the crucial role of the institutional framework but also to the micro-macro relationship and the coherence between micro-rationality and macro-systemic results. Such an opposition is one of the issues studied within the alternative monetary models of capitalism that bring forth endogenous instability of capitalist finance. From this perspective, Iwai (2010, pp. 6–7) argues:

> The key point here is that bubbles and busts look totally irrational at the macroscopic level. Yet the behaviour of individual speculators – buying when they expect prices to rise and selling when they expect them to fall – is perfectly rational on the individual level, and indeed profitable – at least in the short term. Contrary to Milton Friedman's claim, macroscopic irrationality is not necessarily a reflection of individual irrationalities but often an unintended aggregate outcome of individual rationalities.

This "natural feature" of a capitalist economy, the "fallacy of composition" that Iwai terms "the paradox of rationality", is accentuated by the financialisation of economic society since the development of financial markets increase the speed and scale of operations that reinforce the speculative character of rational economic strategies of individuals. In a 2000 book published in Japanese (quoted in Miyazaki, 2013, p. 134), Iwai argues that in a market economy, each individual who produces, consumes and exchanges is naturally a speculator and such behaviour should involve the economy in recurrent crises. A relevant question is therefore: could the use of gift-rules through reciprocity that is mainly resting on societal constraints and that should aim at strengthening macro-stability be a possible direction to make both sides of financial regulation, micro and macro, consistent with each other?

To answer this question one should fix the role of institutions in the organisation of markets. Whatever the (many) shades of capitalism, in economics, markets are considered as an environment (price mechanisms, competition rules, private property and individualistic values) that could lead separate individuals to enter into economic and social transactions in a coherent manner while institutions are usually regarded as social-constraint-structures that are given and aiming at supporting/improving/correcting market transactions (Baumol et al., 2007; Hall and Soskice, 2001, to quote but a few).

Institutions provide the frame in which society evolves in a consistent and "rational" direction. In this, institutions contribute to shape the operating way of societies. Neale (1987, p. 1180) states that institutions "allow people to act with a high degree of confidence in their expectations of how other people will respond to their actions, and that allow other people to interpret actions and to respond intelligently". From this perspective, institutions are the framework that contains written and unwritten rules[10] that should allow a given social group to function in a "normal" and predictable way. Group members would then be enabled to adopt behaviours that would more likely be consistent with each other. This could lead members of society to avoid conflict situations that could provoke crises and challenge the values and references that constitute the societal cement. Consequently, the analysis of economic relations among decentralised individuals is the analysis of an "instituted economy in evolution" (e.g. system-consistent institutional development). Gift-rules, as extra-individual rules, imposed to market participants have then to be fixed on an institutional framework in order to give a consistency with the characteristics of large capitalist societies. Such an assertion might be related to the distinction developed by F. Tönnies (see Cahnman, 1995, for a comprehensive presentation), between *Community and Society (Gemeinschaft and Gesellschaft)*. In large societies, relations are usually more anonymous than in small ones. Therefore, the implementation of gift-engagements between parties seems to be more problematic in large societies since the relevant obligation-scheme is more complex to be framed and to be supervised.[11]

Rooted in the history of "archaic" societies, a gift-based social relationship is usually considered in opposition to market-based individualistic (utilitarian) relationship of capitalist societies. The latter is regarded in terms of individualistic self-interest based on formal contracting while the former is seen as a matter of social informal trust mechanisms that would lie in more holistic dynamics than the individualistic rationality of homo-oeconomicus

(Eisenberg, 1997; Van de Velde, 2003). The market relationship, the so-called commodity exchange schema, rests on the "invisible glue" of the market mechanisms (seeking personal and exclusive alienable wealth accumulation), while the gift stands for moral and collective concerns (with social and inalienable characteristics) which survive after the exchange (Lapavitsas, 2002)[12].

In economics, gift-giving is also studied as a theory of the voluntary public and private redistribution of wealth (Mercier Ythier, 2006). The central object of the theory is altruistic gift-giving, construed as benevolent voluntary redistribution. However, from the perspective of economics, the scope of a gift-economy is much larger since it could be used as an alternative guide for the financial system's organisation as the latter is assumed to be a societal concern determining its domain of viability and not a mere market for some payment services.

In the tradition of Sahlins (1972), the gift allows us to regard the economy as a category of culture and politics related to the material life process of society. In the tradition of Mauss (1954), the threefold social obligation that characterises a gift-exchange[13] enforces the community through some social obligations and can be seen as a source of the formation of social capital (Dolfsma et al., 2008) that might improve social cohesion and strengthen commitments in market exchange relations. Bell (1991) argues that market relations can be embedded in a more general gift-giving schema since they could be thought of as a special (more individualistic) case of social relations globally backed by giving rules.

These different perspectives could improve our understanding of the dynamics of a capitalist economy and its possible viability interval through *societal reforms for market design*. The latter requires some stabilisation rules and tools at a societal level in order to deal with recurrent systemic crises, and then might benefit from the implementation of the reciprocity rule of gift-exchange in market relations. *Therefore, a restatement of the characteristics of a gift relation and its possible implementation as a systemic stabilizer within a capitalist financial framework becomes a relevant issue in search for an alternative financial regulation and supervision system.* This could lead to create a more holistic and comprehensive regulatory framework that could regard the strategies of market actors as the result of complex behavioural phenomena that develop through uncertainty and out of any social optimum that could be previously given by a perfect market equilibrium mechanism. Indeed, the gift relation can be seen as a source of social capital formation, a social infrastructure "which represents shared meanings and interpretations" (Dolfsma et al., 2009, p. 317) that could be used by individuals and groups in a way "that can facilitate an individual or collective action not otherwise possible" (ibid.). Gift-rules might then be regarded as socially recognised means that have the power to transfer, between individuals, between individuals and society and between groups within a given society personal utility as well as social values embedded (and then accepted) in a social structure. Although gifts could be thought of as a unilateral transfer (*I give you something for nothing*, beyond the utilitarian perspective), one might argue that in any exchange relation, exchange should entail reciprocal transfers (*I give you something and something else comes back from you to me*). Rose (1992) shows that the potlatch relationship could be regarded as a form of insurance, a kind of revolving exchange relationship since:

> the kin-group with the most successful annual catch gives away wealth in a kind of rough circle of reciprocity, so that all kin-groups were assured that they would not go hungry in a year of bad luck – though in return, they had given away a great deal during their own lucky years.
>
> (Rose, 1992, p. 299)

Sahlins (1972, p. 150), quoting Mauss, states that the social link is given by "the hau" according to the rule of "giving and receiving in a reciprocal way" in order to fill the common (universal, objective, societal?) obligation of mutual respect of things and values, be they socially or individually evaluated:

> Meanwhile, the Maori hau is raised to the status of a general explanation: the prototypical principal of reciprocity in Melanesia, Polynesia and the American northwest coast, the binding quality of the Roman tradition, the key to gifts of cattle in Hindu India – "What you are, I am; become on this day of your essence, in giving you I give myself"
>
> (Mauss, p. 248, quoted in Sahlins, ibid.)

Indeed, Mauss (1954, p. 14) gives an interpretation of the hau, the spirit of things that might belong to people as private property. In the giving process between individuals within society, the hau is contained in each article given and must be returned back to each person through time. In other case, serious harm might befall individuals who do not respect this "equivalence through given things". Things given between individuals must respect (at least) a recognised equivalence; this equivalence might be an expected social value of the things received or to be received; such an expectation offers the link between the present and the future for the parties and gives the engagement its time-consistency.[14]

In the Preface to Mauss's *Gift*, Douglas (2002, p. xi) maintains that in a gift-giving network the whole society can be described by the catalogue of transfers that maps all the obligations between its members such that the cycling gift system can be regarded as the society:

> The potlatch is an example of a total system of giving. Read this too fast and you miss the meaning. Spelt out it means that each gift is part of a system of reciprocity in which the honour of giver and recipient are engaged. It is a total system in that every item of status or of spiritual or material possession is implicated for everyone in the whole community. The system is quite simple; just the rule that every gift has to be returned in some specified way sets up a perpetual cycle of exchanges within and

> between generations. In some cases the specified return is of equal value, producing a stable system of statuses; in others it must exceed the value of the earlier gift, producing an escalating contest for honour.[15]

From this perspective, one might argue with Douglas that the gift cycle echoes Adam Smith's invisible hand since gift-rules could complement market relations especially when market mechanisms reveal to be weak to ensure the viability of social relations:

> being more directly cued to public esteem, the distribution of honour, and the sanctions of religion, the gift economy is more visible than the market. Just by being visible, the resultant distribution of goods and services is more readily subject to public scrutiny and judgements of fairness than are the results of market exchange. In operating a gift system a people are more aware of what they are doing, as shown by the sacralization of their institutions of giving. Mauss's fertile idea was to present the gift cycle as a theoretical counterpart to the invisible hand.
>
> (ibid., p. xviii).[16]

If one follows Mauss's emphasis on the contractual obligation to reciprocate gift – although gift-giving is not entirely touched by the quantitative equivalence relation of the market between two exchanged things – one could interpret credit relations among enterprises as a specific gift-transaction in a broader sense. As Lapavitsas (2002) argues, in a capitalist economy, enterprises are connected in many production and trade links that create different relations between sellers and buyers, and along with trade credit (a trust relationship between the creditors and debtors) that leads to continuous economic activities. Lapatvitsas (ibid., p. 13) then maintains that, on the one hand:

> ...trade credit tends to emerge among enterprises connected in chains of business that derive from the use value of products and entail frequent buying and selling among participants. Without non-market relations among enterprises, trade credit and its instruments, markets and institutions would be largely impossible.

But, it is worth noting that, on the other hand, once the mechanisms of credit are in place, all the non-market relations (such as trust, commitment and moral obligation among parties) are affected: "For this reason, the trust that underpins capitalist credit relations is profoundly noxious and always likely to turn into outright fraud" (Lapavitsas, ibid.).

Therefore, it should be noted that the logic of gift cannot be reduced to disinterestedness or altruism, or to individualistic and egoist calculation. It seems to be a more complex social phenomenon such that formal contracting is possible with a background of informal trust and values (the "gift component of social life". Van de Velde, 2003, p. 100). There is a kind of mix of values, although not formally describable, going from informal and internal rules to more formal and external statements. In the Durkheimian words, one could assert that formal agreements are only the most visible part of the social iceberg of a set of informal norms, traditions, conventions, etc.

The rationale for the intervention of a non-market societal organisation within the framework of financial markets' regulation rests on the assertion that decentralised and separate individual decisions and strategies cannot ensure a minimal systemic coherence to make society viable through time without any societal constrained framework. In other words, a global equilibrium (or more accurately a globally satisfying viable system) requires a common society-wide organisation of rules and their supervision in a preventive way.

A brief enquiry into gift-relying regulation

Several aspects of gift-economics could be used in order to design financial regulatory rules.

Following Malinowski's and Mauss's extensions of the gift category from the gift to the contract, Miyazaki (2013, p. 149) suggests some extension between arbitrage and gift from a perspective of the anthropology of finance and regards the gift "as an almost eternal point of return and an inexhaustible source of theoretical inspiration and associated humanism, the extensibility of arbitrage lets arbitrage evaporate along with the kind of faith required to recognize its possibility" and argues that

> there is a sense of possibility in re-appreciating the kind of excitement entailed in the logics of finance and their extensibility as a locus of slight expansion of thinking, imagination, and humanity despite all the nightmares such excitement often ends up producing.
>
> (Ibid., p. 150)

Miyazaki then states that such a "broadened" view of finance can also enable dialogue between traders and regulators.

In this section, we seek to look at the issue from a slightly different angle, linked to a holistic stance and based on reciprocity in terms of common rules that should be imposed on the market participants in order to enhance the consistency of their separate actions with overall systemic stability. Could such a view be linked to the holistic analysis developed by Tett (2015) in terms of "blindness to our own blindness", requiring external collective action that could be based on societal constraints gathered around the perspective of the gift-economy. Going beyond the usual opposition between regulation and liberalisation, between regulators and regulatees, between micro-rational individuals and macro-stability-seeking policy-makers, and then breaking out of silos, we suggest some regulatory rules that could use reciprocity as a relevant collective action tool. These rules rest on the assumption that in a large and complex (monetary) capitalist society reciprocity cannot be spontaneously and voluntarily internalised by private profit-seeking players and must be part of a system-wide regulatory framework, organised and supervised through collective action institutions. In other words, reciprocity cannot be ensured in a "natural" way through the so-called market discipline and market incentives that would push individuals to adopt strategies according to society's wishes expressed in the rules of reciprocity. The reason is obvious: capitalism is mainly resting on selfish micro-decision units that seek to achieve private performance in an individualistic way (e.g. capital accumulation).[17] These decision-making units have no way of knowing for sure that if they adopt altruistic strategies they could get back more gain (the so-called Smithian invisible hand reflex). In other words, in a non-cooperative environment, there is no generalisable Pareto-optimal equilibrium and individuals must seek partial and imperfect results for themselves without being able to have control over the whole. This situation often leads to opportunistic behaviour that undermines trust between individuals and then harms collective stability and individual optimum. This implies that while reciprocity can provide some stability, it must be organised by a visible hand through collective action. For instance, Lapavitsas (2002, p. 13) notes that "Extensive institutional mechanisms are necessary to police the edifice of promise and counter-promise that comprises the capitalist credit system".

Reciprocity, as a social rule, could keep separate individuals within societal constraints under the implicit threat of being rejected or not being recognised by the community (whether it is a professional community of monetary interests or a collective community of interests related to status, social recognition, etc.). The gift-rules-based complexity of economic structure might lead to some distinctions between micro-prudential regulation and macro-prudential regulation. Micro-prudential regulation is usually based on the assertion that each individual unit will be aware of the consequences of her/his strategies and will engage in safest strategies to reduce the risk of failure since her/his aim consists in realising high gains. Individuals are therefore concerned with factors that affect their own stability through self-monitoring and legal incentives to ensure regular disclosure and accountability, and rating agencies and banks' own IRB (Internal Ratings Based) models. However, these tools inevitably provoke conflict of interest issues (Crockett et al. 2003; King et al. 2012). Thompson defines conflict of interest as "a set of conditions in which professional judgment concerning a primary interest (such as patient's welfare or the validity of research) is unduly influenced by a secondary interest (such as financial gain)"[18] while Davis (1982, p. 21) brings forth the concept of "judgment" to elaborate a general definition of a conflict of interest:

> A person has a conflict of interest if (a) he is in a relationship with another requiring him to exercise judgment in that other's service and (b) he has an interest tending to interfere with the proper exercise of judgment in that relationship.

In market-related self-regulation systems, conflict of interest is a real concern that arises when the regulator and the regulatee are not well separated from each other. The confusion between these two sides of the process is a common feature of liberal regulation through the rating agencies and IRB mechanisms.

Whatever the supervision mechanisms implemented by public authorities over micro decision units, in a micro-prudential schema the incentives fail to prevent short-sighted individual behaviour which often develops macular degeneration reflecting the very limited horizon of decentralised private expectations and subsequent actions. For instance, the problem of macular degeneration is permitted by the absence of a collective constraint that might be provided by a gift-rule-based anchor. If one can assume that a major gift-rule is reciprocity and respect of mutual engagements, then, the preference order in market decisions of individual actors would not be anymore "First, my interest, second possible nice results for society".[19] In other words, such an alternative organisation would not rest on the Smithian ad hoc hypothesis of the egoist butcher who would finally serve society only by seeking his own profit. There is no direct link between micro-interests and social coherence or invisible hand that would incentivise the butcher to supply the best meat to satisfy his client and get back maximum profits. Furthermore, in a money-based capitalist economy, "money primes individualism: a reluctance to be involved with others, to depend on others, or to accept demand from others" (Kahneman, 2011, p. 55). Since reciprocity requires a reciprocal/mutual respect along with individual objectives, it cannot be generated through market relations. The logic of reciprocity is in an opposite way to market transactions: "Serving community would give me my personal interest thanks to stability and this interest is closely related to the respect for others and myself". Implemented in the financial area, this could prevent society-wide financialisation by directing markets through another regime of accumulation that would not generate speculation-oriented financial products and processes, and transform financing relations into Ponzi schemes (Minsky, 1982, 1986b, 1992). Therefore, the inclusion of the reciprocity rule into market exchange relations might contribute to ensure stability.

Limiting the high-risk operations of financial institutions in order to maintain stability on the basis of general rules is a necessary direction is an alternative regulatory model. This essentially means that the institutions do not receive part of the profit that is transferred to other participants of economic relations in the process of redistribution in order to reduce incentives to undertake speculative activities. Another rule might be more explicitly linked to reciprocity. For instance, reciprocity means you cannot save face if you do not fulfil societal duties (that may be more important than individual interests since "face" means a combination of reputation, honour, dignity, respect, social standing, etc.). Therefore, one of the measures to be included within the financial stability framework could be the interdiction for a failed institution (or person) to undertake similar activities during the next "x" years after the failure if the latter is proved to be due to "collectively irresponsible" (but, maybe, individually rational) strategies. However, this would require some changes in financial regulation and the legal framework according to a set of preannounced social objectives and duties.

The ambivalent nature of money, private and public as mentioned above, is linked both to specific constraints to allow market relations to be developed in a sustainable way. With regard to the private relations, respecting some implicit/explicit accepted standards of behaviour and the rules of good conduct between the parties of a given contract must be observed as an ethical obligation (since in a private property-based society, the respect of the property of a person is a core ethical rule). With regard to the public infrastructure, legal constraints and limitations to individual interests exist in order to prevent individual decisions from generating social crises. For example, the obligation to repay a debt is not only a legal constraint but also an ethical commitment if the debtor expects to remain included in social market relations. However, it is clear that the will and the actual way of doing things may not be compatible with each other.

One of the conclusions that one may draw from this analysis is that the power of reciprocity in an individualistic market society is not as strong as the social constraints and reciprocity that could be in force in a traditional society if it is not resting on collectively imposed formal regulatory rules. *Concerns about the implementation of gift-economy rules in a capitalist society are very similar to the difficulties of effectively considering a self-regulatory framework linked to market-mechanisms through the rule of transparency, disclosure and the so-called market discipline* (the usual arguments of liberal regulation). In a decentralised economy, individuals cannot take into account the systemic instability concerns that are beyond their capacity and will. These concerns must be addressed towards collective rules and principles. The problem endemic to financial markets is that individual borrowers and investors may not always be ideally positioned to evaluate complex risks. To cope with such destabilising evolution and its destructive consequences, the redesign of the regulatory framework is a *sine qua non* condition that requires more voluntarist policies aiming at framing financial markets supervision in a society-viability consistent way. Therefore, collective constraints-based macro-prudential regulation rules that might partly rest on gift-economy rules could be substituted to micro-regulation schemas as they concern themselves with factors that affect the financial system's stability as a whole (Brunnermeier et al., 2009). Macro-prudential regulation holds that micro-regulatory frameworks cannot address the systemic instability issues and take into account counter-cyclical and systemic needs to stabilise the whole economy. That calls for modifications of the institutional structure of financial markets. Stronger macro-prudential regulation framework should be designed instead of market-friendly supervisory approaches, and used to prevent short-sighted speculative activities to offer funds for productive activities, transforming the current crisis into a positive "renaissance opportunity". It seems that the so-called "primitive rules" of a gift-economy may offer us relevant reflections for a renewed way of thinking of our "modern" financial issues. The challenge is, we have to look for means to address it for institutional change.

Conclusion

This article sought to assess whether reciprocity as a gift-economics rule could provide a relevant institutional anchor that could offer a financial regulatory framework able to strengthen the working of financial markets and ensure systemic stabilisation of monetary economies. While the liberal private-interest based agenda tends to ignore the need for consistent embedded institutions, an institutional-evolutionary analysis brings out structural fragilities of the working of financialised capitalism and points to a necessary reframing of markets and institutions. Minsky (1986b, p. 281) maintains:

> If the disrupting effects of banking are to be constrained, the authorities must drop their blinders and accept the need to guide and control the evolution of financial usages and practices. In a world of businessmen and financial intermediaries who aggressively seek profit, innovators will always outpace regulators; the authorities cannot prevent changes in the structure of portfolios from occurring. What they can do is keep the asset-equity ratio of banks within bounds by setting equity-absorption ratios for various types of assets. If the authorities constrain banks and are aware of the activities of fringe banks and other financial institutions, they are in a better position to attenuate the disruptive expansionary tendencies of our economy.

Seemingly paradoxical (but logically natural if Minsky's "endogenous financial instability hypothesis", Iwai's "paradox of rationality" and Kahneman's "planning fallacy" are taken into account), the liberalisation of financial markets increases the need for public oversight since it results in a system-wide financialisation with continuous and permanent effects on the economy: "In a market-based financial system, banking and capital market developments are inseparable, and fluctuations in financial conditions have a far-reaching impact on the workings of the real economy" (Adrian and Shin, 2010, p. 5).

Therefore, a financial system's stability appears to be a general concern that should be considered at a macro level. For this aim, the rule of reciprocity seems to be a relevant source of reflection to provide an alternative model of financial market organisation. However, in a capitalist society, reciprocity needs to be resting on socially given collective rules. It should be relying on a specific financial regulation that should be framed according to a reciprocity-linked-societal-constraints schema that considers the complexity of human decisions (beyond some mere technical models) and strategies (beyond some simplistic optimum calculus). The necessary elaboration of a consistent financial regulatory framework should seek strengthening the trust among market actors but also between markets and society, and between markets and regulators. For this aim, regulation has to oblige market players to respect reciprocity in their market relations through macro-prudential constraints and incentives. In such a schema, reciprocity would play a holistic role beyond legal regulatory restrictions imposed by public authorities while its relevance would be closely related to the strength of those restrictions.

Notes

1 "Give as much you take, all shall be very well" or "My food basket and your food basket will please the people", a Maori *Whakataukī* (proverbe), quoted in Mauss (1954, p. 91). Mauss (Ibid.) precise, at the footnote 14 of Conclusion at page 189, that

> Rev. Taylor, *Te Ika a Maui. Old New Zealand,* p. 130, proverb 42, translates very briefly as "give as well as take and all will be right", but the literal translation is probably as follows: As much as Maru gives, so much Maru takes, and this is good, good. (Maru is the god of war and justice).

2 It is worth noting that in the Anthropology of finance literature, numerous seminal works are available on alternative analyses of financial instabilities in a capitalist economy (see, for instance, Miyazaki, 2013, for a comprehensive presentation on various analytic proposals on related topics). However, an institutionalist framework seeking to use reciprocity/gift-economics in a financial regulation framework is not yet available.

3 See Ülgen, 2013, for a general presentation of the payments system and related issues. The approach developed in this chapter is very close to the arguments developed by the "Modern Monetary Theory" approach. See Tymoigne and Wray, 2013.

4 stock market prices are usually observed as a proxy for this kind of criteria.

5 The debate on the "relevant" financial regulation is very close to the debate on the meaning of democracy since both are related to the same issue about the organisation of society and the role that individual actions and the so-called individual freedom could play within the societal framework with regard to the means and aims of society and its viability concerns. The so-called "third principle" on which democracy could rest, which would differ not only from market transactions but also from state bureaucracy, is a direction suggested by some works (Adloff, 2006). Universalistic politics of justice or recognition that could orient citizens towards the common good and not only act out of utilitarian calculations is one of the expected directions of social organisations.

6 Ülgen (2019, p. 491) defines deregulation as follows:

> Deregulation is an institutional transformation of the public regulation and supervision mechanisms into market-relying, self-regulation mechanisms. There is a retreat of restrictive public rules in order to reduce the constraining character of the supervision in force. This change mainly rests on the assumption that market forces are naturally self-adjusting. However, in most models, market mechanisms are supported by some public rules and laws and require public intervention in order to be re-enforceable and implemental. From this perspective, it might be more suitable to define the financial liberalization as a liberal regulation framework than a deregulation process.

7 See, among others, Ekelund and Hébert (1997) for a presentation of this view from the perspective of the history of economic theory.

8 Saporta (ibid., p. 10) remarks that it is important to evaluate the cost and effect of regulation; however, quantifying financial stability is still a complex issue. Regulatory costs will often be easier to quantify than the financial stability and safety and soundness benefits. And depending on the case, we may need to look beyond the banking system to capture all of the costs and benefits. For instance, unintended consequences of bank regulation might be felt not in the banking sector but in financial markets, financial infrastructures and other parts of the financial system.

9 A further critical consideration is the compatibility of the macro-prudential objective with other economic and financial policy objectives. Given that macro-prudential policy interacts with a range of other policy areas, some tension is probably unavoidable both on the substance of policy and in interinstitutional (and conceivably interpersonal) relationships (Clark and Large, 2011, p. 10). This is most obviously a question in relation to monetary policy where, for example, pursuit of a macro-prudential credit-growth target or ceiling would be likely to have a bearing on the monetary transmission mechanism and on economic growth. But it also applies to other policy areas such as competition, consumer protection and, indeed, fiscal policy (Clark and Large, ibid., p. 13).

10 We will not discuss the respective effectiveness of written and unwritten rules. However, DeHart-Davis, Chen and Little (2013) argue that rule formalisation triggers greater thought and scrutiny about rule design than unwritten rules, and the written nature of formalised rules would convey their legitimacy in ways that unwritten rules cannot: "These possibilities present a paradox: while written organizational rules can be associated with organizational pathologies, they may be a more effective means of achieving managerial objectives than their unwritten counterparts because they are more logically designed and faithfully followed" (ibid., p. 332).

11 We owe this remark to one of the referees. Beyond the scope of this chapter, this issue is however, related to the problems of (ill)working of large, opened and liberalised financial markets that involve huge number of people within their operations without respect to living conditions of these populations that often suffer from the consequences of the crises generated by financial speculation.

12 However, Lapavitsas (ibid.) argues that the use of "commodity versus gift" as metaphor for "market versus non-market" relations in a capitalist society is misleading and the analysis of the interaction between market and non-market relations must be framed on the understanding of capital as a set of social relations in a Marxist political economy way.

13 Namely: giving, receiving and reciprocity.

14 Mauss (1954, p. 14) quotes an example on this issue:

> I will speak to you about the *hau*...The *hau* is not the wind that blows – not at all. Let us suppose that you possess a certain article (*taonga*) and that you give me this article. You give it me without setting a price on it. We strike no bargain about it. Now, I give this article to a third person who, after a certain lapse of time, decides to give me something as payment in return (*utu*). He makes a present to me of something (*taonga*). Now, this *taonga* that he gives me is the spirit (*hau*) of the *taonga* that I had received from you and that I had given to *him*. The *taonga* that I received for these *taonga* (which came from you) must be returned to you. It would not be fair (*tika*) on my part to keep these *taonga* for myself, whether they were desirable (*rawe*) or undesirable (*kino*). I must give them to you because they are a *hau* of the *taonga* that you gave me. If I kept this other *taonga* for myself, serious harm might befall me, even death. This is the nature of the *hau*, the *hau* of personal property, the *hau* of the *taonga*, the *hau* of the forest. *Kati ena* (But enough on this subject).

15 Douglas (2002, pp. xiii–xiv) notes:

> The main strands in Durkheim's opposition to the English Utilitarians were already formulated by French political philosophers. As Larry Siedentrop summarizes a tradition that stemmed from the eighteenth century, from Rousseau and Tocqueville, it made three criticisms of English liberalism: first, that it was based on an impoverished concept of the person seen as an independent individual instead of as a social being; second, that it neglected how social relations change with changes in the mode of production; and third, that it had a too negative concept of liberty and so failed to appreciate the moral role of political participation. Furthermore, early English empiricist philosophy did not explain the role of social norms in shaping individual intentions and in making social action possible; their sensationalist model of the mind allowed no scope for explaining rule-governed action.
>
> (Ibid., pp. xiii–xiv)

16 Indeed, Mauss (1954, p. 17) states:

> It is easy to find many facts concerning the obligation to receive. For a clan, a household, a group of people, a guest, have no option but to ask for hospitality, to receive presents, to enter into trading, to contract alliances, through wives or blood kinship. The Dayaks have even developed a whole system of law and morality based upon the duty one has not to fail to share in the meal at which one is present or that one has seen in preparation. The obligation to give is no less important; a study of it might enable us to understand how people have become exchangers of goods and services. We can only point out a few facts. To refuse to give, to fail to invite, just as to refuse to accept, is tantamount to declaring war; it is to reject the bond of alliance and commonality. Also, one gives because one is compelled to do so, because the recipient possesses some kind of right of property over anything that belongs to the donor.

17 The modern economic theory is based on the assumption that the social organisation around decentralised market rules is the best structure, often called a market economy or a market society, since it would reach – in most efficient way – a social Pareto-optimum under specific competitive conditions. See the two fundamental welfare theorems for this assertion (Hammond, 1998).

18 Thompson, D. 1993. Understanding Financial Conflicts of Interest. *The New England Journal of Medicine*. **329**, pp. 573–576 (quoted in MacKenzie and Cronstein, 2006, p. 198).

19 In an individualistic society, this is rather limited to "I hope so, if possible, even if it's not my explicit intention".

References

Adloff, F. 2006. Beyond Interests and Norms: Toward a Theory of Gift-Giving and Reciprocity in Modern Societies. *Constellations*. **13**(3), pp. 407–427. DOI: 10.1111/j.1467-8675.2006.00399.x

Adrian, T. and Shin, H. S. 2010. Financial Intermediaries and Monetary Economics. *Federal Reserve Bank of New York Staff Reports*, Staff Report no. 398. October 2009, Revised May 2010.

Ahearne, A. G., Ammer, J., Doyle, B. M., Kole, L. S. and Martin, R. F. 2005. House Prices and Monetary Policy: A Cross-Country Study. *International Finance Discussion Papers* Number 841. Board of Governors of the Federal Reserve System, September.

Akerlof, G. A. 1982. Labor Contracts as Partial Gift Exchange. *Quarterly Journal of Economics*. **97**, pp. 547–569. DOI: 10.2307/1885099

Akerlof, G. A. and Dickens, W. T. 1982. The Economic Consequences of Cognitive Dissonance. *The American Economic Review*. **72**(3), pp. 307–319.

Arestis, P. 2009. New Consensus Macroeconomics: A Critical Appraisal. *Levy Economics Institute of Bard College Working Paper* No. 564.

Baddeley, M. 2019. *Behavioural Economics and Finance*. Abingdon: Routledge. DOI: 10.4324/9781315211879

Baker, A. 2013. The New Political Economy of the Macroprudential Ideational Shift. *New Political Economy*. **18**(1), pp. 112–139. DOI: 10.1080/13563467.2012.662952

Baumol, W. J., Litan, R. E. and Schramm, C. J. 2007. *Good Capitalism, Bad Capitalism, and the Economics of Growth and Prosperity*. New Haven, CT: Yale University Press. DOI: 10.2139/ssrn.985843

Bell, D. 1991. Modes of Exchange: Gift and Commodity. *The Journal of Socio-Economics*. **20**(2), pp. 155–167. DOI: 10.1016/S1053–5357(05)80003-4

Bernanke, B. S. 2010. Monetary Policy and the Housing Bubble. Speech of Chairman Ben S. Bernanke at the Annual Meeting of the American Economic Association, Atlanta, Georgia, January 03, 2010. [Accessed 31 May 2019]. Available from: https://www.federalreserve.gov/newsevents/speech/bernanke20100103a.htm

Brunnermeier, M., Crockett, A., Goodhart, C., Persaud, A. D. and Shin, H. 2009. *The Fundamental Principles of Financial Regulation*. ICMB-CEPR, Preliminary Conference Draft. Geneva Reports on the World Economy 11, Geneva.

Buiter, W. H. 2009. The Unfortunate Uselessness of Most 'State of the Art' Academic Monetary Economics. [Accessed 18 September 2016]. Available from: www.voxeu.org/article/macroeconomics-crisis-irrelevance

Cahnman, W. J. 1995. *Weber and Toennies: Comparative Sociology in Historical Perspective*. New Brunswick: Transaction Books.

Clark, A. and Large, A. 2011. Macroprudential Policy: Addressing the Things We Don't Know. *Group of Thirty Occasional Paper* No. 83, Washington, DC.

Crockett, A., Harris, T., Mishkin, F. S. and White E. N. 2003. Conflicts of Interest in the Financial Services Industry: What Should We Do About Them? *Geneva Reports on the World Economy* 5, International Center for Monetary and Banking Studies, Geneva.

Davis, M. 1982. Conflict of Interest. *Business and Professional Ethics Journal*. **1**(4), pp. 17–27.

DeHart-Davis, L., Chen, J. and Little, T. D. 2006. Written Versus Unwritten Rules: The Role of Rule Formalization in Green Tape. *International Public Management Journal*. **16**(3), pp. 331–356. DOI: 10.1080/10967494.2013.825193

Dillard, D. 1987. Money as an Institution of Capitalism. *Journal of Economic Issues*. **21**(4), pp. 1623–1647. DOI: 10.1080/00213624.1987.11504717

Dolfsma, W., Van des Eijk, R. and Jolink, A. 2008. On a Source of Social Capital: Gift Exchange. *Journal of Business Ethics*. **89**, pp. 315–329. DOI: 10.1007/s10551-008-0002-z

Douglas, M. 2002. No Free Gifts. Foreword to Mauss. *The Gift. The Form and Reason for Exchange in Archaic Societies*. Taylor & Francis e-Library, pp. ix–xxiii.

Dugger, W. M. 2005. Dugger's Theorem: The Free Market Is Impossible. Remarks Upon Receiving the Veblen-Commons Award. *Journal of Economic Issues*. **39**(2), pp. 309–324. DOI: 10.1080/00213624.2005.11506808

Eisenberg, M. A. 1997. The World of Contract and the World of Gift. *California Law Review*. **85**(4), pp. 821–866. DOI: 10.15779/Z38FQ5J

Ekelund, R. B, Jr. and Hébert, R. F. 2007[1997]. *A History of Economic Theory and Method*. Long Grove, IL: Waveland Press, Inc.

Epstein, G. A. Ed. 2005. *Financialisation and the World Economy*. Cheltenham: Edward Elgar.

Galbraith, J. K. 2008. The Collapse of Monetarism and the Irrelevance of the New Monetary Consensus. *The Levy Economics Institute of Bard College Policy Note* 2008/1.

Greenspan, A. 1997. Fostering Financial Innovation: The Role of Government. In Dorn, J. A. Ed. *The Future of Money in the Information Age*. Washington, DC: The Cato Institute.

Hake, E. R. 2005. Financial Illusion: Accounting for Profits in an Enron World. *Journal of Economic Issues*. **29**(3), pp. 595–611. DOI: 10.1080/00213624.2005.11506836

Hall, P. A., and Soskice, D. Eds. 2001. *Varieties of Capitalism: The Institutional Foundations of Comparative Advantage*. New York: Oxford University Press.

Hammond, P. J. 1998. The Efficiency Theorems and Market Failure. In: Kirman, A. Ed. *Elements of General Equilibrium Analysis*. Oxford: Blackwell, pp. 211–260.

Harsanyi, J. C. 1980 [1976]. *Essays on Ethics, Social Behavior, and Scientific Explanation*. Dordrecht: D. Reidel Publishing Company.

Harvey, J. T. 2010. Modelling Financial Crises: A Schematic Approach. *Journal of Post Keynesian Economics*. **33**(1), pp. 61–82. DOI: 10.2753/PKE0160-3477330104

Hodgson, G. M. 2009. The Great Crash of 2008 and the Reform of Economics. *Cambridge Journal of Economics*. **33**, pp. 1205–1221. DOI: 10.1093/cje/bep050

Hudson, M. 2010. The Transition from Industrial Capitalism to a Financialized Bubble Economy. *Levy Economics Institute of Bard College Working Paper* No. 627, October.

Independent Evaluation Office of the International Monetary Fund. 2011. *IMF Performance in the Run-Up to the Financial and Economic Crisis, IMF Surveillance in 2004–2007*. Washington, DC.

Iwai, K. 2010. The Second End of Laissez-Faire: The Bootstrapping Nature of Money and the Inherent Instability of Capitalism. June 10, 2011. [Accessed 31 March 2015]. Available from: https://ssrn.com/abstract=1861949 or http://dx.doi.org/10.2139/ssrn.1861949

Janis, I. L. 1982. *Groupthink: Psychological Studies of Policy Decisions and Fiascoes*. 2nd ed. Boston, MA: Houghton Mifflin.

Kahneman, D. 2011. *Thinking, Fast and Slow*. London: Penguin Books Ltd.

Katona, G. A. 1975. *Psychological Economics*. New York: Elsevier.

Keynes, J. M. 1978[1936]. *The General Theory of Employment, Interest and Money*. The Collected Writings of John Maynard Keynes, Volume VII. London: The Macmillan Press Ltd.

King, L., Kitson, M., Konzelmann, S. and Wilkinson, F. 2012. Making the Same Mistake Again –or Is *This Time* Different? *Cambridge Journal of Economics*. **36**, pp. 1–15. DOI: 10.1093/cje/ber045

Lapavitsas, C. 2002. Commodity versus Gift as Metaphor for Market versus Non-Market Relations. *SOAS Working Papers* No 127. Department of Economics, University of London, UK.

Lepper, J. 2011. *An Inquiry into the Ideology and Reality of Market and Market System*. Basingstoke: Palgrave-Macmillan.

MacKenzie, C. R. and Cronstein, B. N. 2006. Conflict of Interest. *Hospital for Special Surgery Journal*. **2**, pp. 198–201.

Mauss, M. 2002[1954]. *The Gift. The Form and Reason for Exchange in Archaic Societies.* Taylor & Francis e-Library, 2002. English edition first published in 1954 by Cohen & West of *Essai sur le don*, first published in 1950 by Presses Universitaires de France in *Sociologie et Anthropologie.* This translation first published 1990 by Routledge: London.

Mercier Ythier, J. 2006. The Economic Theory of Gift-Giving: Perfect Substitutability of Transfers and Redistribution of Wealth. In: Kolm, S. C. and Mercier Ythier, J. Eds. *Handbook of the Economics of Giving, Altruism and Reciprocity.* Volume 1. North-Holland: Elsevier B.V., pp. 227–369.

Minsky, H. P. 1982. *Can "It" Happen Again? Essays on Instability and Finance.* Armonk: M.E. Sharpe, Inc.

Minsky, H. P. 1986a. The Evolution of Financial Institutions and the Performance of the Economy. *Journal of Economic Issues.* **29**(2), pp. 345–353. DOI: 10.1080/00213624.1986.11504505

Minsky, H. P. 1986b. *Stabilizing an Unstable Economy.* New York: McGraw-Hill (2008).

Minsky, H. P. 1991. Financial Crises: Systemic or Idiosyncratic. *The Jerome Levy Economics Institute of Bard College Working Paper* No. 51, April.

Mitchell, W. 1916. The Role of Money in Economic Theory. *American Economic Review.* **6**(1), pp. 140–161.

Miyazaki, H. 2013. *Arbitraging Japan. Dreams of Capitalism at the End of Finance.* Berkeley: University of California Press.

Neale, W. C. 1987. Institutions. *Journal of Economic Issues.* **21**(3), pp. 1177–1206. DOI: 10.1080/00213624.1987.11504700

O'Hara, P. A. 2007. Principles of Institutional-Evolutionary Political Economy – Converging Themes from the Schools of Heterodoxy. *Journal of Economic Issues.* **41**(1), pp. 1–42. DOI: 10.1080/00213624.2007.11506993

Polanyi, K. 2001[1944]. *The Great Transformation: The Political and Economic Origins of Our Time.* Second Paperback edition. Boston, MA: Beacon Press.

Polanyi, K., Arensberg, C. and Pearson, H. Eds. 1957. *Trade and Markets in Early Empires.* Glencoe, IL: Free Press.

Rose, C. M. 1992. Giving, Trading, Thieving and Trusting: How and Why Gifts become Exchanges and Vice Versa. *Yale Law School Faculty Scholarship Series.* Paper 1817.

Sahlins, M. B. 1972. *Stone Age Economics.* Chicago, IL: Aldine Atherton.

Saporta, V. 2018. Prudential Bank Regulation: Present and Future. Speech Given at Westminster Business Forum Keynote Seminar: Building a Resilient UK Financial Sector – Next Steps for Prudential Regulation, Structural Reform and Mitigating Risks. Bank of England. 4 July 2018. [Accessed 15 June 2019]. Available from: www.bankofengland.co.uk/speeches

Tarullo, D. K. 2019. Financial Regulation: Still Unsettled a Decade After the Crisis. *Journal of Economic Perspectives.* **33**(1), pp. 61–80. DOI: 10.1257/jep.33.1.61

Tett, G. 2015. How Tajik Weddings Helped Me Understand Wall Street? *OECD Insights, New Approaches to Economic Challenges.* October 08, 2015. [Accessed 6 February 2020]. Available from: http://oecdinsights.org/2015/10/08/how-tajik-weddings-helped-me-understand-wall-street/

Tymoigne, É. and Wray, L. R. 2013. Modern Money Theory 101: A Reply to Critics. *Levy Economics Institute of Bard College Working Paper* No 778.

Ülgen, F. 2013. Coordination in Economy. An Essay on Money. In: Ülgen, F. Ed. *New Contributions to Monetary Analysis: The Foundations of an Alternative Economic Paradigm*. London: Routledge, pp. 172–187.

Ülgen, F. 2017. Rethinking Monetary and Financial Stability. In: Rochon, L. P. and Rossi, S. Eds. *A Modern Guide to Rethinking Economics*. Cheltenham: Edward Elgar Publishing, pp. 217–239.

Ülgen, F. 2018. Collective Action and the Institutionalist Approach to Financial Regulation. *Journal of Economic Issues*. **52**(2), pp. 541–549. DOI: 10.1080/00213624.2018.1469934

Ülgen, F. 2019. Stabilizing Endogenous Instability. Proposals for an Institutionalist Reform of Financial Regulation. *Journal of Economic Issues*. **53**(2), pp. 488–495. DOI: 10.1080/00213624.2019.1594542

US Congress. 2009. *Special Report on Regulatory Reform*. Congressional Oversight Panel. Washington DC. January 2009.

Van de Velde, T. 2003. Economics and the Social Contract. In: Huegens, P., von Oosterhout, H. and Vromen, J. Eds. *The Social Institutions of Capitalism*. Cheltenham: Edward Elgar Publishing, pp. 97–108.

Veblen, T. 1915[1904]. *The Theory of Business Enterprise*. New York: Charles Scribner's Sons.

Wray, R. 2009. The Rise and Fall of Money Manager Capitalism: A Minskian Approach. *Cambridge Journal of Economics*. **33**, pp. 807–828. DOI: 10.1093/cje/bep024

Wray, R. 2011. Minsky Crisis. *Levy Economics Institute of Bard College Working Paper*, No. 659, March.

10 Principles of exchange and reciprocity in the context of providing care

Anna Zachorowska-Mazurkiewicz

Introduction

In the economy, goods and services are allocated between members of the society. The way in which this allocation is organised could be referred to as a mode of transfer. According to Karl Polanyi (2001[1944]), Jean-Louis Laville (2010a, b), Douglas C. North (1977), among others, there are three such modes: (1) reciprocity and gift-giving, (2) redistribution and central authority, and (3) exchange and market. These modes cannot be understood only as systems of allocation, because they determine institutional structures required to facilitate the process of transfer, which, in turn, shapes economic and social relations. In this chapter the social impact of the application of different modes of transfers, in particular exchange and reciprocity, is discussed in the context of care and care labour. The chapter begins with definitions of the main concepts used, such as modes of transfer, care and care labour. Then the analysis is focused on two modes of transfers – gift-giving and exchange, and their place in contemporary economies. The interaction between these modes and their impact is discussed. The last part of the chapter is devoted to care and care labour in the context of two modes considered. Care is recognised in the chapter as activity crucial for the economic system, and as such shaped by the institutional settings attributed to the modes of transfer. The main question posed in the chapter is: whether the mode, in which care is transferred, determines its place in modern economies. The chapter is an attempt to link institutional thought with feminist theory. Principles of exchange, and reciprocity illustrate the institutional character of economic relations, while the focus on care is one of the main themes of feminist enquiry in economics (Badgett and Folbre, 1999; Folbre and Nelson, 2000; Zachorowska-Mazurkiewicz, 2015a).

Main concepts

Modes of transfer

Approaching a social process from the point of view of economics means beginning with "transfers". In the strict sense, the term "transfer" denotes ordinary transfer of a good from one agent to another, but it can also denote a service provided by one agent for another, and more generally, any exchange in the world that is both costly in some sense for an agent and favourable to another (Kolm, 2000, p. 7; Kolm, 2006, p. 449). Karl Polanyi (2001[1944]) posited three general patterns of integration of economic activity, which he also called principles of behaviour, while Douglas C. North calls them – systems of allocation (1977): reciprocity, redistribution and exchange. Jean-Louis Laville (2010a, b) writes about similar patterns calling them principles applying to exchange – the market principle, the principle of redistribution and the principle of reciprocity. These systems are thus more generally modes of transfers of goods or services (Kolm, 2006, p. 417) – and this term is used most often throughout this chapter.

Exchange refers to a transfer that is dependent on the market and is conducted through prices and interaction between supply and demand. The relationship between buyers and sellers is set through contracts based on information concerning potential benefits. Redistribution is the principle, according to which central authorities are responsible for the allocation of goods, which assumes the procedure of defining fees and taxes and their usage. Redistribution consists of a political central power taking products and redistributing them, or deciding on the allocation of goods and services. In modern times this describes the public sector, and when extended to most of the economy, it is called central planning. Finally, there is reciprocity as a set or interrelated giving. It is linked to relations created between groups and people through activities that are important also as a demonstration of social bonds existing between engaged sides (Laville, 2010a, b, pp. 230–231; Kolm, 2006, p. 417).

Reciprocity denotes movements between correlative points of symmetrical groupings; redistribution designates appropriational movements towards a centre and out of it again; exchange refers to vice-versa movements taking place as between "hands" in a market system. Reciprocity in such a case assumes a background of symmetrically arranged groupings; redistribution is dependent upon the presence of some measure of centricity in the group; exchange in order to produce integration requires a system of price-making markets (Polanyi, 1957, p. 250). According to Karl Polanyi (2001[1944]) reciprocity works mainly in regard to the sexual organisation of society, that is, family and kinship; redistribution is mainly effective in respect to all those who are under a common chief and is, therefore, of a territorial character (p. 50) and it is based on political power (p. 56). These principles were institutionalised with the help of a social organisation which, inter alia, made use of the patterns of symmetry and centricity (p. 56). Exchange is a principle of economic behaviour dependent for its effectiveness upon the market pattern (p. 59). To be effective as integrative mechanisms, reciprocity requires movements between designated symmetrical groupings as in kinship relations; redistribution of goods in and out of a centre requires centricity and is generally accompanied by hierarchy; and exchange requires a system of price-making markets. These patterns of integration do not derive from the summation of individual acts but are conditional on the existence of specific instruments.

Ioana Negru (2009, p. 194) writes that economists, anthropologists and historians have been inclined to pose the spheres of market and gift in complete opposition.[1] According to her, this juxtaposition leads to, or derives from, the conventional linear image of historical development in which market relations systematically displace gift relations. She writes that the usual practice has been to present the gift-economy as an economic system that has been replaced by the development of capitalism as an economic system based on self-regulated, interconnected markets (p. 198). This could be understood as a part of the on-going debate about the presence of the gift in modern societies. The debate, which dates back to Mauss (1954), who has tried to apply his insights concerning gift relationship to contemporary industrial society. Kolm (2006), Polanyi-Levitt (2013), and Polanyi himself (1957, p. 256) could be enlisted as authors claiming that patterns of integration of economic activity – reciprocity, redistribution and exchange – do not represent stages of development, since there is no sequence in time implied. The actual economies are regimes which encompass these three pure systems in various proportions (Kolm, 2006, p. 417). However, they influence one another, and this impact, regarding especially gift-giving and exchange, will be presented in the following parts of the chapter.

Reciprocity and gift-giving

People transfer goods and services between each other, and one of the ways to transfer goods and services, as indicated above, is to give. A transfer of a good, or a service, that intends to benefit someone else and is in some way costly for an actor, is gift-giving, and its result is a gift, if it is not a part of an exchange (Kolm, 2006, s. 398). People tend to provide return-gifts when gifts have been given to them. Giving a return-gift is called reciprocity (Kolm, 2000, p. 1), and reciprocity is thus an in-kind response to certain acts (Fehr and Gächter, 2000, p. 160). Reciprocity consists of gifts – the characteristic aspect is that this should be the case for the return-gift (Kolm, 2006, p. 382). Reciprocity is one mode of transfers – along with market exchange and command. However, the cycle of reciprocity is different than market exchange, since the former one is hard to detach from social connectedness. It needs to be underlined that it is not a question of motives behind reciprocity, but rather it is a matter of structure of human relations. A gift creates the feeling of bonding as a basis for a social system of relationships, while commodity exchange does not (Negru, 2009, p. 197). Thus, gift is a type of transfer that is different from market exchange since its main goal is not utility maximisation (Negru, 2009, p. 195), and it is also different from redistribution, since it is not imposed by central authorities (Polanyi-Levitt, 2013, p. 103).

Most gifting takes place in a context of reciprocity. Anthropologist Marcel Mauss (1954) emphasises the reciprocal nature of gift-giving, even in the subtitle of his essay on *The Gift – Gifts and the obligation to return gifts*. Thus, for Mauss (1954), but also for Akerlof (1982), reciprocity is a major feature of gift exchange. Gift-giving begins with a transfer, for which reciprocity is expected, and reciprocity is usually delayed. Both the value of the reciprocal gesture, and its timing are left to discretion, though often regulated tightly by convention and custom (Offer, 1997, p. 451). Additionally, people tend to give when they are given to, even when the people who gave to them and those to whom they give are not the same ones. It is well documented that people's general behaviour towards others tends to mirror the way they have been treated in childhood (Kolm, 2000). Thus, reciprocity may also have, and often has, an intergenerational character.

Reciprocity instead of analysing it from the Polanyian perspective as one mode of transfer could also be considered as a motivation for gift-giving. It is not a perspective adopted in this chapter; however, it is worth explaining. Ioana Negru (2009, p. 194) defines gifts as transfers motivated by altruism. It is altered once there is an expectation of returning gift. Thus, there are two possible drivers behind gift transfers – altruism and reciprocity. Reciprocity is fundamentally different from altruism. Altruism is a form of unconditional kindness, i.e. altruism given does not emerge as a response to altruism received (Arrow, 1972, p. 346). However, it is important to stress once again that Mauss himself presents gifts as a symbolic form of reciprocity. In such a case, Negru distinguishes between a pure gift, which implies no expectation of reciprocity, and an impure gift that is given in anticipation of return (p. 195).

Care and care labour

In this chapter the modes of transfer are analysed using the context of care and care labour. Care service is transferred between two actors – care giver and care receiver. Care could be broadly defined as an activity that involves looking after the physical, social, psychological, emotional and developmental needs of one or more persons (Standing, 2001, p. 17). "Caring" is an ambiguous notion stretching from physical care, which may, to some extent, be independent of the relation between the carer and the person cared for, to emotional caring, in which the person doing the caring is inseparable from the care given (p. 8). Care could be understood as the provision of personal services to meet those basic physical and mental needs that allow a person to function at a socially determined acceptable level of capability, comfort and safety (Himmelweit, 2007, p. 581). Engster (2005, p. 55) writes that caring includes "everything we do directly to help others to meet their basic needs, develop or sustain their basic capabilities, and alleviate or avoid pain or suffering, in an attentive, responsive and respectful manner". Care is an important source of comfort and support in people's daily lives. Everyone, at different stages of life, is cared for or needs to be cared for. Care that we offer to other people, as well as care that we receive from others, influences our well-being, and without care people would not be able to survive both as individuals and as a society (Esquivel, 2011).

Care could be considered as an important element of social provisioning, and as work. Marilyn Power (2004) writes about economics as the study of social provisioning to emphasise that at its roots, economic activities involve the ways people organise themselves collectively to get a living.[2] Social provisioning may be done through the market, and also within the household or the state, which connects the idea of modes of transfer and their institutional settings with such perspective. Thus the concept allows for a broader understanding of economic activity that includes unpaid and non-market activities. The concept of care as work has been developed by Joan Tronto (1993) or Julie A. Nelson (1999, 2015). In their perspective, care should be recognised as work, since it requires time and effort (Nelson, 2015, p. 3). Nelson (1999 and 2015) claims that care work can be only maintained when it is allocated serious economic resources of time and money. Thus, it may be perceived through the perspective of opportunity costs. Care is work because it requires competence, skills and learning to do it well (Tronto, 1993). The concept of caring labour describes a type of work that requires personal attention, services that are normally provided on a face-to-face or first-name basis (Badgett and Folbre, 1999, p. 312). Lynch et al. (2009), and Himmelweit (1995, 2007) notice that caring labour is relational – it entails not only the performance of physical tasks but also the development of a relationship. Care is relational labour that requires both physical presence which is independent of a relationship between carer and the person cared for, and emotional bond that is inseparable from the person who cares. In time use studies[3] it is often mentioned that it is easier to categorise and measure household activities other than emotional care. Childcare is in fact the only activity that in the US time use survey could be reported as a secondary activity, so the one done while being involved in other activities (ATUS, 2017, p. 30). This particular feature of care work where the main goal of care is building the bond between the carer and the person who is taken care of is a reason that some aspects of care cannot be fully delegated to third persons, and therefore, cannot be completely commodified.

Caring activities might be undertaken in different contexts; however, the family has always been the primary institution providing care (Standing, 2009, p. 122). It is important to recognise who provides care, both within the family and in other contexts, because it is a highly gendered activity. Both within families, as well as outside, care work is done predominantly by women. Women also dominate in care professions such as nurses, teachers, etc. (Folbre and Nelson, 2000; Zachorowska-Mazurkiewicz, 2016). It is also worth mentioning that unpaid caring done for others could be performed on a straightforwardly reciprocal basis but in practice, an equal exchange is not the norm and many people, mostly but not exclusively women, do more caring for others than others do for them (Himmelweit, 2007). Thus, care labour is women's labour.

Reciprocity and exchange in contemporary economies

Elizabeth Anderson (1993) points out that systems of allocation differ not only in forms, but there are also different values and outcomes of these three modes of transfer. Market values (exchange) are different than the values of the gift (reciprocity) and common values (redistribution), which according to her allow grasping the basic differences in social relations, when goods and services are provided by the market or without it. Anderson claims that the values of the gift disintegrate, when they are provided through the market, and this leads to worsening of such social values as trust and mutual obligations. It is also worth adding that market exchange and gift-giving also differ in terms of time requirements. In the case of market exchange every sale is simultaneously a purchase. Any delay is priced by means of an interest rate. In contrast, in the transfer of gifts, the price is indeterminate. "Delivery" and "payment" can be separated by the exercise of discretion and the passage of time. (…) A gift transfer is a good in itself, a "process benefit", usually in the form of a personal relationship (Offer, 1997, p. 451).

Despite these differences between market exchange and the transfer of gifts, non-monetary aspects of the economy seem to become more and more subordinate to the market. Markets step into the spheres of life that seem to lie outside their range, or used to be dominated by non-monetary relations (Sandel, 2013). Due to its tendency to marketise more and more goods and services – that is, make them exchangeable for money – capitalism constantly enlarges the sphere of monetary measurement and thus the ease of direct comparison. Thinking in terms of the market assumes that everything could be priced – expressed by identical units – without losing value. More and more things we value are "priced" and thus enter the sphere of relational competition. A cognitive simplification is at work in such circumstances, which among other things simplifies proportionality of different things by creating market evaluation, which ignores the dimension of values that cannot be translated into money (Carvalho and Rodrigez, 2008, pp. 273–274).

A well-known description of such changes is provided by Titmuss (1972) in his book concerning human blood. When the market for blood was created the social attitudes towards the problem changed. Giving blood stopped being the gift of life, and started to be a market transaction. Titmuss (1972, p. 245) in his final paragraphs writes that "the commercialization of blood and donor relationships repress the expression of altruism, erodes the sense of community, lowers scientific standards, limits both personal and professional freedoms, (…)". There are more examples of changes related to modes of transfer. Skidelsky and Skidelsky (2012, p. 41) provide the example of education that is increasingly seen not as a preparation for the good life but as a means for increasing the value of "human capital". Carvalho and Rodrigues (2008) give examples of reforms in education (especially at the university level) and healthcare. And finally Debra Satz (2010, p. 211) uses the example of the environment and the introduction of pollution fees.[4]

There is another aspect of monetisation – by increasing the sphere of money measurement, capitalism inflames the love of money for its own sake. Money has become a final good, the one that people desire the most. Money opens the doors to power, attention, status, prestige and even love and emotions (Peterson, 1996, pp. 157–158; Tool, 2001, p. 97). Traders in futures, derivatives and other financial products need to know nothing at all of the actual goods that lie at the bottom of their transactions. Living in the world of pure money, they lose the feeling for the value of things (Skidelsky and Skidelsky, 2012). Interestingly, Veblen in 1891 (p. 350) wrote that the value of human beings may also be presented in terms of money.

> When we say that a man is "worth" so many dollars, the expression does not convey the idea that moral or other personal excellence is to be measured in terms of money, but economic success is the most widely accepted as well as the most readily ascertainable measure of esteem.

Markets influencing the evolution of values, tastes and identities shape the culture, policies, support or limit social development and support defined structures of power, they even shape our identities (Bowles, 1998, p. 75; Bowles, 1991, p. 11; Satz, 2010, p. 4). Additionally, Bowles (1991, p. 13) points out that in market exchange the creation of human bonds is not necessary, even the use of language communication is not necessary, since it is money that speaks. Features linked to market exchange are: anonymity, indifference, mobility, lack of responsibility and independence. He also states that markets are a school, in which people learn particular skills that are later valued. In the long run it may lead to a corrosion of such skills and features like solidarity with others, empathy, ability to use complex communication and common decision making. And it is possible to paraphrase Sahlins (1972), who writes that gifts make friends, while market exchange makes strangers. However, the later one to some extent, depends on some features of the market, like the size of it. Nelson and Folbre (2000) write that real markets are characterised by dimensions of provisioning, relationships and incomplete commodification that should also be accounted for.

According to Polanyi (2001) a society cooperating only through the markets will lose the ability to reproduce itself. According to Debra Satz (2010) such a vision was also shared by classical economists, because they believed that markets cannot become the only institutions around which the society is organised, because it will lead to the destruction of that society. Moreover, they believed that markets should be limited if a society based on ideas of freedom and equality of its members was to survive. From this perspective, the dominance of the market in contemporary economies and societies creates problems. If value is measured in money, the lack of such a measure implies the lack of value. Social perception of activities taking place outside the market is based on such conviction, and that, in turn, leads to a number of rather negative consequences. The inappropriateness of the market in certain spheres has important implications for the allocation of resources necessary to produce goods and services. The market economy is not able to produce enough non-market goods and services in sufficient amounts for a sustainable society (Segerson, 2017, p. 3).

But market exchange is only one type of integrating mechanism. Another is the transfer of gifts – when for some reason the market "fails", the most common correctors are efficient substitutes relying on a variety of reciprocal motives (Kolm, 2006, p. 378). The persistence of non-market exchange on such a scale indicates that gifting may be at the very least a viable alternative to the market system. This preference arises out of the intrinsic benefits from social and personal interaction. Reciprocal exchange has been preferred when trade involves a personal interaction, and foremost gifting is a transfer within the household (Offer, 1997, p. 450). The co-existence of markets and gifts of different forms within different economic systems requires recognition of the complexity of economic systems and the varying degrees of importance that should be attached to markets and other institutions, such as gifts, in seeking to understand different economies (Negru, 2009, p. 202). If we conceive of markets and gifts as being the product of the institutional context from which they spring, then this places institutions such as values and norms at the central loci of economic activity (Negru, 2009, p. 201).

Care and modes of transfer

Gift-giving often takes place within the family. Thus, the family is a dense and intense network of various reciprocities in sentiments and conduct (Kolm, 2006, p. 378). Since the family is a domain for collective and mutual giving, family economics is an important application of the economics of reciprocity and giving (Kolm, 2000, p. 28). Care is a service that has been and still is predominantly transferred as a gift between family members, and is based on the expectation of reciprocity. But care takes place in different contexts, mostly but not exclusively, in the domestic sector, where it is usually unpaid, but also in various sectors of the paid economy. In the private-for-profit sector, care is allocated by market forces and paid for by its customers. The state may subsidise such care or may purchase it directly. Alternatively, the state may employ wage labour to provide care as a public service, funded by general taxation, national insurance or user fees (Himmelweit, 2007, p. 582). Nevertheless, the traditional mode of transfer impacts the place of care and care labour in contemporary economies.

As described above a large proportion of care is provided on an unpaid basis by family members, making the domestic sector a highly significant part of all economies (Himmelweit, 2007, p. 586). However, due to historical developments the significance of care has disappeared from economic considerations. The economic concept of labour and employment was established during industrialisation and the process of urbanisation. Development of wage labour that separated people from traditional family-based production brought a new understanding of productive labour. In such circumstances care labour performed predominantly within a family, taking the form of a gift transfer constitutes a puzzle for economists and policy makers. Folbre (2009, pp. 252–253) describes the process of redefining the place of women performing unpaid work, including care work, within their own households. In the seventeenth century women, whose work consisted mainly of caring for their own families, were perceived as productive workers. During the census conducted in England in 1851 women working for their own households were acknowledged as a separate category (another category included dependents), in the census conducted in 1881 they were added to a category consisting of unskilled workers. However, by the end of the nineteenth century a special parliamentary commission included remarks made by Alfred Marshall, who suggested to adopt German traditions and move women working for their own households to a category of dependent persons. In this way, by 1900 women were formally moved to the category of dependents, which apart from women consisted of children, elderly and the disabled (Folbre, 1991, p. 464). In this process, goods and services that were meant for the market, amounts that could be expressed in money, have become new arbiters of value (Folbre, 1991, p. 465). And today labour, both in theory and in statistics, is linked to the market (Beneria, 1999, p. 288). In the twentieth century the performance of labour has become a locus of social rights, and care performed within household without monetary remuneration, has vanished statistically. But not only this, it has become an impediment to norm-based entitlements, a "barrier to work", something to be minimalised so that we could do more market work. To be performing care work became a source not just of low status but of pity (Standing, 2009, p. 316).

There are many activities paid and unpaid, which could be classified as care. Care is transferred using all three modes, but it is regulated to a large extent by ideological and normative mechanisms. Monetary value is assigned to it only, if its substitutes could be found in the market (Campillo, 2003, p. 106). And since personal and relational aspects of care do not have market equivalents, it is difficult to valuate it (Folbre, 2001; Sikorska, 2003). Feminist economists point that as a consequence, care in some degree seems to be invisible labour (Folbre, 2001; Himmelweit, 1995), ignored in economic analysis (van Staveren, 2005, p. 567) and not paid well, if performed in the market place[5] (Lynch et al., 2009; Nelson, 1999). Some work is remunerated and a lot of work that is done is not remunerated,[6] but economics students are taught that non-remunerated work has no value (Polanyi-Levitt, 2013, p. 16). Thus the significance of transferring care within families as a gift determines the situation of care workers in the market.

There is another issue arising from the non-monetary character of most of the caring activities. Veblen argued that although capitalist pecuniary incentives had become powerful, modern productive labour still depended on a degree of attention and care that would be inadequately promoted by monetary

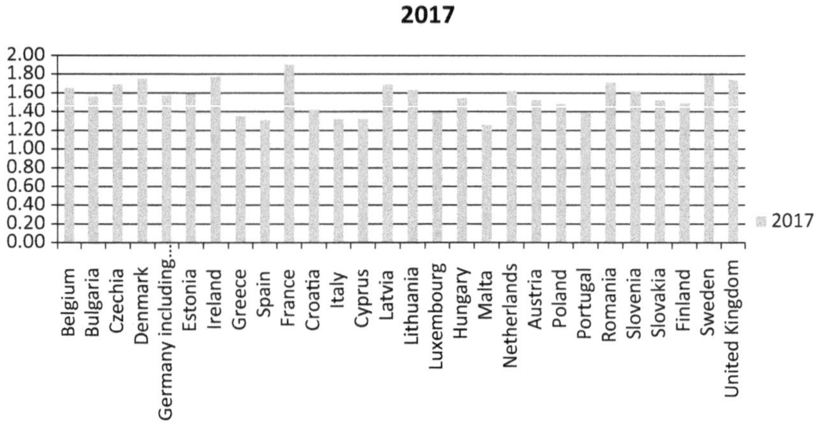

Figure 10.1 Total fertility rate in European Union member states in 2017.
Source: Eurostat, extracted 19 November 2019.

incentives (Hodgson, 2004, p. 196). Also Joseph Schumpeter (2008[1950]) noticed, that when women and men learn their lesson regarding utility well, and start to question traditional societal roles assigned to them, as soon as they start weighing benefits and costs of each and every activity they are involved in, they will surely recognise that maintaining family ties is no longer profitable (especially between parents and children, in the situation when children are no longer seen as an investment for their future[7]) (Gilbert, 2008). An additional problem is caused by recent changes in the labour market and family structure that led to breaking down of the reciprocity relationship, due to intensified mobility and fragility of households and families (Standing, 2009, p. 123). The consequences of these changes are well illustrated by the overall fertility rates in EU member states that are presented in Figure 10.1.

In 1944, Karl Polanyi predicted that an economy and society will lose their ability to reproduce themselves. Polanyi's vision nowadays takes a form of care crises – a significant drop in birth-rates in the developed world, fastest in Japan and Southern and Eastern Europe (Himmelweit, 2005, p. 26; United Nations, 2005). Data gathered in graph 1 shows that current European fertility rates do not reach the replacement level of 2.1 children per woman. This situation could be understood as an outcome of the transformation taking place in current economies, as a consequence of the dominance of one mode of transfer – exchange, over another – gift-giving, as one of the possible reasons for such a situation.

Conclusions

The gift is a type of transfer that takes place between people who know each other well, usually family and friends. Giving is linked to ceremonies and customs, among which reciprocity seems to be the most important. Care labour is distributed to a great degree between family members, and it is done not for immediate reward but rather for the expectation of the reciprocal activity to be performed in the future (like in a parent – child relationship). Care, however, could also be purchased in the market or provided by the state. So there are different modes of transfer involved in providing care. But care activities are not allocated equally between sectors and/or members of society, with a predominant role played by households and women.

In the contemporary world, care work is undervalued and not appreciated by society. One of the reasons for it could be the association of care with women (England and Folbre, 1999). But arguments collected in this chapter point at another reason – dominance of market exchange over two other modes of transfer, gift-giving in particular. Such a structure, promoting one system of allocation, shapes our culture and policies, according to the rules and values present in the market. Gifts that are transferred outside of the market are undervalued both by the market itself and by members of society, who believe that what is not priced lacks value. However, the work of carers is crucial for the reproduction of markets and societies. In order to make the process of provisioning effective, and our societies sustainable, all forms of transfer are necessary while promoting only one may have negative consequences for everyone. Reciprocity and gift-giving needs to find a more visible place in contemporary economics.

Notes

1 She mentions Hicks (1969), Sahlins (1972) and Polanyi (1957) in this context.
2 Interestingly defining economics as the study of social provisioning is a common feature of institutional and feminist economics (Zachorowska-Mazurkiewicz, 2015b).
3 Time use data are quantitative summaries of how individuals allocate their time over a specific period of time – typically 24 hours (ATUS, 2017).
4 It is worth noting that there is an on-going debate concerning the "crowding out effect" between monetary incentives and moral incentives (Bowles, 2012; Gintis 2012; Sandel, 2013). Paolo Silvestri (2019) is pointing at this debate.
5 Around 50% of domestic workers lack minimum wage protection, and more than 50% of them have no legal limits on their work hours, additionally an estimated 90% of domestic workers have no access to social security (Oxfam, 2020).
6 Oxfam (2020) estimates that the monetary value of unpaid care work globally for women aged 15 and over is worth at least 10.8 trillion USD annually.
7 Due to the introduction of old-age pension systems and legal limits to child labour.

References

Akerlof, G. A. 1982. Labor Contracts as Partial Gift Exchange. *Quarterly Journal of Economics*. **97**(4), pp. 543–569. DOI: 10.2307/1885099

Anderson, E. 1993. *Values and Ethics in Economics*. Cambridge, MA: Harvard University Press.

Arrow, K. J. 1972. Gifts and Exchange. *Philosophy and Public Affairs*. **1**(4), pp. 343–362.

ATUS. 2017. American Time Use Survey User's Guide, Bureau of Labor Statistics and US Census Bureau. [Accessed October 2017]. Available from: https://www.bls.gov/tus/

Badgett, M. V. L. and Folbre, N. 1999. Assigning Care: Gender Norms and Economic Outcomes. *International Labour Review*. **138**(3), pp. 311–326. DOI: 10.1111/j.1564–913X.1999.tb00390.x

Beneria, L. 1999. The Enduring Debate Over Unpaid Labour. *International Labour Review*. **138**(3), pp. 287–309. DOI: 10.1111/j.1564–913X.1999.tb00389.x

Bowles, S. 1991. What Markets Can – and Cannot – Do. *Challenge*. **34**(4), pp. 11–16. DOI: 10.1080/05775132.1991.11471518

Bowles, S. 1998. Endogenous Preferences: The Cultural Consequences of Markets and other Economic Institutions. *Journal of Economic Literature*. **36**(1), pp. 75–111.

Bowles, S. 2012. How Markets Crowd In Morals. *Boston Review*. June 25. [Accessed May 1st, 2020]. Available from: http://bostonreview.net/bowles-markets-crowd-in-morals

Campillo, F. 2003. Unpaid Household Labour: A Conceptual Approach, Chapter 6. In: Gutierrez, M. Ed. *Macroeconomics: Making Gender Matter: Concepts, Policies and Institutional Change in Developing Countries*. London and New York: Zed Books, pp. 106–121.

Carvalho, L. F. and Rodrigues, J. 2008. Are Markets Everywhere? Understanding Contemporary Processes of Commodification. In: Davis, J. B. and Dolfsma, W. Eds. *The Elgar Companion to Social Economics*. Cheltenham: Edward Elgar, 2008, pp. 267–286.

England, P. and Folbre, N. 1999. The Cost of Caring. *The Annals of the American Academy of Political and Social Science*. **561**, pp. 39–51. DOI: 10.1177/000271629956100103

Engster, D. 2005. Rethinking Care Theory: The Practice of Caring and the Obligation to Care. *Hypatia*. **20**(3), pp. 50–74. DOI: 10.1111/j.1527–2001.2005.tb00486.x

Esquivel, V. 2011. Sixteen Years After Beijing: What Are New Policy Agendas for Time-Use Data Collection? *Feminist Economics*. **17**(4), pp. 215–238. DOI: 10.1080/13545701.2011.616947

Fehr, E. and Gächter, S. 2000 Fairness and Retaliation: The economics of reciprocity. *Journal of Economic Perspectives*. **14** (3), pp. 159–181.

Folbre, N. 1991. The Unproductive Housewife: Her Evolution in Nineteenth-Century Economic Thought. *Signs: Journal of Women in Culture and Society*, **16**(3), pp. 463–484.

Folbre, N. 2001. *The Invisible Heart: Economics and Family Values*. New York: The New Press.

Folbre, N. 2009. *Greed, Lust & Gender. A History of Economic Ideas*. Oxford: Oxford University Press.

Folbre, N. and Nelson, J. A. 2000. For Love or Money – or Both? *Journal of Economic Perspectives*. **14**(4), pp. 123–140. DOI: 10.1257/jep.14.4.123

Gilbert, N. 2008. *A Mother's Work*. New Haven and London: Yale University Press.

Gintis, H. 2012. Giving Economists Their Due. *Boston Review*. June 25. [Accessed May 1st, 2020]. Available from: http://bostonreview.net/gintis-giving-economists-their-due

Hicks, J. R. 1969. *A Theory of Economic History*. Oxford: Oxford University Press.

Himmelweit, S. 1995. The Discovery of "Unpaid Work": The Social Consequences of the Expansion of "Work." *Feminist Economics.* **1**(2), pp. 1–19. DOI: 10.1080/714042229

Himmelweit, S. 2005. Can We Afford (Not) To Care: Prospects and Policy. New Working Paper Series. London School of Economics, Gender Institute. Issue **15**, July.

Himmelweit, S. 2007. The Prospects for Caring: Economic Theory and Policy Analysis. *Cambridge Journal of Economics.* **31**(4), pp. 581–599. DOI: 10.1093/cje/bem011

Hodgson, G. M. 2004. *The Evolution of Institutional Economics; Agency, structure and Darwinism in American Institutionalism.* London and New York: Routledge.

Kolm, S.-Ch. 2000. Introduction: The Economics of Reciprocity, Giving and Altruism. In: Gerard-Varet, L. A., Kolm, S.-Ch. and Mercier Ythier, J. Eds. *The Economics of Reciprocity, Giving and Altruism.* Houndmills, Basingstoke and Hampshire: Macmillan Press Ltd., pp. 1–43.

Kolm, S.-Ch. 2006. Reciprocity: Its Scope, Rationales, and Consequences. In: Kolm, S.-Ch. and Mercier Ythier, J. Eds. *Handbook of the Economics of Giving, Altruism and Reciprocity.* Amsterdam: Elsevier.

Laville, J. L. 2010a. Plural Economy, Chapter 7. In: Hart, K., Laville, J. L. and Cattani, A. D. Eds. *The Human Economy.* Cambridge: Polity, pp. 77–83.

Laville, J. L. 2010b. Solidarity Economy, Chapter 21. In: Hart, K., Laville, J. L. and Cattani, A. D. Eds. *The Human Economy.* Cambridge: Polity, pp. 225–235.

Lynch, K., Baker, J. and Lyons, M. 2009. *Affective Equality: Love, Care and Injustice.* Basingstoke: Palgrave MacMillan.

Mauss, M. 1954. *The Gift: Forms and Functions of Exchange in Archaic Societies.* London: Cohen and West.

Negru, I. 2009. The Plural Economy of Gifts and Markets, Chapter 14. In: Garnett, R., Olsen, E. K. and Starr, M. Eds. *Economic Pluralism.* London: Routledge, pp. 194–204.

Nelson, J. A. 1999. Of Markets and Martyrs: Is It OK to Pay Well for Care? *Feminist Economics.* **5**(3), pp. 43–59. DOI: 10.1080/135457099337806

Nelson, J. A. 2015. Husbandry: A (feminist) Reclamation of Masculine Responsibility for Care. *Cambridge Journal of Economics.* **40**(1), pp. 1–15.

North, D. C. 1977. Markets and Other Allocation Systems in History: The Challenge of Karl Polanyi. *Journal of European Economic History.* **6**(3), pp. 703–716.

Offer, A. 1997. Between the Gift and the Market: The Economy of Regard. *Economic History Review.* **50(3)**, pp. 450–476. DOI: 10.1111/1468-0289.00064

Oxfam. 2020. Time to Care; Unpaid and Underpaid Care Work and the Global Inequality Crisis. [Accessed 21 January 2020]. Available from: https://oxfamilibrary.openrepository.com/bitstream/handle/10546/620928/bp-time-to-care-inequality-200120-en.pdf

Peterson, W. C. 1996. Macroeconomics and the Theory of a Monetary Exchange, Chapter 8. In: Whalen, Ch. J. Ed. *Political Economy for the 21st Century.* Armonk: M.E. Sharpe, pp. 151–170.

Polanyi, K. 1957. The Economy as Instituted Process. In: Polanyi, K., Arensberg, C. M. and Pearson, H. W. Eds. *Trade and Market in Early Empires.* Glencoe: The Free Press, pp. 243–270.

Polanyi, K. 2001[1944]. *The Great Transformation. The Political and Economic Origins of Our Time.* Boston, MA: Beacon Press.

Polanyi-Levitt, K. 2013. *From the Great Transformation to the Great Financialization*. London: Zed Books.

Power, M. 2004. Social Provisioning as a Starting Point for Feminist Economics. *Feminist Economics*. **10**(3), pp. 3–19. DOI: 10.1080/1354570042000267608

Sahlins, M. P. 1972. *Stone Age Economics*. Chicago, IL: Aldine Pub. Co.

Sandel, M. J. 2013. *What Money Can't Buy: The Moral Limits of Markets*. London: Penguin Books.

Satz, D. 2010. *Why Some Things Should Not Be for Sale. The Moral Limits of Markets*. New York: Oxford University Press.

Schumpeter, J. A. 2008[1950]. *Capitalism, Socialism and Democracy*. New York: Harper Perennial Modern Thought.

Segerson, K. 2017. Valuing Environmental Goods and Services: An Economic Perspective, Chapter 1. In: Champ, P. A., Boyle, K. J. and Brown, T. C. Eds. *The Economic of Non-Market Goods and Resources; A Primer on Nonmarket Valuation*, second edition. Dordrecht: Springer, pp. 1–26.

Sikoska, T. 2003. Measurement and Valuation of Unpaid Household Production: A Methodological Contribution, Chapter 7. In: Gutierrez, M. Ed. *Macroeconomics: Making Gender Matter*. London: Zed Books.

Silvestri, P. 2019. The All Too Human Welfare State: Freedom Between Gift and Corruption. *Theory and Criticism of Social Regulation*. **2**(12), pp. 123–146.

Skidelsky, R. and Skidelsky, E. 2012. *How Much Is Enough? Money and the Good Life*. New York: Other Press.

Standing, G. 2001. Care Work: Overcoming Insecurity and Neglect. In: Daly, M. Ed. *Care Work; The Quest for Security*. Geneva: ILO, pp. 15–32.

Standing, G. 2009. *Work after Globalization. Building Occupational Citizenship*. Cheltenham, Northampton: Edward Elgar.

Titmuss, R. 1972. *The Gift Relationship: From Human Blood to Social Policy*. New York: Vintage Books.

Tool, M. R. 2001. *The Discretionary Economy; A Normative Theory of Political Economy*. New Brunswick and London: Transaction Publishers.

Tronto, J. 1993. *Moral Boundaries: A Political Argument for an Ethic of Care*. New York: Routledge.

United Nations. 2005. *World Population Prospects: The 2004 Revision: Highlights*. New York: United Nations.

Van Staveren, I. 2005. Modelling Care. *Review of Social Economy*. **63**(4), pp. 567–586. DOI: 10.1080/00346760500364429

Veblen, Th. 1891. Some Neglected Points in the Theory of Socialism. *Annals of the American Academy of Political and Social Sciences*. **2**(3), pp. 345–362.

Zachorowska-Mazurkiewicz, A. 2015a. The Concept of Care in Institutional and Feminist Economics and Its Impact on Public Policy. *Journal of Economic Issues*. **49**(2), pp. 405–413. DOI: 10.1080/00213624.2015.1042747

Zachorowska-Mazurkiewicz, A. 2015b. Institutional and Feminist Challenges to Neoclassical Economics. *Economic Studies*. **87**(4), pp. 493–510.

Zachorowska-Mazurkiewicz, A. 2016. *Praca kobiet w teorii ekonomii – perspektywa ekonomii głównego nurtu i ekonomii feministycznej*. Kraków: Jagiellonian University Press.

11 Afterword

The puzzle of the gift

Wilfred Dolfsma

The phenomenon of the gift – the transfer of a symbolic good from one individual or group to another, the good being material or immaterial – is a puzzle for many different reasons – reasons that have become abundantly clear after reading this volume, and that I will present some additional thoughts on. It is a key puzzle because gift-giving goes to the heart of how we understand human beings and their behaviour, and how we understand society.

Gifts – pure and mixed

The puzzle begins by how to conceive of gifts. Some favour the strict or pure definition of a gift being a transfer of a symbolic good without (the expectation of) a reciprocal gift, of some symbolic value, at some stage in the future. This reasoning relates to a view of human beings and what motivates their decisions and behaviour that de-emphasises self-interest as a motivator. Some actions, and the more important ones in particular, it is claimed, are not even slightly taken for self-interested reasons. Care taking in a family, in particular towards one's children, is given as example oftentimes. Gift-giving in this view is because of a deep bond that (already) exists. Supporters of this point of view speak of pure gifts. In this view, the Marshall Plan was not a gift (the chapter by Kesting).

Others, following Mauss (1990), argue that a return-gift is essential, but that the return-gift needs or is likely to be of a different symbolic value than the initial or prior gift. If and when an imbalance in gift and return-gift-giving exists, the relationship between two individuals or groups continues. Gift-giving in this view constitutes and maintains a deep bond that starts or exists.

The two different views of gift-giving are quite antagonistic and cannot be reconciled even when bringing the factor of time or a broader definition of (return) gift into the equation. For if one would conceptually allow for a return-gift to be handed long after a prior or initial gift was handed, the two views could approach one another. The longer a return-gift may be expected to be given, the less likely it is to actually happen, and the more likely a prior or initial gift is given for altruistic reasons as the initial giver will take into account that legitimate reasons for not returning the gift may have arisen. Will one's child, set on this world and raised at sometimes great cost, actually care and provide for you when you are unable to do so yourself? Maybe the child has fallen ill themselves, maybe the labour market circumstances for younger generations are much more bleak than before leaving less room to combine a job with care-tasks. If a return-gift can also include a "thank you", appreciation expressed, status or valued (aspiring) role confirmed, a seemingly pure gift can turn out to be (seen to be) reciprocated. With definitions thus stretched, the pure and the mixed views of gifts merge, and the discussion can easily come to be seen as a semantic one: of no consequence to the real world. The truth is a very different one: in a study of how a daycare centre tried to reduce the number of parents picking up their children too late by starting to fine them if they did. Gneezy (2000) found that this increased the number of parents who picked up the children later than daycare regulations allow. No longer were parents desperately trying to avoid feeling guilty for arriving too late and thus becoming indebted to the daycare professionals who gave their time beyond what was agreed to and paid for. A debt they might not be able to repay. By simply paying the penalty (price) for daycare professionals delivering their services longer, many no longer tried their utmost to be there in time.

The logic of the mixed gift is not a straightforward one. Yet, however intuitive it might be, it is worth spelling it out, following Mauss (1990) closely (cf. Dolfsma et al., 2009). In order to establish a relationship, for instance, between two individuals, one must initiate by giving a gift, the other has the obligation to accept the gift, and to reciprocate the gift. A gift – material or immaterial – has a symbolic value even if not a market value. When a balance of the value of gifts exchanged between people is reached, the grounds for maintaining the relation disappear and a relation may end. The value of a (counter) gift is constituted between the individuals involved, with reference to group norms and relevant societal institutions. People in hierarchically higher positions may, objectively measured, give less, but what they give can be perceived by the recipients as valuable.

The mixed view of gifts explains too why someone might not want to accept what many would see as a gift. In case one does not want the relationship that starts or exists due to accepting a gift, one does not accept. What is more, if one cannot reciprocate a gift in a way that is close to the value of the prior gift received, in the near and even distant future, one would remain indebted and subjugated to the giver.

In the chapter by Zachorowska-Mazurkiewicz it becomes very clear that this discussion of what constitutes gifts, and in general how the exchange of gift (-like) things is conceived of by the participants in a practice themselves has implications for their behaviour. There are no clearer (set of) practices where this performative aspect of how to conceive of gift vs. market exchange becomes clearer than in the context of care.[1]

The form of the gift

The mixed view of gifts allows for a differentiated view about the forms that gift-giving might take. In the pure understanding of gift-giving the status of the givee should not matter for the giver. With reference to Figure 11.1(I), a return-gift to the initial giver from the givee should not be expected. No indirect return-gift through a known third party (Figure 11.1(II)) nor an (implied) return-gift from the same community (Figure 11.1(III)) can be expected to motivate the giver to give. Refereeing submitted manuscripts for journals is often argued as a form of generalised gift-giving by a referee. Refereeing is then argued to keep in place a system to assess quality of the work to be published from which the referee will also profit if everybody in the community takes part. In terms of Figure 11.1(III), a referee can thus not predict or know who has paid their gift of refereeing forward.

The three forms of gift-giving pictured in Figure 11.1(I)–(III) have very different dynamics and persistence conditions, yet cannot be analysed in a gift-giving logic that the view of the pure gift entails. This also depends on the extent of institutionalisation of the gift exchange: if more institutionalised, indirect and generalised forms of gift exchange can also persist. The gift

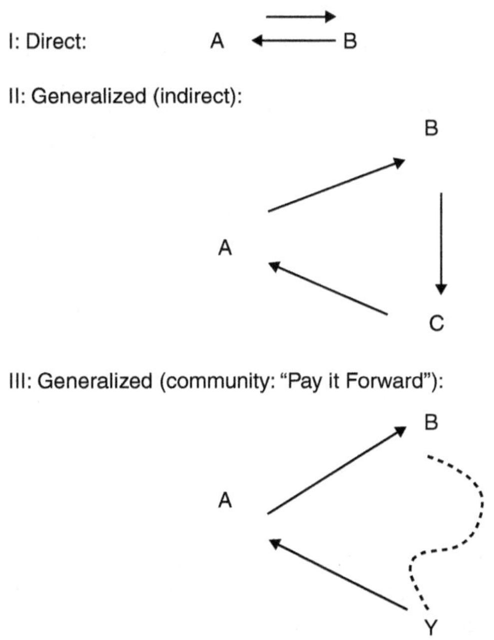

Figure 11.1 (I), (II), and (III) Direct, indirect and generalised gift-giving (Dolfsma et al., 2009).

of the Marshall plan from the United States to post-war Europe was extensively institutionally encapsulated and resulted in a number of return-gifts to this date. Generalised gift exchanges are much more vulnerable for breakdown than direct or even indirect kinds of gift exchange are. In generalised gift-giving there is much more need of support of auxiliary institutions – academics who are assessed by their line-manager about refereeing activities in their annual personal development review to see to what extent their views are held in regard in their domain. On a supra-human scale the strength of civil society organisations and support for multinational organisations such as NGOs (Non-Governmental Organisations) and also an organisation such as the WHO (World Health Organisation) are indicative.

What motivates people (to give)?

The phenomenon of the gift puzzles social scientists and people generally. Clearly there is a lot of gift-giving going on, including of the pure kind, which stupefies those who believe people are best understood as being motivated by pursuing their self-interest. What makes people "waste" so much money during Christmas, for instance (Waldfogel, 1993)?

At the same time quite a bit of what people themselves, and quite a few social scientists too, would call behaviour gift-giving also when it is done with at least a whiff of self-interest involved, because, perhaps without making it explicit and without having the purpose on top of their mind, a counter-gift is expected. Dowry is commonly seen as a gift, yet a counter-gift is explicitly expected (chapter by Khanal and Sen). Other motives can motivate gift-giving, even status seeking, as Arvanitidis and Strolonga explain in their chapter by re-reading Homer's Odyssey.

The pure view of gifts thus separates motives people might have for behaviours strongly – gifts are motivated by altruism, and other exchanges are motivated by self-interest and therefore take place on a market. The mixed view of the gift would rather suggest that engagement in all kinds of exchanges of goods between individuals or groups can be instigated by different and likely multiple motives. Walraevens' chapter shows this has been Adam Smith's view all along. There thus is no categorical distinction between gifts and market exchange in the mixed view of gift-giving. Care-giving straddles this blurred line, sometimes uncomfortably, as Anna Zachorowska-Mazurkiewicz explains in her chapter.

The chapter by Dolfsma and Van der Eijk follow the lead of influential sociologist of science Robert Merton. Merton in a much referred article in Science (1968) takes what adherent of the pure view of gifts would label as a dim view of science: whoever ends up being seen as a key actor in a scientific field will end up receiving all kinds of gifts, so that the givee may expect at some stage to benefit by a return-gift. A return-gift could consist of having an acknowledged link to the person perceived as influential. Dolfsma and

Van der Eijk show this is largely true for a commercial, applied engineering setting as well. They do make a point of distinguishing the structural part of the argument Merton makes (a contact in a network structure) from the individual attitude.

The social, the market and the gift

The different views of gifts – pure and mixed – relate also to views on how market and society relate. Figure 11.2 illustrates views on how market and society relate (see Dolfsma et al., 2005). The view illustrated in Figure 11.2(I) is one where the market is fully separate from society – it is a view held not only by mainstream economics, but also by Marxist economics, for instance. A strict separation of market and society, albeit connected, is in line with a pure view of what gifts are. Despite what many economists in particular believe, this was not founder of economics Adam Smith's view (see Walraevens' chapter).

Figure 11.2(II) and (III) see the market and the social (society) as related, albeit emphasising different types of connections. The chapter by Viana explores this point in much more detail. These latter two views are not mutually exclusive – I would argue here that they might connect in cases. When one sees the market as part of society (Figure 11.2(II)), one emphasises how market activities can be undertaken for reasons not governed by market logic, which market activities are subject to constraints imposed and presented opportunities from outside of the market, yet that, in turn, market activities can impact society. Some firms might feel required to engage in Corporate Social Responsibility (CSR) (i.e. society imposing its expectations on the market with its economic logic), yet at the same time, the manner in which it does CSR is subjected to the kinds of efficiency norms a market or economic logic Ülgen and Sakovich take this position in their chapter and even make the point that the gift logic should determine the market logic. In an argumentative move that seems to then assume pure altruist motives for and

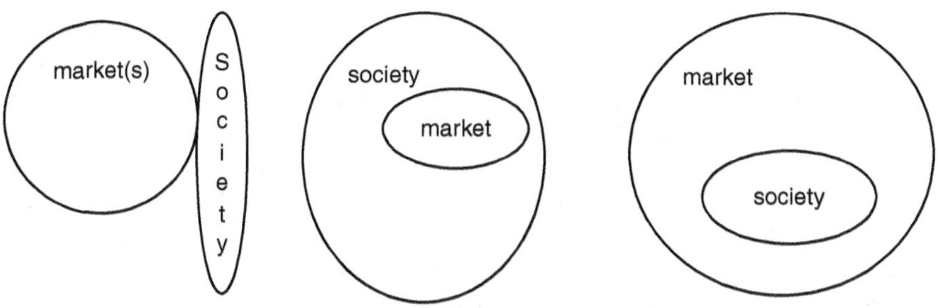

Figure 11.2 (I), (II), and (III) The separate, embedded and impure views of how market and society relate (from Dolfsma et al., 2005).

beneficial consequences of gift-giving, they claim that the gift logic determining the (financial) market logic will lead to a more stable economy. Gift and market logics in this view are more closely connected than some believe – this is also what Adloff argues, among other things, in his chapter. Surely the social impacts the economic or market logic and vice versa.

When one sees the social as part of the market, one acknowledges that market interactions can involve social dimensions. One may even argue that commerce and trade sprang from family exchanges (Dolfsma and Spithoven, 2008; Polanyi, 1963). The claim by Williamson that "in the beginning there were markets" (Williamson, 1975, p. 20) does not sound convincing and does not hold up to empirical scrutiny (Dolfsma and Spithoven, 2008). North is not much more detailed about the logic nor the empirics of how trade emerged and developed over time (cf. North, 1955, 1991). Indeed still, family businesses remain a large part of what constitutes the market. In making deals, a personal relationship between the individuals involved can often play a big part. Good business persons know how to mingle market and gift logic, even if sometimes perhaps with a view one might say to enhance their self-interest. Yet in the meantime they cannot ignore the logic of the gift, creating the trust that markets are fond to rely on. Gift exchange creates relationships one cannot ignore when opportunity presents itself.

Can groupings (firms, countries) give?

How one is apt to understand the phenomenon of the gift not just relates to how one thinks about people's motives and behaviour, what one thinks about how market and society relate, but also how one believes the choices and actions of individuals and groups come about. Khanna and Sen in their chapter make this point very convincingly.

Can groupings such as a community, a firm, a country give gifts? In taking a view on what constitutes a gift, this question is answered with a resounding "no!", or a careful "yes". A pure view of the gift, where gifts are given for altruistic reasons only, where gift-giving is spontaneous and ungoverned by mores and institutions, groupings cannot give as groupings almost by definitions have mixed reasonings for their routinised actions. The Marshall plan would in this view not be a gift. The mixed view of gifts that I, admittedly, favour would argue that groupings including firms can give. This is because gifts can be co-motivated by self-interest, status seeking and what not – social groupings will always have some individuals included in them who agree to giving a gift for other than the motive of altruism. This latter, mixed view of the gift also is accepting of the view that giving gifts can be (highly) institutionalised, such as gift-giving during Christmas. A period when I happen to be writing the core of this chapter. Arguing that firms too can give does mean that one must acknowledge that firms are not solely motivated by self-interest, that a semblance of social resides in firms. And as firms give, they will do so in view of appropriate institutions for gift-giving in society.

The gift, in short, has puzzled and continues to puzzle many social scientists. The chapters brought together in this volume will not fully resolve this puzzle, but they do bring out clearly why the gift is such a puzzle, what is at stake, and what studying the economy and society from the perspective of gift-giving allow one to understand that would otherwise remain utterly opaque.

Note

1 On performativity and economics, most dramatically see MacKenzie and Yonal (2003).

References

Dolfsma, W., Finch, J. and McMaster, R. 2005. Market and Society: (How) Do They Relate, and Contribute to Welfare? *Journal of Economic Issues.* **39**(2), pp. 347–356. DOI: 10.1080/00213624.2005.11506811

Dolfsma, W. and Spithoven, A. 2008. Silent Trade and the Supposed Continuum between OIE and NIE. *Journal of Economic Issues.* **42**(2), pp. 517–526. DOI: 10.1080/00213624.2008.11507161

Dolfsma, W., Van der Eijk, R. and Jolink, A. 2009. On a Source of Social Capital: Gift Exchange. *Journal of Business Ethics.* **89**(3), pp. 315–329. DOI: 10.1007/s10551-008-0002-z

Gneezy, U. and Rustichini, A. 2000. Pay Enough or Don't Pay at All. *Quarterly Journal of Economics.* **115**(3), pp. 791–810.

MacKenzie, D. and Yuval, M. 2003. Constructing a Market, Performing Theory: The Historical Sociology of a Financial Derivatives Exchange. *American Journal of Sociology.* **109**(1), pp. 107–145. DOI: 10.1086/374404

Mauss, M. 1990[1924]. *The Gift.* London and New York: Norton.

Merton, R. K. 1968. The Matthew Effect in Science. *Science.* **159**, pp. 56–63.

North, D. C. 1955. Location Theory and Regional Economic Growth. *Journal of Political Economy.* **63**(3), pp. 243–258.

North, D. C. 1991. Institutions. *Journal of Economic Perspectives.* **5**(1), pp. 97–112. DOI: 10.1257/jep.5.1.97

Polanyi, K. 1963. Ports of Trade in Early Societies. *Journal of Economic History.* **23**(1), pp. 30–45. DOI: 10.1017/S002205070010333X

Waldfogel, J. 1993. The Deadweight Loss of Christmas. *American Economic Review.* **83**(5), pp. 1328–1336.

Williamson, O. E. 1975. *Markets and Hierarchies.* New York: Free Press.

Index

Note: **Bold** page numbers refer to tables; *italic* page numbers refer to figures and page numbers followed by "n" denote endnotes.

For Product Safety Concerns and Information please contact our EU
representative GPSR@taylorandfrancis.com
Taylor & Francis Verlag GmbH, Kaufingerstraße 24, 80331 München, Germany

www.ingramcontent.com/pod-product-compliance
Lightning Source LLC
LaVergne TN
LVHW021127300926
849160LV00010B/888

9780367510879